Cambridge English

EMPOWER

COMBO A
STUDENT'S BOOK

B1

Adrian Doff, Craig Thaine
Herbert Puchta, Jeff Stranks, Peter Lewis-Jones
with Graham Burton

This page is intentionally left blank

STUDENT'S BOOK

Map of Student's Book	4
Unit 1 Communicating	7
Unit 2 Travel and Tourism	17
Unit 3 Money	27
Unit 4 Social Life	37
Unit 5 Work	47
Unit 6 Problems and Advice	57
Communication Plus	127
Vocabulary Focus	133
Grammar Focus	142
Audioscripts	166
Phonemic symbols and Irregular verbs	171

WORKBOOK

Map of Workbook	2
Unit 1 Communicating	4
Unit 2 Travel and Tourism	10
Unit 3 Money	16
Unit 4 Social Life	22
Unit 5 Work	28
Unit 6 Problems and Advice	34
Vox pop video	76
Audioscripts	82
Answer key	87

Lesson and objective	Grammar	Vocabulary	Pronunciation	
Unit 1 Communicating				
Getting started Talk about sharing things on your phone				
1A Ask and answer personal questions	Question forms	Common adjectives	Syllables and word stress Sentence stress	
1B Talk about how people communicate	Present simple and present continuous	Adverbs	Long and short vowels	
1C Greet people and end conversations			Sentence stress	Greeting people; Ending a conversation
1D Write a personal email				
Review and extension More practice		WORDPOWER *like*		
Unit 2 Travel and Tourism				
Getting started Talk about holiday activities				
2A Talk about past holidays	Past simple	Tourism	*-ed* endings	
2B Describe difficult journeys	Past continuous	Travel collocations	Sentence stress: vowel sounds	
2C Ask for information in a public place			Joining words	Asking for information in a public place
2D Write a travel blog				
Review and extension More practice		WORDPOWER *off*		
Unit 3 Money				
Getting started Talk about shopping				
3A Talk about experiences of generosity	Present perfect or past simple	*make / do / give* collocations		
3B Talk about spending and saving money	Present perfect with *just*, *already* and *yet*	Money	Sound and spelling: /dʒ/ and /j/	
3C Talk to people in shops			Sentence stress	Talking to people in shops; Paying at the till
3D Write an update email				
Review and extension More practice		WORDPOWER *just*		
Unit 4 Social Life				
Getting started Talk about weddings				
4A Talk about your plans for celebrations	Present continuous and *going to*	Clothes and appearance	Sound and spelling: *going to*	
4B Plan a day out in a city	*will / won't / shall*	Adjectives: places	Sound and spelling: *want* and *won't*	
4C Make social arrangements			Sentence stress	Making arrangements
4D Write and reply to invitations				
Review and extension More practice		WORDPOWER *look*		
Unit 5 Work				
Getting started Talk about people at work				
5A Talk about what people do at work	*must / have to / can*	Work	Word stress	
5B Talk about your future career	*will* and *might* for predictions	Jobs	Sound and spelling: /ʃ/	
5C Make offers and suggestions			Sentence stress: vowel sounds	Offers and suggestions
5D Write a job application				
Review and extension More practice		WORDPOWER *job* and *work*		
Unit 6 Problems and Advice				
Getting started Talk about being afraid				
6A Give advice on common problems	*should / shouldn't*; imperatives	Verbs with dependent prepositions	Sound and spelling: /uː/ and /ʊ/	
6B Describe extreme experiences	Uses of *to* + infinitive	*-ed / -ing* adjectives	*-ed* endings Word stress	
6C Ask for and give advice			Main stress	Asking for and giving advice
6D Write an email giving advice				
Review and extension More practice		WORDPOWER verb + *to*		
Communication Plus p.127	**Grammar Focus** p.142		**Vocabulary Focus** p.133	

Contents

Listening and Video	Reading	Speaking	Writing
Three conversations at a party	Article: *Small Talk*	Getting to know each other	Personal questions
Four monologues about technology and communication	Article: *The Fast and the Furious*	Ways of communicating	Sentences about communicating
Meeting an old friend		Meeting people and ending conversations; Showing interest	Unit Progress Test
Conversation: keeping in touch	Three personal emails	Keeping in touch	Personal email Correcting mistakes
Audio diary: *Yes Man changed my life*	Diary article: *Yes Man changed my life*	Types of holiday; A holiday you enjoyed	
Monologue: a bad flight	Two news stories about problems on journeys	Retelling a news story; Problems on journeys	
At the train station		Asking for information in a public place; Asking for more information	Unit Progress Test
Conversation: travelling to Indonesia	Travel blog	Writing blogs and diaries	Travel blog Linking words
Radio biography: Philip Wollen	Web forum: *Generosity Day*	Experiences of generosity	
Three monologues: spending habits	Quiz: *What kind of spender are you?*	Spending and saving money	Sentences about spending
Shopping for a present		Talking to people in shops; Changing your mind	Unit Progress Test
Four monologues: raising money for charity	Email: update on raising money for charity	Charities	Update email Paragraphing
Interview: May Ball; Audio blog: Indian wedding	Article: *Life in numbers*	Future plans; Preparations for special occasions	
Conversation: Mike and Harry in Tokyo		Tokyo highlights; Planning a day out in a city	Notes on a city you know well
Arranging to meet; birthday dinner		Making arrangements; Making time to think	Unit Progress Test
Three monologues: socialising	Two emails: invitations		Invitations and replies
Three monologues: work	Infographic: *The happiest jobs*	What makes people happy at work; Job qualities and requirements	Workplace rules
Three interviews: future careers	Article: *Planning a safe future career*	Your future career; The future world of work	Predictions: finding a job / world of work
Leaving work early		Offers and suggestions; Reassurance	Unit Progress Test
Conversation: a summer job	Email: Job application	Summer jobs	Job application Organising an email
	Article: *How to deal with life's little problems*	Common problems and possible solutions; Advice for people who are always late	Advice on a common problem
Two interviews: *Sharks saved my life* (Part 2) / *Skydiving accident*	Article: *Sharks saved my life* (Part 1)	Emotional experiences; Stories about dramatic events	Notes about a dramatic event
Advising a friend		Asking for and giving advice; Showing sympathy	Unit Progress Test
Three monologues: problems	Wiki: *Advice for learners of English*	Advice	Message giving advice; Linking: ordering ideas and giving examples

Audioscripts p.166   **Phonemic symbols and Irregular verbs** p.171

This page is intentionally left blank

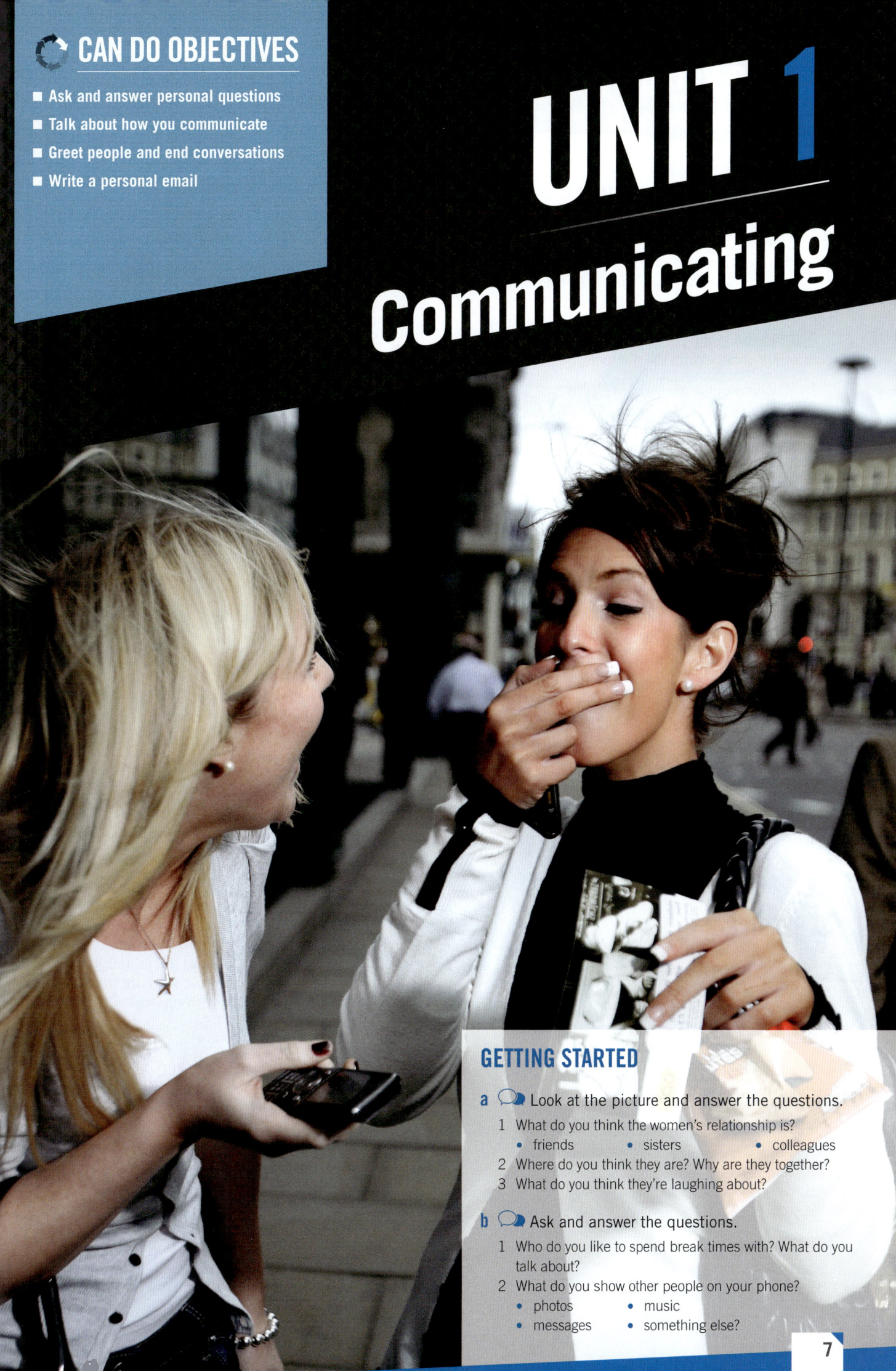

CAN DO OBJECTIVES

- Ask and answer personal questions
- Talk about how you communicate
- Greet people and end conversations
- Write a personal email

UNIT 1
Communicating

GETTING STARTED

a Look at the picture and answer the questions.
1 What do you think the women's relationship is?
   • friends   • sisters   • colleagues
2 Where do you think they are? Why are they together?
3 What do you think they're laughing about?

b Ask and answer the questions.
1 Who do you like to spend break times with? What do you talk about?
2 What do you show other people on your phone?
   • photos   • music
   • messages   • something else?

7

1A Do you play any sports?

Learn to ask and answer personal questions
G Question forms
V Common adjectives

1 SPEAKING AND LISTENING

he spotted the film for her the twist

a 💬 Look at pictures 1–3 and answer the questions.
1 What event are the people at?
2 Do you think each pair are meeting for the first time? Why/Why not?

b ▶1.2 Listen to the people's conversations 1–3. What do they talk about? Write the numbers.
- the party — 1, 2, 3
- work — ✓
- people they know — 2
- their interests — 3
- money — 2
- education — 1
- where they live — 1, 2

c ▶1.2 Listen again. Which speakers are not enjoying their conversations? Why?

2 VOCABULARY Common adjectives

a ▶1.3 Complete the sentences with the adjectives the speakers used in the listening. Then listen and check.

alright   awful   strange   delicious   perfect   boring

1 It's a _perfect_ day for a birthday party.
2 The pizza is _delicious_.
3 It's _alright_ but the music is a bit _boring_.
4 It's an _awful_ film.
5 It's a really _strange_ story.

b Which of the adjectives from 2a are positive? Which adjectives are negative? Which adjective means 'OK'?

c ▶ Now go to Vocabulary Focus 1A on p.133

3 READING

a 💬 Talk to a partner. Answer the questions together.
1 Where do you usually meet new people?
2 Do you usually start conversations or wait for others to speak?
3 What's the first question you usually ask someone?

b Read the first paragraph of *Small Talk*. Who is the article for? What problem does it help with?

c Read the article. Complete gaps 1–8 with the questions.

How do you know Ana?   What do you do?
How much do you earn?   How's the food?
Do you live near here?   Do you play any sports?
How much rent do you pay? Where did you buy them?

d 💬 Read the article again with a partner. Do you both agree with the advice?

SMALL TALK

Do you have problems when you meet people for the first time?

Is it difficult to think of what to talk about? Don't worry. You don't need to talk about yourself; ask the right questions and you can make the other person talk.

When you start a conversation with a new person, ask about the situation you're in and the people who are there:
What do you think of the party?
1 _How do you know Ana_
2 _How's the food?_
Say something positive and follow it with a question:
This music's brilliant. Do you know what it is?
The match was great last night. Do you watch the football?
I really like your shoes. 3 _Where did you buy them_
Then, ask personal questions about interests and hobbies to show you are interested:
Did you see the film? What was it like?
4 _Do you play any sports_ **Which ones?**
What was the last album you bought?
What kind of music is that?

8

UNIT 1

4 GRAMMAR Question forms

a Complete the tables with the questions in the box.

> Where did you meet? Are you married?
> Who do you know at this party? Why were you late?
> Do you like the music? Is she your sister?

Questions with the verb *be*

Question word	Verb *be*	Subject	Adjective, noun, etc.
Why	were	you	late?
	Are	you	married
	Is	she	your sister

Questions with other main verbs

Question word	Auxiliary verb	Subject	Main verb	
Where	did	you	meet?	
Who	do	you	know	at this party?
	Do	you	like	the music?

b Look at the two tables in 4a and answer questions 1 and 2.
   1 In questions with the verb *be*, which word is first, *be* or the subject?
   2 In questions with other main verbs, what kind of word goes before the subject?

c ▶ Now go to Grammar Focus 1A on p.142

d ▶1.8 **Pronunciation** Listen to the questions in the tables in 4a. Underline the stressed words.

e Put the words in the correct order to make questions.
   1 do / like / what kind of music / you ?
   2 do / what / your parents / do ?
   3 grow up / did / you / in this area ?
   4 are / you / how old ?
   5 have / you / do / any hobbies ?
   6 speak / any other languages / you / do ?

f ▶1.9 Listen and check. Underline the stressed words.

g 💬 Ask and answer the questions in 4e.

5 SPEAKING

a Write down six questions that you would like to ask other people in the class. You can use questions from this lesson or your own. Think about:

- home
- relationships
- education
- work
- interests
- people you know
- the weekend
- travel
- something else?

b 💬 Work in small groups. Ask the other students the questions you wrote in 5a. Then ask for more information.

> Do you live near here?
> No, I live 20 km away.
> Oh, how do you get here?
> By car.

When you feel more relaxed, ask personal questions about relationships and home life:
**Where did you grow up?
Are you married? Do you have any children?**
5 *Do yo live near here?*
Holidays are always a good topic if the conversation slows down:
**Do you have any holiday plans?
Where did you go for your last holiday?**
You can ask about work and studies anytime:
6 *What do you do?*
or **Where do you study?**
But be careful – sometimes people don't want to talk about work at a party!

There are also some topics that are never a good idea.
Money – people usually think talking about money is rude. So unless you know people very well, don't ask:
7 *How much do you earn?*
or
8 *How much rent do you pay?*
Politics and religion – you don't want to start an argument!
Age – never guess anyone's age. They won't be happy if you get it wrong!

1B I'm really into Facebook

Learn to talk about how you communicate
- **G** Present simple and present continuous
- **V** Adverbs

THE FAST AND THE FURIOUS

Communication is quick and easy with digital technology. But is it making us lazy? Should some things be more personal?

1 READING AND LISTENING

a 💬 How do you communicate? Do you do these things with your friends and family? If not, what do you do instead?
- send birthday cards to friends
- write a blog
- send postcards from abroad
- write letters by hand
- make plans with friends by email
- cancel plans by text or instant message
- telephone friends to invite them somewhere

> I always send birthday cards.

> I don't. I write 'happy birthday' on Facebook instead.

b Read the introduction to the article and the line in green under each photo. What do you think the missing words are?

c Read the article and check your answers to 1b. Answer the questions.
1. Why does Julie think her friend will cancel?
2. What does Facebook help Gin to remember?
3. Why is Marc writing a blog?
4. Why does Claudio prefer sending instant messages?

d ▶ 1.10 Listen to four speakers. Match them with the topics they talk about.

Tara	blogs and emails
Magda	relationships and text messages
Chris	important days and Facebook
Mike	plans and text messages

e ▶ 1.10 Listen again. Is each speaker happy or unhappy about the use of technology? Why/Why not?

f 💬 Which ideas do you agree with?
- It's rude to cancel by text.
- It's alright to finish a relationship by text.
- Facebook is the perfect place to say 'Congratulations!'
- I love to get postcards and letters.

Gin

'Facebook means I don't _____ anything.'

I'm really into Facebook. It's especially useful for birthdays, that kind of thing. When I check my Facebook page, it tells me whose birthday it is. So I never forget and I can just write a message on their wall. And when people have big news – maybe a new baby or something – you can write a comment straight away.

Julie

'I'd prefer a phone call to a _____.'

I absolutely hate it when friends cancel by text message. It's so rude. My friend Sara and I planned to go to the cinema tonight. But I'm pretty sure she'll cancel – she generally does. I'm waiting for her text message now.

'Writing a blog is a lot easier than sending _____.'

I'm studying in New York, away from my family. And while I'm here I'm writing a blog so my friends and family at home know my news. I particularly like putting all my photos on there because people leave comments. Most of my friends use Facebook but I prefer writing a blog. It's fairly easy to do and it's quicker than writing 50 separate emails.

Marc

Claudio

'I just send an _____.'

I normally communicate with people by instant message because they're free. I've even finished relationships with girlfriends by IM. In fact, I mainly do that. I know it's not the best thing to do – but it's better than a lot of shouting and crying. Some of my friends don't even send a message. They just stop all communication and wait for her to realise they're not interested.

10

UNIT 1

2 VOCABULARY Adverbs

a Look at the highlighted adverbs in the text. Answer the questions.

1 Which adverbs make another word stronger?
___ ___ ___ ___

2 Which adverbs make another word less strong?
___ ___

b Look at the sentences and complete 1–4 with the frequency adverbs.

I **generally** just send a text.
I **hardly ever** get cards or presents from friends.
I **mainly** finish relationships by IM.
My daughter **rarely** calls me.

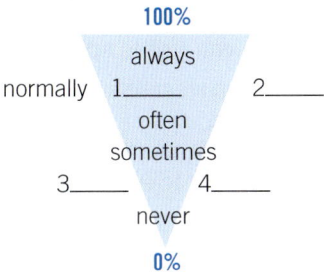

c ▶ 1.11 **Pronunciation** Look at the words in the table. Do the letters in **bold** make **long** or **short** vowel sounds? Complete the table headings. Listen and check. Repeat the words.

___ vowels	___ vowels
always	pr**e**tty
n**o**rmally	esp**e**cially
h**a**rdly	part**i**cularly
awful	**o**ften
g**o**rgeous	s**o**metimes
alright	n**e**ver
r**u**de	l**o**vely

d ▶ 1.12 Listen and repeat the sentences.

1 I absolutely hate rude people.
2 I particularly enjoy getting letters.
3 I think Facebook is fairly good.
4 I hardly ever send postcards.
5 I generally text my friends.
6 I'm really into blogs.
7 I'm pretty sure my mum can't use Skype.
8 I mainly see my family at weekends.

e 💬 Change the sentences in 2d so they are true for you. Then compare your sentences with a partner.

3 GRAMMAR
Present simple and present continuous

a Look at these sentences. Which are present simple? Which are present continuous?

present _____
1 I like putting all my photos on my blog.
2 When I plan something, I send a text.

present _____
3 I'm waiting for her text message.
4 She's writing a blog so we know what she's doing.

b Match sentences 1–4 with these uses of present simple and continuous.

> We use the present simple to talk about:
> • habits and routines ☐
> • feelings and permanent situations ☐
>
> We use the present continuous to talk about:
> • actions right now ☐
> • temporary actions around now ☐

c ▶ Now go to Grammar Focus 1B on p.142

4 SPEAKING

💬 Ask and answer the questions. Give reasons for your answers.
How often do you …?
• send a message to your boss or teacher to say you are sick
• share important news on Facebook
• read English-language websites
• send an e-card instead of a real card
• buy presents for people online
• start conversations with new people
• write emails in English
• call friends and relatives on Skype
• send video by instant message

> How often do you read English-language websites?

> Not very often. But, I'm planning a holiday in America…

> How often do you send 'e-cards'?

> Never. I absolutely hate them!

1C Everyday English
It was really nice to meet you

Learn to greet people and end conversations
- **P** Sentence stress
- **S** Showing interest

1 LISTENING

a In your country, what do you normally say and do when you …
- first meet somebody new?
- meet someone you know well?

We hug and kiss.

We shake hands and say …

b Look at the photographs. Do you think the people in each photo know each other well? Why?

c ▶1.15 Watch or listen to Part 1 and check your answers to 1b.

d ▶1.15 Watch or listen again. Are sentences 1–5 true (*T*) or false (*F*)? Correct the false sentences.
1. ☐ The last time Rachel and Annie saw each other was six years ago.
2. ☐ Annie lives a long way from the town centre.
3. ☐ Rachel and Mark got married a year ago.
4. ☐ Annie has a boyfriend.
5. ☐ Rachel, Mark and Annie decide to go to a restaurant together.

2 USEFUL LANGUAGE Greeting people

a ▶1.16 Complete the sentences from Part 1 with the words in the box. Listen and check your answers.

meet you	no see	to see you	by the way	are you	these days

1. Long time _no see_!
2. How _are you_?
3. Great _to see you_
4. Where are you living _these days_
5. My name's Mark, _by the way_
6. Nice to _meet you_

b Look at the phrases in 2a. Which can you use to speak to … ?
1. someone you know   2. someone you are meeting for the first time

c ▶1.17 Listen and note down some possible replies to the phrases in 2a. Do you know any different ways to reply to each phrase in 2a?

d Work in pairs. Take turns saying the phrases in 2a and replying.

3 CONVERSATION SKILLS Showing interest

a ▶1.18 Listen and complete the conversations from Part 1 with the adjectives in the box.

| fantastic | lovely | good | nice |

1. Long time no see! How are you?
   I'm great. What a _lovely_ surprise! Great to see you.
2. We live on Compton Road.
   Oh – how _nice_!
3. Mark's my husband!
   Husband – wow! That's _fantastic_ news.
4. Would you both like to come?
   Yeah, that sounds _good_.
   Brilliant! Let's go.

b Look at the conversations in 3a. Do the highlighted phrases give information or show interest?

c What kind of word completes each phrase 1–4? Choose the correct form from the box.

| adjective + noun | adjective |

1. What a _nice_!   2. How + _lovely_!
3. That sounds + _great_.   4. That's + _great_ + news.

d Work in pairs. Take turns to tell your partner about yourself. Reply using the phrases in 3c.

Tell your partner:
- where you live
- something you did at the weekend
- some news
- what job you do / what you are studying these days

12

UNIT 1

4 PRONUNCIATION Sentence stress

a ▶1.19 Listen to the sentences. Notice the words with stressed syllables.

I think it was about six years ago!
I live on Hampton Street.
My name's Mark, by the way.
Mark's my husband!
I'm going to the café down the street now...
...to meet Leo, my boyfriend.

b Look at the sentences in 4a. Which words have stressed syllables – grammar words or words that give information?

5 LISTENING

a 💬 Look at the picture from Part 2. Who is the fourth person at the café? Does he know Rachel and Mark?

b ▶1.20 What do you think they will talk about in the café? In pairs, think of three things. Then watch or listen to Part 2. Were you right?

c ▶1.20 Watch or listen again. Answer the questions.
1 Do Rachel and Mark have plans for next week? *No, work*
2 What job does Rachel do? *florist*
3 Who helps Rachel at the shop? *yes Tina*
4 What does Annie say about her job? *boring*
5 What does Mark do? *He works in marketing*
6 What is Annie doing at the weekend? *visit her bo*
7 Why do Rachel and Mark leave? *work*
8 What suggestion does Annie make before they leave?
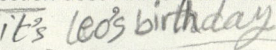
It's Leo's birthday

6 USEFUL LANGUAGE Ending conversations

a ▶1.21 Listen and complete the phrases for ending a conversation.
1 We really must _go_.
2 It was really nice to _meet_ you.
3 It was great to _see_ you again, Annie.
4 Yeah! We must _meet up_ soon.
5 _Say_ hello to Dan for me!

b Which phrase in 6a do you use when you say goodbye to somebody you have just met? _2_

c Put the sentences in the correct order to make a conversation.
B [6] Oh, that's fine. It was great to see you.
A [5] Not far from here. Look, I'm sorry, but I really must go. I'm late for a meeting.
A [1] Dan, is that you?
A [3] Yeah! I think I last saw you at John's wedding. How are you?
A [7] You, too! I'll give you a call!
B [4] I'm fine. And you? Where are you living these days?
B [2] Hi Sarah! Long time no see!

7 SPEAKING

a ▶ **Communication 1C** Student A: go to 7b below.
Student B: go to p.129.

Student A

b Read card 1. Think about what you want to say.

c Start the conversation with Student B. Use your own name.

> 1 You are walking down the street and you see your friend.
> • say hello
> • give your news:
>   • you've got a new job
>   • *your own idea*
> • listen to your friend's news and respond
> • say goodbye

d Now look at card 2. Listen to Student B and reply. Use your own name.

> 2 You meet a colleague for the first time.
> • say who you are
> • give some information:
>   • your office is in building C
>   • *your own idea*
> • listen to what your new colleague says and respond
> • say goodbye

🔄 **Unit Progress Test**

CHECK YOUR PROGRESS

You can now do the Unit Progress Test.

13

1D Skills for Writing
I'm sending you some photos

Learn to write a personal email
W Correcting mistakes

1 SPEAKING AND LISTENING

a Read the messages 1–3 and answer the questions.
1. What do the highlighted phrases mean?
2. Do you ever send or receive these kinds of message? Who to/from? Why?

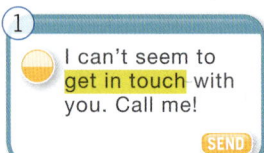
1. I can't seem to **get in touch** with you. Call me!
SEND

2. Did you **get** my last text?
SEND

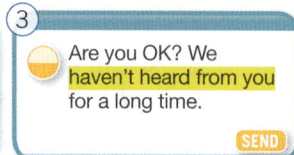
3. Are you OK? We **haven't heard from you** for a long time.
SEND

b ▶1.22 Listen to Nina and Chris talking about keeping in touch with friends and family. Who is better at keeping in touch: Nina or Chris?

c ▶1.22 Listen again and answer the questions.
1. Why doesn't Nina send many emails?
2. Why does Chris phone his mother so often?
3. How often does Nina phone her parents?
4. When does Nina prefer to tell her friends her news?
5. When does Chris send photos by email?

d How often do you keep in touch with family and friends? Circle the correct adverb for you.

always   generally   sometimes   rarely

Think about:
1. a family member who lives in a different place
2. a friend who you don't see very often

Which of these do you do with each person?
Write the first letter of their name.
- talk on the phone or Skype
- send emails or messages
- send pictures, video or web links
- hardly ever keep in touch
- meet for a chat

e Work in pairs. Talk about your answers to 1d.

> I rarely keep in touch with people. I never have time to …

> I generally keep in touch with my family. I enjoy sending …

> I sometimes send photos to my sister Jane. Usually pictures of…

> I send my friend Alex web links to interesting articles.

f Which of these opinions do you agree with?
1. 'It's nice to see photos of what your friends are doing.'
2. 'You don't have to keep in touch with people all the time.'
3. 'If your parents worry a lot, you should phone them.'

2 READING

a Simon is a student from England. Look at his pictures from Salamanca in Spain. What do you think he is doing there?

b Read the emails and check your ideas in 2a. Which email is to his … ?
- 2 friend Blake
- 1 uncle and aunt
- 3 younger sister Mika

c Who does Simon write to about these subjects?
- the weather
- what he does in the evenings
- the family he is staying with
- learning to speak Spanish
- the other students

d Answer the questions about Simon's emails.
1. What does he say about speaking Spanish?
2. Why do you think he says different things about this to each person?

What's Mexico City like?

Hope you're both well and you're enjoying the summer.
I'm in Salamanca, in Spain. This is a photo I took of the old centre.
It's a beautiful old town, as you can see.
As you know, I'm learning Spanish at the moment. I'm doing a two-month Spanish course here, so my Spanish is slowly improving. The classes are very good and we also watch Spanish films.
It's pretty hot here, but it's nice and cool in the evenings.
Love to all,
Simon *uncle*

How's it going? Are you having a good time in Berlin?
Here are some photos of my group on the Spanish course. We're all from different countries, so we usually speak English when we're together – not very good for my Spanish! Anyway, I'm having a great time here and the time's going much too quickly. There are lots of good cafés here and we usually all go out in the evening together.
What's Berlin like? Send me some photos! See you back at college next month.
Simon *friend*

I'm sending you some photos of the family I'm staying with in Salamanca. They've got a daughter the same age as you (her name's Blanca). She speaks English quite well, but we usually speak Spanish together. She introduced me to some of her friends and I speak Spanish to them, too … some of the time, not always! How's your job in the supermarket? Hope you're not working too hard and you're saving lots of money?!
See you next week.
Love
Simon xx *sister*

UNIT 1

3 WRITING SKILLS
Correcting mistakes

a Look at the pairs of sentences A–D. Which pair has mistakes in … ?

- [C] grammar
- [A] punctuation marks
- [D] spelling
- [B] capital letters

A 1 Hope youre both well and youre enjoying the summer.
  2 Are you having a good time in Berlin.
B 1 i'm in salamanca, in spain.
  2 the classes are very good and we also watch spanish Films.
C 1 I having a great time here and the time going much too quickly.
  2 She speak English quite good, but we are usually speaking Spanish together.
D 1 Her are some fotos of my group on the Spanish corse.
  2 We're all from diferent countrys, so we usually speak English.

b Match the rules with mistakes in five of the sentences in 3a (A1–D2).

1 The present continuous is formed *be* + verb + *-ing*. C1
2 When we leave out a letter, we write an apostrophe A1
3 We use the present simple to talk about habits. C2
4 If a word ends in *-y*, we change it to *-ies* in the plural. D2
5 Place names start with a capital letter. B1

c Correct all of the mistakes in the sentences in 3a. Check your answers in Simon's emails.

4 WRITING

a Write an email to a friend or family member who you don't see very often. Write about:
- how you are
- what's new for you (the place you're living or the people you're spending time with)
- what you're doing these days

b Work in pairs. Exchange emails and read your partner's email. Circle their mistakes and write these letters at the end of the line.
- grammar **G**
- punctuation marks **P**
- spelling **Sp**
- capital letters **L**

c Work in pairs. Correct the mistakes in your emails together.

d Read other students' emails. Which email is the most interesting? Why?

15

UNIT 1
Review and extension

1 GRAMMAR

a Put the words in the correct order to make questions.
1 night / did / go / out / you / last ?
2 where / you / last / weekend / go / did ?
3 kind of / like / you / what / do / TV programmes ?
4 do / this school / know / who / at / you ?
5 you / how / play / sport / often / do ?
6 you / do / what / at weekends / do / usually ?
7 tired / you / are / today ?

b Ask and answer the questions in 1a.

c Complete the conversation with the present simple or present continuous forms of the verbs.

JACKIE Hi Mum.
MUM Oh, hi Jackie. Nice of you to call. You ¹_____ (not call) very often!
JACKIE Oh come on, Mum! I ²_____ (work) really hard at university at the moment. I never ³_____ (have) time to call! And I ⁴_____ (send) you emails all the time.
MUM I ⁵_____ (like) to speak to you and hear your voice, that's all. Your sister ⁶_____ (call) me every weekend.
JACKIE Well, we ⁷_____ (speak) now. But the world ⁸_____ (change), Mum! Some of my friends never ⁹_____ (phone) home. They just ¹⁰_____ (email) or send a text.
MUM I preferred how things were in the past.

2 VOCABULARY

a Complete the sentences with the correct adjectives.
1 The film was a b r i g h t at the beginning, but I didn't like the ending.
2 We ate some really d e l i c i o u s food at the party.
3 They've got a nice house, but they live in a really u g l y part of town.
4 It was a l o v e l y day, so we decided to go to the beach.
5 I bought a g o r g e o u s new dress to wear to my friend's wedding.
6 He listens to really s t r a n g e music – I don't know any of the bands.
7 This summer, the weather here was h o r r i b l e – it rained all the time.
8 This is a p e r f e c t day for a walk in the park – it's so warm and sunny.

b Choose the correct answers.
1 I *absolutely* / *fairly* love football.
2 My parents live abroad. I *rarely* / *mainly* see them.
3 I think American films are *absolutely* / *really* good, but they're not brilliant.
4 I *normally* / *particularly* go for a run once or twice a week.
5 I *really* / *fairly* hate rock music.
6 I love all sports, but tennis is *especially* / *normally* good.

c Which sentences in 2b are true for you?

3 WORDPOWER *like*

a Match sentences (1–4) with replies (a–d).
1 [c] I've got a jacket **like** yours.
2 [d] **What was** the film **like**?
3 [b] I enjoy visiting countries with a lot of history, **like** Greece.
4 [a] We can go for a walk later **if you like**.

a Yes, that would be great.
b And Italy! Me too.
c Yes, this style's popular at the moment.
d I thought it was alright, but my friend hated it.

b Match the expressions in **bold** from 3a with the meanings (a–d).
a what was your opinion of 2   c if you want 4
b similar to 1   d for example 3

c Complete the sentences with the words in **bold** from 3a.
1 A Is your university different from others in your country?
   B No, it's *like* most of the others.
2 A We can meet tomorrow *if you like*.
   B OK – come to my flat for a coffee.
3 A Do you want me to bring something to the dinner party?
   B Yes. Bring something sweet, *like* some ice cream.
4 A We went to that new restaurant yesterday.
   B *What was* it *like*?

d We often use *like* with the verbs *look* and *sound*. Look at the examples.

• saying people or things are similar
  John **looks like** his brother – they're both tall with black hair.
  I think this new song **sounds like** The Beatles.

• saying what you think will happen
  It **looks like** it might rain – it's very cloudy.

• giving your opinion from what you heard or read
  I spoke to Sara yesterday. It **sounds like** she had a really good holiday.

Complete the sentences with the correct forms of *look like* or *sound like*.
1 It *sounds like* their first album. I really like it!
2 Sam invited Tom to the party. So it *looks like* he'll come.
3 You don't *look like* your sister. She's very tall.
4 That was the last bus. It *looks like* we'll have to walk.

REVIEW YOUR PROGRESS

How well did you do in this unit? Write 3, 2 or 1 for each objective.
3 = very well   2 = well   1 = not so well

I CAN ...

Ask and answer personal questions ☐
Talk about how you communicate ☐
Greet people and end conversations ☐
Write a personal email ☐

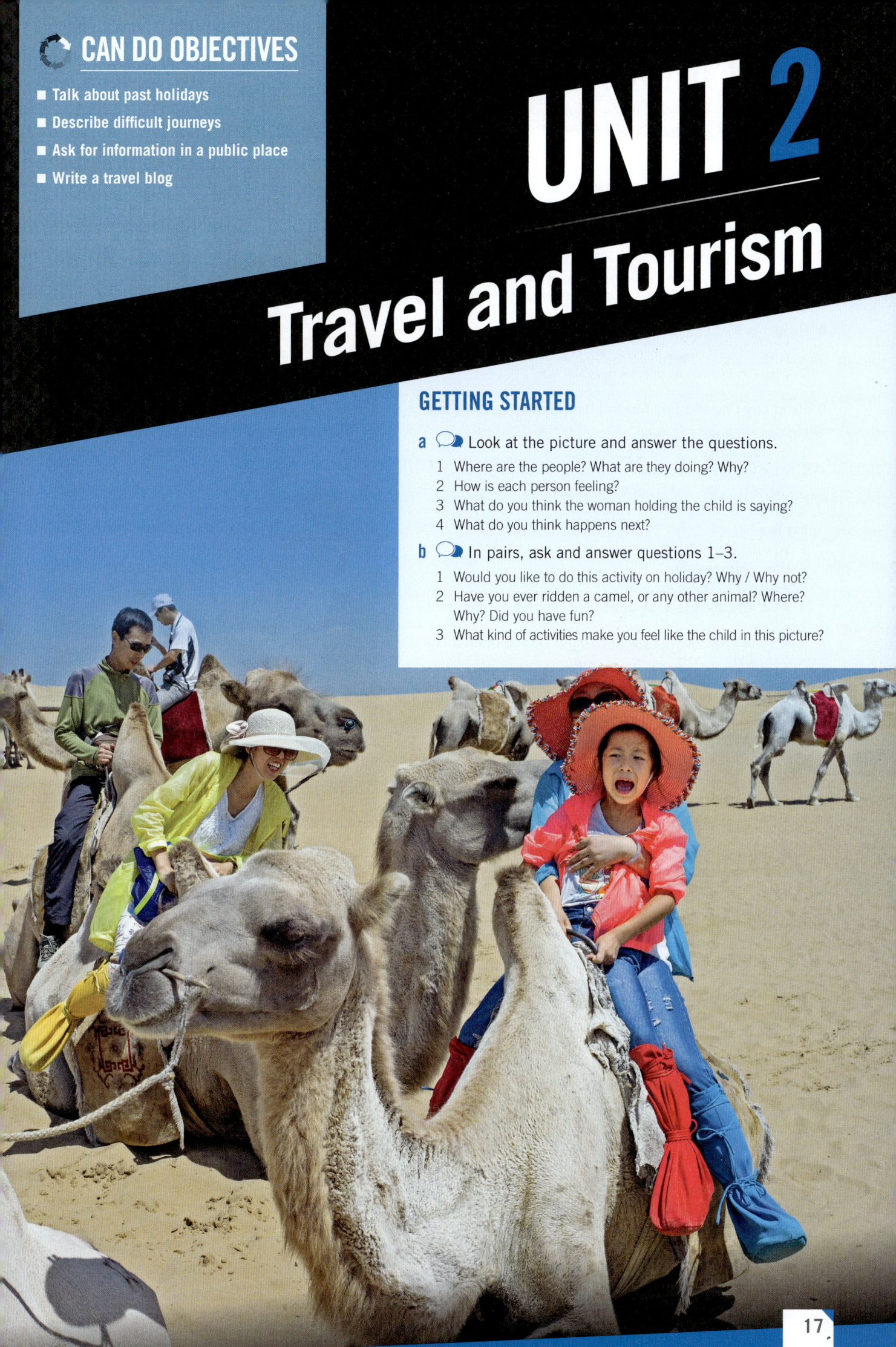

UNIT 2
Travel and Tourism

CAN DO OBJECTIVES
- Talk about past holidays
- Describe difficult journeys
- Ask for information in a public place
- Write a travel blog

GETTING STARTED

a Look at the picture and answer the questions.
1 Where are the people? What are they doing? Why?
2 How is each person feeling?
3 What do you think the woman holding the child is saying?
4 What do you think happens next?

b In pairs, ask and answer questions 1–3.
1 Would you like to do this activity on holiday? Why / Why not?
2 Have you ever ridden a camel, or any other animal? Where? Why? Did you have fun?
3 What kind of activities make you feel like the child in this picture?

17

2A We had an adventure

Learn to talk about past holidays
- G Past simple
- V Tourism

1 READING AND LISTENING

a Ask and answer the questions.
1 Where do you like to go on holiday?
2 Do you like to try new things on holiday? What?
3 Can you think of any kind of holiday you wouldn't enjoy?

b Read *Yes Man changed my life* and answer the questions.
1 What is Danny Wallace's book, *Yes Man* about?
2 What did Richard do after he read *Yes Man*?

c Read *Day One* and *Day Two* and then answer the questions.

Day One
1 Why did Richard go into the travel agent's?
2 What holiday did he book?
3 Did he book the kind of holiday he usually likes?
4 When was his flight?

Day Two
1 Why did Richard go to the beach?
2 How was the weather?
3 What did he buy at the beach?
4 What is he going to do on Day Three? How does he feel about it?

d Would you like to try water skiing? Do you think Richard will enjoy it?

e 1.23 Listen to Richard describing day three. Are sentences 1–5 true (*T*) or false (*F*)? Correct the false sentences.
1 The class began with a lesson before they went out to sea.
2 Richard felt fine when they went out on the boat.
3 He found it difficult to stand up on the water skis.
4 He hated water skiing.
5 When he got back to the hotel, he went to bed.

f Can you think of a time when you were surprised you enjoyed something?

2 GRAMMAR Past simple: positive

a Underline the past simple form of these verbs in the article.

| become | feel | decide | start | ask | do | change |
| have | want | get | see | sleep | go | arrive | give |

b Which verbs in 2a end in *-ed* in the past tense? How do the other verbs change?

You can find a list of irregular verbs on p.176

c Complete the sentences with the past simple form of the verbs in brackets.
1 I _____ as a waiter for a day, for no money. (work)
2 I _____ a day fishing with five Greek fishermen. (spend)
3 I _____ at a beach party until six in the morning. (stay)
4 I _____ a dancing competition. (win)
5 I _____ the same boat trip three times. (take)
6 I _____ swimming at midnight. (go)

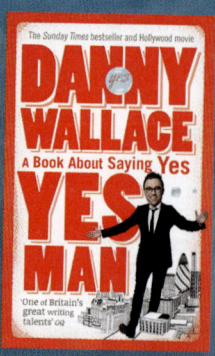

YES MAN CHANGED MY LIFE
by Richard Collins

Yes Man is the best book I've ever read. It's the true story of a year in the life of author, Danny Wallace. Before Danny Wallace became the 'Yes Man', his life was boring and he felt old. So he decided to make things more exciting. He started saying "yes" to every question people asked him. And he did it for a whole year. From the day he started, it completely changed his life and he had all kinds of adventures.
It's a fantastic story. When I finished the book, I wanted to change my life like Danny Wallace. So I took some holiday from work, and became a 'Yes Man' for a week. This is what happened.

3 LISTENING

a 1.24 Which of the activities in 2c do you think Richard enjoyed? Tell a partner. Listen and check.

b 1.24 Listen again. What is Richard's last question? Do you think he will say *yes* or *no*? Why?

c Ask and answer the questions.
1 Do you ever say yes when you don't want to? When?
2 Would you like to be a 'Yes Man' for a week? Why / Why not?

UNIT 2

Day One

I started on Saturday morning. At 10 am, I got my first question. I saw a poster in the window of a travel agent's. It said, "Tired?" (Yes – I slept badly the night before, so I was tired). Under this, it said, "Do you need a holiday?" (Yes, definitely.) So I went in. The travel agent asked me where I wanted to go. But before I could answer, she said, "Somewhere hot?"
I don't like hot weather, but I said, "Yes."
"A beach holiday? Maybe in Greece?"
I don't like the beach. I prefer cities. But I said, "Yes."
"What kind of accommodation? A hotel? Or a … "
I hate hotels, but before she could continue, I said, "Yes."
Five minutes later everything was ready. My flight was the next day.

Day Two

I arrived at my hotel on the island of Zante at lunchtime. It was very, very hot. I just wanted to check in and unpack my suitcase, but the receptionist said, "We have a minibus to the beach in ten minutes. Do you want to go?"
You know the answer I gave her.
It was about 40°C at the beach. Luckily, I brought suntan lotion. A man came towards me: "Sunglasses? Do you want sunglasses?"
I had some in my bag, but I said, "Yes."
Five minutes later, another man came: "Beautiful hat, sir?" I tried not to look at him.
Three hours later, I had two pairs of sunglasses, three hats, a watch and a woman's necklace.
It was difficult to carry all my new things back to the minibus.
I decided: no trips tomorrow, just rest. When I got back, the receptionist asked, "Did you like the beach?"
I didn't, but I said, "Yes."
"Oh, there's a water skiing course tomorrow. Do you want me to book a place for you?"
I can't swim very well and I don't like the sea. I wanted to cry …

4 GRAMMAR

Past simple: negative and questions

a Complete the sentences with the words in the box.

> was   didn't   did   weren't

1 Some of my experiences ____ very good.
2 I ____ like the mosquitoes that bit me.
3 ____ you have a good week?
4 What ____ your favourite thing?

b Look at the sentences in 4a and answer the questions about the past simple.
1 Which sentences include the verb *be*?
2 How do we make negatives and questions …
 • with the verb *be*?   • with other verbs?

c ▶ Now go to Grammar Focus 2A on p.144

5 PRONUNCIATION -ed endings

a ▶1.27 Listen and tick (✓) the verbs which have an extra syllable when we add -ed.

change	>	changed	□	play	>	played	□
need	>	needed	□	ask	>	asked	□
decide	>	decided	□	want	>	wanted	□
start	>	started	□				

b Complete the rule with two sounds.

> *-ed* endings are pronounced with an extra syllable /ɪd/ after ___ and ___ only.

c ▶1.28 Which of the verbs + -ed in the box have the extra /ɪd/ syllable? Listen and check.

| waited | included | arrived | looked | watched |
| shouted | smiled | stopped | ended | believed |

6 VOCABULARY Tourism

a 💬 What useful holiday items can you see on these pages? What else do people normally take?

b ▶ Now go to Vocabulary Focus 2A on p.133

7 SPEAKING

a Think of a holiday you enjoyed. Think about your answers to these questions.
• When did you go?
• Where did you go?
• Was it your first time?
• How long did you go for?
• Who did you go with?
• What kind of accommodation did you stay in?
• Did you do any sightseeing?
• Who did you meet?
• Did you bring back any souvenirs?

b 💬 Tell your partner about your holiday. Listen to your partner and ask questions.

19

2B Everyone was waiting for me

Learn to describe difficult journeys
- **G** Past continuous
- **V** Travel collocations

1 VOCABULARY Travel collocations

a 💬 Look at the list of ways to travel. Which do you prefer? Why?
- car
- bus
- train
- plane
- coach
- on foot

b 💬 Look at the travel problems in the pictures. Which situation do you dislike most?

c ▶ Now go to Vocabulary Focus 2B on p.134

2 LISTENING

a 💬 Look at the picture and the headline. What do you think happened?

Woman angry after flight in toilet

b ▶1.33 Listen to the woman describing her experience. Were your ideas in 2a correct?

c ▶1.33 Listen again. What does the woman say about … ?
- her journey to the airport
- boarding the plane
- what the flight attendant said
- what happened when she was in the toilet
- how she feels about what happened now

d 💬 Do you believe the woman's story? Why? / Why not?

20

UNIT 2

3 GRAMMAR Past continuous

a ▶1.34 Listen and complete the past continuous verbs in the sentences.
1 It _____ when I left the house.
2 When I boarded the plane, all the other passengers _____ for me.
3 I _____ my book, when one of the flight attendants spoke to me.
4 I _____ on the toilet when the turbulence started.

b Underline the past simple verbs in sentences 1–4 in 3a.

c Look at the sentences in 3a again and answer the questions.
1 Which action started first in every sentence? (past simple or past continuous?)
2 Think about when and why the past continuous action stopped in each sentence. Write the sentence numbers (1–4).
   The past continuous action
   … stopped because of the past simple action. ☐
   … stopped some time after the past simple action. ☐

d ▶ Now go to Grammar Focus 2B on p.144

e ▶1.36 **Pronunciation** Listen to the sentences. Notice which words are stressed.
1 It was <u>rain</u>ing.   4 We were <u>driving fast</u>.
2 It <u>wasn't rain</u>ing.   5 We <u>weren't driving fast</u>.
3 Was it <u>rain</u>ing?   6 Were we <u>driving fast</u>?

f ▶1.36 Listen to the sentences in 3e again. Do the vowel sounds in *was* and *were* sound the same in all the sentences?

g ▶1.37 Listen to five more sentences. Do you hear *was*, *wasn't*, *were* or *weren't* in each?

h Complete the sentences with the past continuous or past simple forms of the verbs in brackets.
1 The train *was leaving* (leave) the station, when I *realised* (realise) I was on the wrong train.
2 When I *was travelling* (travel) around Australia, I *lost* (lose) my passport.
3 I *was running* (run) for the bus when my bag *opened* (open) and all my things *fell* (fall) out.
4 I *was driving* (drive) to a family wedding when my GPS *stopped* (stop) working.
5 Someone *stole* (steal) my bag when I *was standing* (stand) in the queue for a ticket.

i 💬 Have you had any similar experiences to those in 3h?

> I lost my passport when we were moving house.

> What did you do?

4 READING AND SPEAKING

a 💬 Read the headlines and look at the pictures. What do you think happened to the travellers?

Did you mean Capri?
Swedish tourists miss their destination by 600 km

Coach passengers asked to get out and push

b ▶ **Communication 2B.** Student A: go to page p.127. Student B: go to p.128.

c 💬 Tell your partner your story. Use the questions to help you.
• Where were they going?
• How were they travelling?
• What was the problem?
• Who helped solve the problem? How?
• What happened in the end?

> Two Swedish tourists were on holiday in Italy. They …

d 💬 Which journey do you think was worse for the travellers?

e Think of a time you had a difficult journey. Think about your answers to these questions.
• Where were you going?   • What went wrong?
• How were you travelling? • What happened in the end?

f 💬 Work in small groups. Tell the group about your journey.

> When I was travelling to Florida, we waited for ten hours in the airport. Then they sent us to a hotel.

> Was it free?

g 💬 Who in your group has had the worst experience on … ?
• a plane   • a train   • a bus or a coach

21

2C Everyday English
What time's the next train?

Learn to ask for information in a public place
- **P** Joining words
- **S** Asking for more information

1 LISTENING

a 💬 What kind of information do people ask for in these places? Think of two kinds of information for each place.
- train stations
- tourist offices
- airports

b 💬 Look at the picture. Where is Annie? What information do you think she is asking for?

c ▶ 1.38 Watch or listen to Part 1 and check your ideas in 1b.

d ▶ 1.38 Watch or listen to Part 1 again. Answer the questions.
1 When does the next train to Birmingham leave? four minutes   every
2 How often do the trains leave? 30 mins
3 Which platform does the Birmingham train leave from? 12
4 Which day will Annie come back? Sunday
5 How much is Annie's ticket? £26.30
6 What does Annie want to get from the newsagent's? magazine

2 USEFUL LANGUAGE Asking for information in a public place

a ▶ 1.39 Match 1–6 with a–f to make questions from Annie's conversation. Then listen and check.
1 [d] What's time's
2 [e] How often
3 [c] Could you tell me where
4 [a] How much
5 [b] Can I
6 [f] Where can I

a is a ticket?
b pay by card?
c the ticket office is?
d the next train?
e do the trains leave?
f buy a magazine?

b ▶ 1.40 Listen and complete the questions the assistant asks.
1 Yes, how _can I_ help you?
2 Is there _anything else_ I can help you with?

c Complete the dialogue with words from the box.

| what time   where can I   can I   how much   could you tell me |

A Hi, ¹_could you tell me_ where the museum is, please?
B Yes, it's not far. It's by the river. Look on the map – here.
A I see. And ²_what time_ does it open?
B From 8 am till 4 pm.
A ³_how much_ is a ticket?
B For adults, it's £14.
A ⁴_where can_ I buy a ticket?
B I can sell you a ticket here, or you can buy one at the museum.
A Oh, I'll buy one here. ⁵_Can I_ pay by card?
B Of course – that's no problem.

d ▶ 1.41 Listen and check. Practise the dialogue.

3 PRONUNCIATION Joining words

a ▶ 1.42 Listen to the questions and look at the letters in **bold**.
- Where ca**n I** buy a magazine?
- How mu**ch i**s a ticket?

1 Underline the correct word to complete the rule.

> There *is* / *isn't* a pause between words when a consonant sound comes before a vowel sound.

2 What sound exactly do the letters in **bold** in each question make?

b Underline the letters and spaces where there isn't a pause.
1 Is anyone sitting here?
2 Could I sit next to you?
3 What are you reading?
4 Do you want a drink?
5 Where do you get off?
6 Can I have your email address?

c ▶ 1.43 Listen and check.

d 💬 In pairs, ask the questions in 3b and answer with your own ideas.

22

UNIT 2

4 CONVERSATION SKILLS
Asking for more information

a Look at the underlined phrases. Do the phrases show that the speaker wants to … ?
 1 end the conversation
 2 ask something else

ANNIE	<u>Sorry, just one more thing.</u>
ASSISTANT	Yes, of course.
ANNIE	Could you tell me where the ticket office is?
ASSISTANT	Is there anything else I can help you with?
ANNIE	<u>Actually, there is one more thing</u>. Where can I buy a magazine?

b ▶ 1.44 Listen to the phrases and repeat.

c 💬 Work in pairs. Student A: you are a tourist officer. Student B: you are a tourist in town. Use the dialogue below, and ask two more questions.

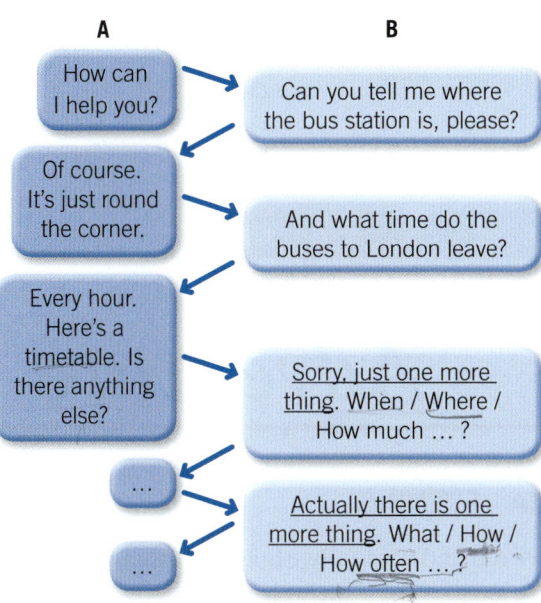

d 💬 Swap roles. Do the dialogue again.

5 LISTENING

a 💬 Look at the picture from Part 2. Why do you think Annie runs back to the assistant?

b ▶ 1.45 Watch or listen to Part 2 and check your ideas. What mistake did Annie make? What is her last question?

c 💬 Have you ever made a silly mistake like Annie? What happened?

6 SPEAKING

a ▶ **Communication 2C** Student A: go to 6b below. Student B: go to p.128.

Student A

b Look at Card 1. Think about what you want to ask.

① You need to book a train ticket.
 • 🕐 – first train to Manchester / in the morning?
 • how often / trains to Manchester?
 • £ two adult tickets?
 • pay by card?
 • where / leave luggage?
 • where / the waiting room?

c Listen to Student B and reply. Find out the information you need.

d Now look at card 2. Start the conversation with Student B. Say 'How can I help you?'

② You are a tourist guide in Warwick.
 • castle is in the centre of town
 • opening hours 10 am–6 pm
 • prices: adult £30.60, child £25.80
 • buy tickets at the castle or online
 • tours every hour
 • visitors can bring food, but many places to buy food

Unit Progress Test

CHECK YOUR PROGRESS

You can now do the Unit Progress Test.

23

2D Skills for Writing
This city is different, but very friendly

Learn to write a travel blog

W Linking: and / but / so / because / when

1 SPEAKING AND LISTENING

a 💬 Look at the pictures of Indonesia. Ask and answer the questions.
1 What can you see in the photos?
2 What do you know about Indonesia?
3 Have you been there? Would you like to go there? Why / Why not?

b ▶ 1.46 Listen to Karen talking to her nephew Tim about Indonesia. Answer the questions.
1 Why is Tim phoning Karen?
2 When did she travel to Indonesia?
3 Which of the things in the photographs (a–e) in 1a does Karen describe to Tim?

c ▶ 1.46 Listen again and answer the questions.
1 How is Tim planning to get to his hostel?
2 What were the problems with Karen's flight to Jakarta?
3 How does Karen describe Indonesian traffic jams?
4 How did Karen feel about the storms in Indonesia?
5 Why didn't Karen write a blog?

d 💬 Ask and answer the questions.
1 Do you write a blog or diary when you travel? Do you know someone who does?
2 Do you like reading other people's blogs? Why / Why not?

2 READING

a Read Tim's travel blog about arriving in Jakarta, Indonesia. Tick (✓) the topic he does not write about.
- his flight to Jakarta
- animals
- the weather
- the traffic
- the people
- food
- tourist places

MY BLOG | ABOUT ME

Indonesian Adventure

TUESDAY 22ND APRIL
JAKARTA – EVENING

We've arrived and it's really exciting! It was a long flight, but I slept most of the way, so I'm not tired. When I got off the plane, I noticed the heat first – 32 degrees! It's really humid, because this is the rainy season.
Everything they say about the roads in Jakarta is true! When we left the airport, there was a huge traffic jam. It took a very long time to get to the centre of town.
We got a taxi to the hostel (where we're staying). The taxi driver was very friendly, but he didn't speak much English. I just showed him the address of the hostel on a piece of paper and he brought us here. I think we paid him too much, because he seemed very happy when he drove away! Sam's telling me to get ready to go and eat, so I have to finish now – more tomorrow.

24

UNIT 2

b Read the blog again and answer the questions.
1 What did Tim do on the flight?
2 Why was the journey to the city centre slow?
3 Why did Tim think the taxi driver was happy?
4 What did he think of the food at the restaurant?
5 What did he see in the Old Town?

3 WRITING SKILLS Linking words

a Read the examples and answer the questions about the linking words in **bold**.
1 I slept most of the way, **so** I'm not tired.
2 **When** I got off the plane, I noticed the heat first.
3 It was really fresh **and** full of flavour.
4 The taxi driver was very friendly, **but** he didn't speak much English.
5 I decided to have *nasi goreng* **because** it's the Indonesian national dish.

Which word do we use to … ?
a say two things happen at the same time
b add a similar idea
c add a different idea
d give the reason for something
e give the result of something

b Find and underline more examples of the linking words in Tim's blog.

c Put *but*, *when*, *so* or *because* where you see ∧ in the sentences.
1 We were very tired, ∧ we went straight to bed.
2 ∧ we got to the hotel, I unpacked.
3 It was the middle of the night, ∧ the streets were completely empty.
4 The restaurant looked small and cheap, ∧ the food was amazing.
5 We gave the waiter $5 ∧ the service was excellent.
6 We ran into a shopping centre ∧ the storm began.
7 We went to the National Museum ∧ we wanted to understand more about the country's history.
8 We tried to check in, ∧ we were very early and the desk was closed.

4 WRITING

a You're going to write a blog. Choose one of the topics.
• a holiday experience
• your first day doing something new (for example, starting a new course or job)
• a new place you visited recently

b Make notes. Think about:
• where you were
• how you felt
• what you saw and did
• who you talked to

c Write your blog. Use some linking words from 3a.

d Work in pairs. Read your partner's blog. Do they use linking words? Is it similar to your blog?

WEDNESDAY 23RD APRIL
JAKARTA – THE NEXT DAY!

Sam and I had a delicious meal last night in a small local restaurant – we were the only tourists there, so it seemed to be a place for local people. I decided to have *nasi goreng* because it's the Indonesian national dish. It was really fresh and full of flavour. I felt tired when I got back to the hostel and fell asleep immediately.
Today we visited the Old Town. There are lots of old buildings in different styles. They're very attractive and very different from anything you see in the UK. I took a lot of photos …

UNIT 2
Review and extension

1 GRAMMAR

a Complete the sentences with the past simple forms of the verbs in the box.

ask   not get   learn   meet   need   not spend   wear

1 We _____ a lot of money, because everything was very cheap.
2 She _____ the bus driver for directions.
3 I _____ to change my ticket before I got on the train.
4 I _____ the bus home, because I didn't have any money.
5 He _____ his new shirt to the party.
6 _____ you _____ any interesting people on holiday?
7 I _____ how to surf when I lived in California.

b Choose the correct verb forms.

I had a terrible journey. I [1]*walked / was walking* to the train station and it started raining. And then the train was twenty minutes late. When it [2]*came / was coming*, I [3]*found / was finding* a seat by the window. Some girls [4]*played / were playing* music on their mobiles, but it was great music. That was OK, but I [5]*read / was reading* my book when the train [6]*arrived / was arriving* at the next station. Two people got on and a man [7]*sat / was sitting* down next to me and he started talking loudly on his mobile. He [8]*told / was telling* someone about his new car, his job – everything! He was still talking when the train [9]*got / was getting* in to the station.

2 VOCABULARY

a Match the clues (1–5) to the words.

| suntan lotion   sunglasses   backpack   foreign currency |
guidebook   map   passport   suitcase

1 You wear or use these two things when it's sunny.
2 This is money from another country.
3 These two things give you ideas of where to go.
4 You normally need this to travel internationally.
5 You pack clothes in these two things when you go away.

b Complete the sentences with the verbs in the box.

| change   check out   do   get |
go away   set off   travel around

1 We hope to _____ the world next year.
2 You need to _____ a visa if you want to visit China.
3 You will have time to _____ some sightseeing later.
4 You need to _____ trains at Frankfurt for Berlin.
5 We want to _____ for the weekend later this month.
6 We _____ very early, because our train was at 6.30 am.
7 We need to _____ of our hotel before 10 am.

3 WORDPOWER off

a Match the general meanings of *off* (a–c) with the groups of sentences (1–3).

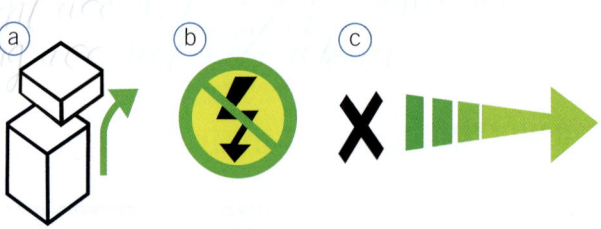

1 We booked an early ferry, so we **set off** at 5 am.
   OK, **I'm off**. My train leaves in ten minutes.
   The traffic lights turned green and they **drove off**.
   I asked a man for directions, but he just **walked off**.
   The plane **took off** half an hour early.

2 The airline has 20% **off** tickets to New York.
   He **fell off** the chair and hurt his back.
   Can you **cut off** a piece of that cheese for me?
   Why don't you **take off** your coat? It's not cold here.

3 I hate it when people don't **switch off** their phones in the cinema.
   I tried to call him, but his phone **was off**.
   I was tired, so I **turned off** the TV and went to bed.

b Match sentences (1–8) with replies (a–h).

1 There's 10% off if you buy today.
2 Is that your phone? What happened to it?
3 Why is it so cold in here?
4 When are you off?
5 Can I try some of that sausage?
6 Can you turn off the radio, please?
7 We took off an hour late.
8 So, do you know who hit your car?

a It fell off the table.
b Of course. I'll cut off a piece for you.
c Great! I'll take two, please.
d In five minutes.
e What time did you land?
f No, they drove off before I saw them.
g No. I'm listening to it.
h The heating's off.

c 💬 Work in pairs. Cover a–h in 3b and try to remember the replies.

⟳ REVIEW YOUR PROGRESS

How well did you do in this unit? Write 3, 2 or 1 for each objective.
3 = very well   2 = well   1 = not so well

I CAN ...

Talk about past holidays   ☐
Describe difficult journeys   ☐
Ask for information in a public place   ☐
Write a travel blog   ☐

26

CAN DO OBJECTIVES

- Talk about experiences of generosity
- Talk about spending and saving money
- Talk to people in shops
- Write an update email

UNIT 3
Money

GETTING STARTED

a 💬 Look at the picture and answer the questions.
  1 What kind of shop are the people in? What products does it sell?
  2 What is the relationship between the people? What do you think they are saying to each other? What do you think happens next?

b 💬 Which shops do you like to go into? Are there any kinds of shop you dislike? Do you think men and women shop differently? Why / Why not?

c 💬 What are your three favourite things to spend money on? Here are some ideas:

- fashion
- holidays
- education
- beauty
- food and drink
- charity
- health
- home
- something else?

Explain your answers to a partner.

27

3A Have you ever helped a stranger?

Learn to talk about experiences of generosity
- G Present perfect or past simple
- V *make / do / give* collocations

1 READING

a 💬 Look at the picture. What are the people doing? How do you think they're feeling? Why?

b 💬 Read about Generosity Day. Do you think it's a good idea? Would you like to try it? What would you like to do?

c Read the *Share the LOVE* forum. Which people mention … ?
- helping other people
- receiving help from other people

What kind of help did each person mention?

d Work in pairs. Read the text again. What do the highlighted words and phrases mean?

e 💬 Which writer in the forum do you think is the most generous? Why?

GENEROSITY DAY

Everyone knows that 14 February is Valentine's Day, a day when people spend money on cards, flowers and romantic meals for the people they love. But did you know that 14 February is also Generosity Day? It's a chance to do something nice for someone you don't know. For example, buy a stranger a coffee, smile at ten people you see on the street or give someone who looks sad a hug! So this year, why not do something a bit different?

Share the LOVE

Home   About   Message board   Search

Have you ever done something nice for a stranger? What did you do?
Has a stranger ever helped you in any way? Write and let us know.

1 SALLY_TM
POSTS 102
Last week while I was running, I fell and hurt my knee quite badly. A few moments later, an older woman stopped in her car. She helped me to stand up and drove me to the corner shop to get some ice. Then she waited until my husband came to get me. It was the nicest thing `a stranger` has ever done for me.

2 @HELPHAITI
POSTS 1024
I have been to Haiti three times to `do volunteer work` and I am paying for a young man to finish his high school there. He's doing really well. He just needed someone to give him a chance. I am not rich, but with my credit card anything is possible.

3 NEIL50
POSTS 24
On my fiftieth birthday, I was in a queue in a café and I noticed that everyone looked really stressed. I decided to buy drinks for everyone in the queue and I `gave the waitress a big tip`, too. It was great to see everyone's faces – I `made them all smile`!

4 THATGEORGEKID
POSTS 2868
Strangers have helped me lots of times, and I've helped them too. I've `given people directions`, I've picked up hitchhikers … A few weeks ago, I made a new friend when I called 999. I saw this guy lying on the street and I tried to wake him up, but I couldn't. The ambulance came and he's OK now. He thinks I'm `a hero`, but I just did what was right.

5 MAYA_FLOWER
POSTS 67
I've never seen a serious accident, so I've never had the chance to `save someone's life`, like George. But I often help strangers: for example, I buy meals for `homeless` people and I `give away` my old clothes to charity. I try to be generous in small ways that don't cost anything, like listening to people when they are lonely, or making a joke when people look bored.

28

2 GRAMMAR
Present perfect or past simple

a Complete the sentences with the verbs in the box. Check your answers in the forum.

> saw   do   decided   been   done   seen

1 I have _____ to Haiti three times.
2 A few weeks ago, I _____ a man lying in the street …
3 I've never _____ a serious accident.
4 On my fiftieth birthday, I _____ to buy drinks for everyone.
5 Have you ever _____ something nice for a stranger?
6 What did you _____ ?

b Which sentences in 2a are present perfect? Which are past simple?

☐☐☐ present perfect   ☐☐☐ past simple

c <u>Underline</u> the time expressions in the sentences in 2a. Complete the rules with the time expressions from the sentences.

> We can use the present perfect to talk about past experiences in our whole lives, not at a particular time. We often use adverbs like _____ _____ _____
>
> We use the past simple to talk about a particular time in the past. We often use time phrases like _____ _____

d ▶ Now go to Grammar Focus 3A on p.146

e Complete the questions with present perfect and past simple forms of the verbs in brackets.

1 _____ you ever _____ anything for a charity? (do)
  What _____ you _____ ? (do)
2 _____ you ever _____ a stranger somewhere? (drive)
  Where _____ you _____ them? (drive)
3 _____ you ever _____ food for a homeless person? (buy)
  What _____ you _____ for them? (buy)

f ▶1.48 Listen and check. Ask and answer the questions with a partner.

3 VOCABULARY
make / do / give collocations

a Complete the phrases with the verbs make, do or give.

1 _____ a friend   3 _____ volunteer work
  someone smile   something nice
  a joke   well (at school/work)
2 _____ someone directions
  something away
  someone a tip
  someone a hug

b Check your answers to 3a in the Generosity Day text and forum. Try to guess the meaning of new phrases. Check your ideas in a dictionary.

c 💬 Which of the things in 3a have you done this week?

> I haven't given anyone directions.
>
> I gave my sister a hug this morning.

4 LISTENING

a ▶1.49 Read the information about Philip Wollen and answer the questions.
1 What was Philip Wollen's job?
2 Why did he leave his job?
3 What do you think Philip Wollen has done with his money?
Listen and check your answer to question 3.

Philip Wollen was once a very successful banker. However, after he became rich, he had a life-changing experience. On his fortieth birthday, he left his job in banking and decided to give away all his money. It is Philip's ambition to spend all his money before he dies.

b ▶1.49 Listen again and answer the questions.
1 What size are the charities that Philip helps?
2 How many charities has he helped?
3 How did the Morning Star orphanage begin?
4 How did Philip's money help Morning Star?
5 What does the Morning Star's first child do now?
6 What kind of animals do Edgar's Mission help?
7 What do they try to teach people?

c 💬 Would you like to give money to the Morning Star or Edgar's Mission? Why / Why not?

5 SPEAKING

a 💬 You are going to find out about the generosity in your class. Walk around the class and find someone who has done each thing in the grid. Ask more questions.

buy something for a stranger	carry a heavy bag for a stranger
send someone a surprise gift	leave a big tip in a restaurant
smile at a stranger to make them smile	take a lost object back to the owner
do volunteer work	help someone who was hurt
give money to charity	show the way to a lost stranger
pay for all your friends' food or drinks	give away something you like to a friend

> Have you ever bought something for a stranger?
>
> Why did you buy him a ticket?
>
> Yes, I have. Once I paid for a man's train ticket.
>
> He needed to get home to his family.

b 💬 What was the most generous thing you heard?

UNIT 3

29

3B I've already spent my salary this month

Learn to talk about spending and saving money
- G Present perfect with *just*, *already* and *yet*
- V Money

current account / pay interest on
saving account / a loan

1 VOCABULARY Money

a 💬 Do you think saving money is easy? Why / Why not?

b Work in pairs. Read the saving tips. What do the highlighted words and phrases mean?

c ▶ Now go to Vocabulary Focus 3B on p.135

2 READING AND SPEAKING

a Read *What kind of spender are you?* and choose the answers (a, b or c) which are true for you.

b 💬 In pairs, compare your answers. Are they similar?

c 💬 Check your results on p.130. Do you agree with the results?

---

www.moneythings.co.uk

SAVING TIPS

Maureen, Wigan
"Always look for special offers on food in the supermarket and go shopping for clothes during the sales."

Paul, Brighton
"Don't lend money to people – sometimes they don't pay it back!"

Jane, Manchester
"Open a second bank account and put some money into it every month."

WHAT KIND OF SPENDER ARE YOU?

1 What do you think about credit cards?
a They're great. I can buy what I want even when I don't have any money.
b They can be useful if you are careful with them.
c They're a bad idea. It's better not to have them.

2 You want to go on holiday. What's the best idea?
a Forget about the cost. Holidays are only once a year!
b Look around for special offers on the Internet.
c Go just for two or three days and sleep in a tent.

3 You've lost your camera. What do you do next?
a Buy a new one. It was a bit old anyway.
b Look for a good second-hand one.
c Use the camera on your mobile phone.

4 You're at the supermarket check-out. Which statement is true for you?
a Your basket is full of expensive food for dinner tonight!
b You have fifteen packs of coffee. It was on offer!
c You've chosen the basic things and nothing more.

5 Do you know how much money you have in the bank?
a Not really. If my credit card works, then I'm happy.
b Not exactly, but I know I have enough for the month.
c Yes, of course. I checked my balance five minutes ago.

6 Are you a saver?
a What do you mean?
b I save about 10% of my money every month.
c I save all my spare money every month.

Do you agree

30

3 LISTENING

a 💬 Look at the pictures of the three people. Who do you think is a ... ?

- [3] big spender
- [2] non spender
- [1] smart spender

1   2   3

b ▶ 1.51 Listen to the people being interviewed. Check your ideas in 3a. What has each person bought?

c ▶ 1.51 Listen again and answer the questions about each speaker.
1 What is he/she saving for? food save car
2 How does he/she feel about borrowing money? always save generally he doesn't like it. never lend money

d 💬 Look at the ideas from the listening. Do you agree with the speakers? Do you agree
1 'I don't want to owe money to a bank.' 2
2 'Everyone should save for when they're older.' 2
3 'Life's too short to worry about money!' 3

4 GRAMMAR We've just taken

Present perfect with just,

a Complete the sentences with the past
1 I've **just** bought my food for the week. (bu
2 I've **already** spent my salary this month.
3 I **haven't** paid it back **yet**. (pay)

b ▶ 1.52 Listen and check. What tense

c Look at the sentences in 4a. Then co
already and *yet*.
Use ~~just~~ already to say something is complete,
we expected. just
Use ~~already~~ just to say something happened a short time ago.
Use *not* + yet to say something is not complete.

d ▶ Now go to Grammar Focus 3B on p.146

e ▶ 1.54 **Pronunciation** Listen to how the following words spelt with *j* and *y* are pronounced. Then listen again and repeat.

/dʒ/	/j/
just	**y**et
enjoy	**y**ou
join	**y**oung

f ▶ 1.55 Put the adverbs in brackets in the correct places in the sentences. Then listen and check.
1 I've spent a lot of money on a new pair of glasses. (just)
2 I've bought a new mobile last month, but I've lost it. (already)
3 I need some winter clothes, but I haven't had time to go shopping. (yet)
4 I've bought a card for Mother's Day. (already)
5 I've bought some amazing shoes last year, but I haven't worn them. (yet)
6 I've seen a special offer on a holiday online, but I haven't decided to buy it. (just, yet)

g Change four sentences in 4f to make them true for you.

h 💬 Compare your sentences with a partner.

> I've just spent a lot of money on my phone bill.

> Really? I've just spent a lot of money on my car. It broke down.

---

you can
could
should   haggle
would
must
will

to be able
يستطيع، يقدر على

UNIT 3

31

3C Everyday English
Do you have anything cheaper?

Learn to talk to people in shops
- P Sentence stress
- S Changing your mind

1 LISTENING

a 💬 Do you enjoy going shopping? Which of these things do you like shopping for? Why?
- food • gifts • clothes • books

> I like shopping for clothes. It's fun.

> I hate it. I think it's really boring, but I like buying books.

b 💬 Look at the pictures of Mark and Rachel shopping. What do you think they are shopping for?

c ▶1.56 Watch or listen to Part 1 and check your ideas.

d 💬 In pairs, look at the products 1–4. Answer the questions.
1. What do you think each product is used for?
2. Would you buy any of the products for someone you know?
3. Would you like to receive any of them as a present?

e ▶1.57 Watch or listen to Part 2. Which of the products in the pictures do they buy?

f ▶1.57 Watch or listen again. Answer the questions.
1. Why does Mark think 'Football in a tin' is a good present?
2. Why does Rachel disagree about the 'Football in a tin'?
3. Why doesn't Mark like the weather station?
4. Why does Mark decide not to buy the book money bank?

g 💬 Work in pairs. What do you think of the present they chose? Do you think Leo will like it?

2 USEFUL LANGUAGE
Talking to people in shops

a ▶1.58 Complete the phrases from Part 2 with the words in the box. Then listen and check.

| anything | sort | cheaper | looking |
| take | do | help | show |

1. Can I _help_ you?
2. We're _looking_ for a present for a friend.
3. Are you looking for _any_ in particular?
4. What _sort_ of thing does he like?
5. What does it _do_ ?
6. Do you have anything _cheaper_ ?
7. Could you _show_ us something else?
8. We'll _take_ it.

b Answer the questions about the phrases in 2a.
1. Which phrases did the shop assistant say?
2. Which phrase explains why they are in the shop?
3. Which phrases mean they want to see another product?
4. Which phrase asks for information about a product?
5. Which phrase means 'We want to buy this one'?

32

UNIT 3

3 PRONUNCIATION
Sentence stress

a ▶1.59 Listen to the sentences. Notice the stress.
1 This looks perfect.
2 We're only here for Leo.

b ▶1.59 Listen again. Answer the questions.
1 How many syllables does each sentence have?
2 How many stressed syllables does each sentence have?
3 Do we say the unstressed syllables in sentence 2 quickly or slowly?

c ▶1.60 Listen and complete the sentences. The missing words are all unstressed.
1 I'd like to look at a different one.
2 Can you show me the first one again?
3 I'm looking for a present for my brother.
4 Do you have this in a different size?
5 It'll cost a lot of money to fix.

4 USEFUL LANGUAGE
Paying at the till

a ▶1.61 Watch or listen to Part 3. What does Mark change his mind about?

b ▶1.61 Watch or listen again. Complete the questions with the words in the box.

| put your   receipt   enter your |
| you like   next, please |

1 Who's next please?
2 How would you like to pay?
3 Can you put your card in, please?
4 Can you enter your PIN, please?
5 Here's your receipt.

c 💬 Practise the conversation from Part 3. Take turns to be the shop assistant and the customer (Mark).

5 CONVERSATION SKILLS Changing your mind

a Look at the underlined phrases in the sentences. Do the two phrases mean the same or are they different?
On second thoughts, I really think we should get something sporty.
Actually, I think I'll put it on my credit card.

b 💬 Work in pairs. Take turns to change your mind. Start with I'd like.
1 a coffee – a cup of tea
2 take the bus – get a taxi
3 a sandwich – a salad
4 go for a drive – go for a walk
5 watch TV – put some music on
6 a first-class ticket – a normal ticket

> I'd like a coffee.
> OK.
> On second thoughts, I'd prefer a cup of tea.
> Fine.

6 SPEAKING

▶ **Communication 3C** Work in groups of three. Students A and B: you are buying a present – go to p.130. Student C: you are a shop assistant – go to p.127.

Unit Progress Test

CHECK YOUR PROGRESS

You can now do the Unit Progress Test.

33

3D Skills for Writing
We've successfully raised £500

Learn to write an update email
W Paragraphing

1 LISTENING AND SPEAKING

a 💬 Look at the names of the charities. What do you know about the charities? What do they do?

Match the charities with the sentences.

This charity …
1 protects animals and the environment.
2 protects historic buildings, gardens and the countryside.
3 helps people in poorer countries.

What other large charities do you know? What do they do?

b 💬 Work in pairs. How do people raise money for charity? Add ideas to the list.
– collect money in the street
– sponsor someone to do a sports event, for example, run a marathon
– make and sell food, e.g. cakes at work or school

c ▶ 1.62 Listen to four people talking about giving money to charity. Do they support a charity? Which one?
1 Shona   2 Jack   3 Jessica   4 William

d ▶ 1.62 Listen again. Why do/don't the people in 1c support a charity? How do they help? Listen and make notes.

e Work on your own. Make notes on these questions.
1 What charity do you prefer to give money to? Why?
2 Have you ever raised money for charity? What did you do? Who gave you money?

f 💬 Work in small groups. Talk about your answers to 1e.

UNIT 3

2 READING

a Anita and her team at work support the National Trust. Read Anita's email. Why is she sending the email? Tick the correct reasons.

1. ☐ to say thank you
2. ☐ to apologise
3. ☐ to tell people how much money they have raised
4. ☐ to tell people about how the team raised money
5. ☐ to tell people about what the National Trust do
6. ☐ to ask people for money

Hello everyone,

(a) We'd like to thank everyone for their help over the past few months raising money for the National Trust. We've successfully raised £500.

(b) Most of you know one of the ways we raised money, because you bought our cakes every Wednesday! But we'd just like to let you know about the different things we did. We also sold our old books, DVDs and clothes online. And, every Friday, we each paid £1 to wear casual clothes to work.

(c) The National Trust will use the money to repair historic buildings and keep them open for the public to visit. It's interesting to see how people lived in the past – some of the rooms and furniture in these buildings are beautiful. Visiting a historic building is a really enjoyable thing for a family to do at weekends, and another way to help the National Trust continue their excellent work.

(d) Thanks again for all your help. Please look out for our next event.

Anita Webb (and team)
Resources Manager

b Read the email again and answer the questions.
1. How did the team raise £500?
2. How will the National Trust spend the money?
3. What is another way Anita's colleagues can help the National Trust?

3 WRITING SKILLS Paragraphing

a Match the descriptions with paragraphs a–d in Anita's email.
1. ☐ closing the email
2. ☐ the introduction
3. ☐ how the team raised money
4. ☐ information about the National Trust

b What information does Anita include in the introduction? What does she mention in the closing paragraph?

c Put the paragraphs below in the correct order to make an email.

☐ Oxfam will use the money on projects around the world to help people have happier and healthier lives. Last year, they helped 13.5 million people. A small amount of money can make a big change. For example, just £15 can give free health care to a mother and her baby.

☐ Many of you have bought tickets to our 'Quiz and Pizza' nights. Others gave their unwanted clothes to the very successful 'Clothes Market' in March. We really hope you enjoyed these events. Your money and time will help Oxfam to continue their important work.

☐ Would you like to help us raise more money for Oxfam? Just email me and I'll tell you what we're planning next. Thanks again for all your help.

☐ This email is to say a big 'Thank you!' to everyone who has helped us to raise money for Oxfam over the last few months. We have now raised £750.

4 WRITING

a Choose one of these emails to write.
1. Write about a real experience of raising money for charity. Write to the people who gave you money to thank them. Tell them about how much money you raised, how you raised the money and about the charity.
2. You and some friends have raised £1,000 for a charity at work/school. Write to everyone who helped you to say thank you. Tell them about how much money you raised, how you raised the money and about the charity.

b Plan the email. Use four paragraphs. What information will you put in each paragraph?

c Write the email.

d Swap emails with a partner. Read your partner's email. Are there four paragraphs in the email? What information is in each paragraph?

35

UNIT 3
Review and extension

1 GRAMMAR

a Put the words in the correct order to make questions.
1 you / bought / ever / have / something you didn't need ?
2 given / you / a stranger / have / money / to ?
3 ever / to / a very expensive restaurant / have / you / been ?
4 ever / driven / you / an expensive car / have ?
5 lost / ever / you / money / have / on the street ?

b 💬 Ask and answer the questions in 1a.

c Complete the text with the present perfect forms of the verbs in the box.

do   go   have   help   raise   run   spend

My colleague Andrea is really generous. She ¹_____ a lot of work for charity. She ²_____ two marathons and from that she ³_____ lots of money for different charities. She ⁴_____ some time in foreign countries – she ⁵_____ to India to help build a school. At work, she ⁶_____ me a lot when I ⁷_____ problems.

d Put the adverb in brackets in the correct place.
A Have you spoken to John? (yet)
B Yes, he's called me. (just)
A Did you ask him about the party?
B Yes, he's bought the food. (already)
A Great. I haven't been to the shops. (yet)
B Have you decided what music to play? (already)
A Yes, I've made a list. (just)

e 💬 Practise the exchange in 1d.

2 VOCABULARY

a Complete the sentences with the words in the box.

directions   hug   joke   something   volunteer

1 My mum was very upset, so I gave her a _____.
2 I gave the woman _____ to the tourist office.
3 I want to do some _____ work for a charity this summer.
4 He made a _____ and everyone laughed.
5 I always try to do _____ nice at weekends.

b Match questions (1–5) with answers (a–e).
1 ☐ Can you lend me ten euros?
2 ☐ How did you afford your new car?
3 ☐ What are you saving up for?
4 ☐ Did you get a discount on your new bike?
5 ☐ Have you got the money you owe me?

a A new laptop. I want to buy one in the sales.
b Sorry, no. I just spent it on my electricity bill.
c I got a loan!
d No, you won't pay me back!
e Yes, it was on special offer.

3 WORDPOWER just

a Look at the different meanings of just (in 1–4). Read the example sentences. Match the meanings of just in sentences a–d with meanings 1–4.
1 ☐ = a short time ago
I've just got home from work. I need a rest!
2 ☐ = only
He doesn't understand money. He's just a child.
3 ☐ = almost not
I ran to the station and I just caught my train.
4 ☐ = soon
Hang on! I'm just coming.

a The tickets cost just a few dollars.
b I'm just finishing this email – I'll be ready in one minute.
c Sorry, he's just left – he was here a minute ago.
d You can just see the sea from my window, but it's very far away.

b Match sentences (1–5) with replies (a–e).
1 ☐ She looks just like her sister.
2 ☐ I think the books cost just under £10.
3 ☐ The flight is three hours long.
4 ☐ I've just about finished my work.
5 ☐ Look at that rain.

a Yes, they're £9.80. I checked.
b Yes – we got home just in time!
c That's good. We need to leave in five minutes.
d Really? It was just over two hours when I went.
e Of course – they're twins!

c Complete the sentences with expressions from 3b.
1 Michele leaves home at 8 am and arrives at work at 8.25. It takes him _____ half an hour to get there.
2 Steven looks _____ his brother – they're both tall and they've both got black hair.
3 I normally arrive _____ when I get a train or plane. I never arrive early!
4 My electricity bill is always _____ €50. This time it's €51.20.
5 The new university building is _____ ready – we'll have our lessons there next month.

d 💬 Work in pairs. Make sentences about your life with the expressions in 3b.

◌ REVIEW YOUR PROGRESS

How well did you do in this unit? Write 3, 2 or 1 for each objective.
3 = very well   2 = well   1 = not so well

I CAN ...

Talk about experiences of generosity ☐

Talk about spending and saving money ☐

Talk to people in shops ☐

Write an update email ☐

CAN DO OBJECTIVES

- Talk about your plans for celebrations
- Plan a day out in a city
- Make social arrangements
- Write and reply to an invitation

UNIT 4
Social Life

GETTING STARTED

a Look at the picture and answer the questions.
1 What country do you think the people are from? Why are they together? How are they feeling? What are the relationships between the people?
2 What food can you see? Who do you think prepared it? What other activities do you think they'll do on this day?
3 Who is speaking? What are they saying?
4 Which guests are missing from this picture? Where are they? What do you think they're doing?

b In pairs, describe a typical wedding photograph from your country.

4A I'm going to the hairdresser's tomorrow

Learn to talk about your plans for celebrations
- **G** Present continuous and *going to*
- **V** Clothes and appearance

1 VOCABULARY Clothes and appearance

a Look at the pictures on these pages. Answer the questions with a partner.
1. What clothes and accessories can you see?
2. Would you like to wear any of the clothes?
3. Are there any clothes that you would never wear? Why?

b Now go to Vocabulary Focus 4A on p.135

2 LISTENING

a Look at the pictures of Marta and Craig below. What events are they at? What are they doing in the pictures?

b 1.65 Work in pairs. Read sentences 1–6. Do you think Marta or Craig is speaking? Write *M* or *C*. Listen and check.
1. ☐ We're going to stay the whole night – until they serve breakfast!
2. ☐ This year one of my favourite DJs is playing.
3. ☐ They're going to make a special cream from turmeric.
4. ☐ I'm not going to see Monisha until the ceremony begins.
5. ☐ I'm meeting the others at 7 pm so we can start queuing.
6. ☐ My friends are arriving early tomorrow to help me get ready.

c 1.65 Listen again and answer the questions.
1. Why does the college organise the May Ball?
2. What is special about Marta's dress?
3. Why is Marta going to stay at home on Saturday?
4. What happens at the end of the May Ball?
5. What are Craig's guests going to do with the special cream?
6. When do the wedding day celebrations start and finish?
7. How does Craig describe the clothes he's going to wear?
8. What happens at the beginning of the wedding day?

d Ask and answer the questions.
1. What's the biggest party you've ever been to?
2. What's the best wedding you've ever been to?

3 GRAMMAR
Present continuous and *going to*

a Read the sentences. Are Craig and Marta talking about the present or the future?
1. My friends **are arriving** early tomorrow.
2. I**'m not going to leave** the house on Saturday.
3. I**'m going to stay** the whole night.
4. A beautician **is doing** our make-up.

b Look at the verb forms in **bold** in the sentences in 3a. Answer the questions with present continuous or *going to*.
1. Which sentences are about future plans with other people?
2. Which future plans are just ideas, not already arranged?

c Now go to Grammar Focus 4A on p.148

d 1.67 **Pronunciation** Listen to five speakers. Which speakers pronounce *going to* /ˈɡəʊɪŋ tə/? How do the other speakers say it?

e Answer questions 1 and 2 for each future time in the box.

> today   this week   this weekend
> this summer   this month   next year

1. What are your plans? Who are they with?
2. Have you arranged anything yet?

f Tell your partner about your plans.

> I'm going to Brazil this summer.
>
> When are you going?

Marta at the University of Cambridge May Ball

Craig at his Indian wedding

LIFE IN NUMBERS

VIETNAM

Imagine sharing your birthday with the whole country! That's exactly what happens every year in Vietnam. The Vietnamese don't celebrate on the day they were born. Instead everyone gets one year older on the same day – Vietnamese New Year's day or 'Tet'. People don't give birthday presents, but children receive red envelopes with money inside. Children greet older people with the phrase, 'Long life of 100 years!'

Tet is the biggest celebration of the year in Vietnam – and it can last for a week. Everyone takes to the streets to make as much noise as they can and there are fireworks and lion dances.

LATIN AMERICA

Becoming an adult is a very special day for girls in South America and it happens on their fifteenth birthday – the Quinceañera.

In some places, such as parts of Mexico, the father or another relative gives the girl her first pair of high heels as a symbol of becoming a woman. The birthday girl, or quinceañera, often gives out fifteen candles, one to each of the fifteen most important people in her life.

Then there is a meal and dancing. The quinceañera's first dance is always with her father.

JAPAN

In Japan everyone has a day off to celebrate the world's biggest twentieth birthday party.

The second Monday of January every year is 'Coming of Age Day' or 'Seijin no hi' – the day all twenty-year-old Japanese become adults.

Men wear suits and girls dress in beautiful kimonos, which they often have to rent or borrow because they're so expensive. A ceremony is held in the local government office and afterwards the new adults can party with their friends and family.

THE UK

Your 100th birthday is a big day in any country, but it's even more special in the UK – you get a card from the Queen! Don't forget to let her know though – the Queen is a busy woman, so you or your family should apply before the big day.

Each card she sends contains a personal greeting – when twins reach 100 years old together, each one gets a slightly different message. The oldest person who has ever received a birthday card from the Queen was 116 years old.

4 READING

a 💬 Ask and answer the questions.

1. Do you celebrate your birthday? What do you do?
2. Do people in your country celebrate any specific ages? Which ones?

b Read the article. What do the numbers refer to? (Sometimes there is more than one possible answer.)

1 15 20 100

c Read the article again and answer the questions.

For which celebration do people … ?
1. wear clothes they can't afford to buy
2. need to request something
3. both give and receive something
4. have a party that goes on for several days
5. wear special shoes
6. not go to work so they can celebrate

d 💬 Work in pairs. Answer the questions.

1. Which celebration in the text did you find most interesting? Why?
2. What other celebrations are important in your country? Which is your favourite?
   - weddings
   - local festivals
   - family celebrations
   - work/school/university events
   - birthdays
   - religious festivals and new year

5 SPEAKING

a Work on your own. Write down three events you are going to in the future. Use the list in 4d for ideas.

1. *My best friend's wedding in August*
2. *21st September – Grandfather's 80th birthday*

b 💬 Now work in a small group. Ask each person questions. Try to guess the three events they are going to. (You can't ask: *What is the event?*)

When is the event happening? — *In August.*
Who are you going with? — *I'm going with my boyfriend.*
What are you going to wear?

4B Shall we go to the market?

Learn to plan a day out in a city
G will / won't / shall
V Adjectives: places

1 LISTENING

a 💬 Ask and answer the questions.
1 What do you know about Tokyo? Have you ever been there? Would you like to go? Why / Why not?
2 Look at the places 1–5 in *Tokyo Highlights*. Which would you like to visit?

b ▶1.68 Mike is visiting his friend Harry in Tokyo for one day. Listen and answer the questions.
1 Which places in *Tokyo Highlights* do they decide to visit?
2 Which three other places do they decide to visit?

c ▶1.68 Listen again and answer the questions.
1 Why do they decide not to go to the Imperial Palace?
2 How does Harry describe the noodle restaurant?
3 Why do people do *cosplay*?
4 Why is Akihabara a good place for Mike's shopping?
5 Where will they do karaoke?
6 Why does Harry want to go to the fish market at night?

d 💬 Do you think they chose good places to visit? Did they choose any places you would not like to visit?

2 GRAMMAR will / won't / shall

a ▶1.69 Listen to the sentences. Complete the sentences with the words in the box.

'll   won't   shall

1 So we _____ go to Disneyland then!
2 _____ we start with something to eat?
3 **M** I want to look for a new camera.
   H I _____ take you to Akihabara, then.
4 Don't worry – you _____ miss your flight!
5 _____ I come to your hotel in about an hour?

b Are Mike and Harry talking about the present or the future? What are the full forms of *'ll* and *won't*?

TOKYO HIGHLIGHTS

1 Go to the top of Tokyo Tower for a great view of the city

c Match the sentences in 2a with the uses of *will* and *shall*. Write the numbers.

We use *will* and *won't* to:
☐ make promises
☐ ☐ make decisions while we are speaking

We use *shall* to:
☐ make offers
☐ make suggestions

d ▶ Now go to Grammar Focus 4B on p.148

e ▶1.72 **Pronunciation** Listen to the sentences. Is the vowel in **bold** pronounced /ɒ/ or /əʊ/?
1 I w**a**nt to visit the museum.
2 We w**o**n't have time to see everything.

f ▶1.73 Listen to the sentences. Circle the correct answers.
1 We *want to / won't* come back next year.
2 They *want to / won't* stay in the same hotel again.
3 I *want to / won't* go for a walk in the park.
4 They *want to / won't* see the market.
5 You *want to / won't* find a table at that restaurant.
6 I *want to / won't* take you to see the castle.

g ▶1.73 Listen again and repeat.

h ▶ **Communication 4B** Work in pairs. Student A: go to p.128. Student B: go to p.129.

2 Enjoy a day out at Disneyland Tokyo

3 Walk around the beautiful Yoyogi Park and see people doing cosplay

4 Visit Kyokyo – the Imperial Palace

5 Go shopping in Akihabara

3 VOCABULARY
Adjectives: places

a Look at the sentences. What are the opposites of the highlighted adjectives? Choose the adjectives in the box.

tiny   quiet   ugly

1 The palace is nice but it's so crowded. _____
2 It's a huge park so it's always really nice. _____
3 Everyone goes to look at the pretty flowers. _____

b Match the opposite adjectives.

1 ☐ modern   a peaceful
2 ☐ high   b wide
3 ☐ indoor   c ancient
4 ☐ magnificent   d outdoor
5 ☐ narrow   e low
6 ☐ noisy   f ordinary

c ▶1.74 Listen and check. Underline the stressed syllables.

d ▶1.74 Listen again. Repeat the words.

e 💬 Work in a small group. Think about places you all know. Can you think of one place for each adjective in 4b?

There's an outdoor swimming pool near the river.

The market in the town centre is really noisy.

4 LISTENING

a ▶1.75 Listen to Mike and Harry's conversation. What was Mike's favourite part of the day?

b ▶1.76 Listen to the last part of the conversation. What is the problem? What does Harry suggest?

c 💬 Would you stay another day? Why / Why not?

d 💬 Are there any cities in another country that you would like to visit? Is there any city you would like to live in? Which?

5 SPEAKING

a Your partner is going to visit you for one day in a city you know well. Make notes on:
• places to visit   • where to eat   • what to do in the evening

b 💬 Student A: describe the places to your partner.
Student B: choose which places you want to visit. Agree on a plan for the day. Then swap roles.

Shall we go to an art gallery first?

I don't really like art galleries.

OK – I'll take you to the National Cinema Museum. It's huge.

That sounds good.

c 💬 Describe each day out to the class. Vote for the day out you like the most.

4C Everyday English
Are you doing anything on Wednesday?

Learn to make social arrangements
- P Sentence stress
- S Making time to think

1 LISTENING

a 💬 Do you make arrangements with people by phone? What kind of things do you arrange?

b ▶1.77 Watch or listen to Part 1. Why does Annie call Rachel?

c ▶1.77 Watch or listen again. Answer the questions.
1 Why can't Rachel come on Wednesday? *meeting friend*
2 What is she doing on Thursday? *work*
3 Which day do they agree to have the meal? *on monday*
4 What time do they decide? *dinner*
5 What does Annie want Rachel to bring? *Nothing*

2 USEFUL LANGUAGE
Making arrangements

a Look at the phrases. Which phrases are for inviting? Which are for responding to invitations? Write I (inviting) or R (responding).
1 [I] Would you like to come round for a meal?
2 [I] Are you doing anything on Wednesday?
3 [R] We can't do Wednesday.
4 [I] How about Thursday? Is that OK for you?
5 [R] This week's really busy for us.
6 [I] What are you doing on Monday?
7 [R] What time shall we come round?
8 [R] Would you like us to bring anything? *No, nothing*

b ▶1.78 Listen to how Rachel and Annie replied to each question. Make notes. What different replies could you give?

c ▶1.79 Complete the gaps with words from the box. Listen and check.

> how about   shall I   are you doing (x 2)
> is that OK   would you like   can't do   busy

A ¹*Are you doing* anything tomorrow? ²*would you like* to come round for a coffee?
B I ³*can't do* tomorrow. ⁴*How about* the weekend? ⁵*is that OK* for you?
A No, the weekend's really ⁶*busy* for me. What ⁷*are you* on Monday next week?
B Nothing – I'm free. What time ⁸*what time shall I* come round?
A Any time in the morning.

d 💬 Work in pairs. Practise the conversation in 2c. Change the details.

> Are you doing anything on Friday? Would you like to go to the cinema?

> I can't do Friday.

3 CONVERSATION SKILLS
Making time to think

a Look at the examples from Part 1. Underline the phrases Rachel uses to give herself time to think.
1 Oh, that sounds nice. I'll just check. No, we can't do Wednesday. Sorry.
2 Thursday … hang on a minute … no, sorry.
3 Just a moment … Nothing! We can do Monday.

b ▶1.80 Listen and repeat the phrases in 3a.

c 💬 Work in pairs. Take turns to make an invitation. Check your phone / diary before you reply. Use the phrases in 3a.

> Do you want to come to the cinema on Saturday?

> Saturday … hang on a minute … yes, that would be great!

UNIT 4

4 LISTENING

a ▶ 1.81 Look at the pictures. Where are they? Do you think Leo likes his present? Watch or listen to Part 2 and check your ideas.

b ▶ 1.81 Watch or listen again. Answer the questions.
1 Why does Mark want to go for a run tomorrow?
2 What does Rachel find out about Leo?
3 What do Mark and Leo arrange to do and when?

c 💬 Ask and answer the questions.
1 Do people in your country usually open their presents when the giver is there? Why / Why not?
2 Do you ever receive presents you don't like?
3 Do you think you are good at choosing presents for people?

5 PRONUNCIATION Sentence stress

a ▶ 1.82 Listen to two sentences from Part 1. Answer the questions.
We can do Monday.
We can't do Wednesday.
1 Which word is stressed more – *can* or *can't*?
2 Is the vowel in *can't* long or short?

b ▶ 1.83 Listen to the sentences. Complete the rule.
I <u>don't</u> really <u>like</u> <u>sport</u>.
I <u>can't</u> <u>stand</u> <u>football</u>.
You <u>really</u> <u>didn't</u> <u>need</u> to.

Negative auxiliary forms are *sometimes* / *always* stressed.

c ▶ 1.84 Listen and repeat.
1 I can't do next week.
2 We don't have time.
3 I won't be late.
4 I could see you tomorrow.
5 We didn't go to the party.
6 We can come at six o'clock.

6 SPEAKING

a ▶ Communication 4C Work in pairs. Student A: go to 6b below. Student B: go to p.129.

Student A

b You want to invite Student B for dinner one evening. Look at your diary. Complete your diary with plans for three evenings. Decide what you want Student B to bring to the dinner.

c 💬 Call and invite Student B to dinner. Arrange an evening for dinner. Try to arrange it this week. If you can't, arrange it for next week. Tell Student B what to bring.

🔄 **Unit Progress Test**

CHECK YOUR PROGRESS

You can now do the Unit Progress Test.

43

4D Skills for Writing
Are you free on Saturday?

Learn to write and reply to an invitation
W Inviting and replying

1 SPEAKING AND LISTENING

a How often do you do the things in this list? Who do you do them with?
- have a party
- go out for a coffee or a meal
- go out and do something (for example, see a film)
- do sport (for example, go swimming or play football)
- invite people for a meal at your home
- go for a walk

b Which of the activities in 1a do you do to … ?
- celebrate a birthday
- celebrate the end of term
- meet new friends
- spend time with old friends
- spend time with colleagues

c ▶1.85 Listen to three people. What is each person going to do this weekend?
1 Susanna
2 Barbara
3 Sven

d ▶1.85 Listen again and answer the questions.

Susanna
1 Why doesn't Susanna like parties at home? *I don't like having a lot of stress*
2 Where is she going to celebrate her 21st birthday?
3 What is she going to wear?

Barbara
4 Why doesn't Barbara like cooking for people at home?
5 Why does she prefer cooking things together?
6 What's Barbara going to make for the barbecue on Saturday?

Sven
7 What does Sven say people do at parties?
8 What does he prefer to do with friends? Why?
9 What is he going to do at the lake?

e Which person are you most similar to? Why?

2 READING

a Barbara sent emails inviting people to her barbecue. Read the emails and answer the questions.
1 Has Barbara seen Martina recently?
2 When is the barbecue?
3 What do Martina and Bill need to bring to the barbecue?

b Who do you think Barbara sees more often? How do you know?

Hi Martina,

How are you? We haven't seen you for ages! Hope you're well and you're enjoying your new job. This is just to say that we're having a barbecue at the weekend. Are you free on Saturday and, if so, would you like to come? People are going to arrive around eight o'clock. Everyone's bringing something for the barbecue. Do you think you could bring something?

It would be lovely to see you and have a chance to chat.

Best wishes,

Barbara

Inbox

Hi Bill,

How are things? I hope the cycling trip went well – you had good weather for it!

Are you doing anything on Saturday evening? We're having a barbecue and inviting a few people. Can you come? It'd be great to see you!

Everyone is bringing something. We'll make some salads, but could you bring some meat for the barbecue?

Love,

Barbara

44

UNIT 4

3 WRITING SKILLS Inviting and replying

a Look at the emails in 2a again and complete the table.

Type of phrase	Email to Martina	Email to Bill
Asks how the other person is	1 How are you?	5 How _____ ?
Asks if he/she is free	2 Are you _____ on Saturday?	6 Are you _____ on Saturday?
Invites him/her	3 _____ to come?	7 _____ come?
Says she wants to see him/her	4 It _____ to see you.	8 It'd _____ to see you!

b Read the replies to Barbara's emails. Which is from Martina and which is from Bill? How do you know? Who is coming to Barbara's BBQ?

Hi Barbara,

Nice to hear from you. Yes, I'm fine, but I'm very busy. The job's great, but I have to work very long hours. Thanks for inviting me on Saturday. I'm free that evening and I'd love to come. Is it OK if I bring my daughter, Stephanie? We don't eat meat, but we'll bring some vegetables for the barbecue.

I'm looking forward to seeing you and having a good chat.

All the best,

Hi Barbara,

Yes, we had a great time, but my legs still hurt! I'm really sorry, the BBQ sounds great, but I'm afraid I can't come. Thanks for asking. I'd love to, but I'm staying with my sister at the weekend.

See you soon anyway. Hope you have a nice time!

xx

c Underline the phrases in the replies that each person uses to:
1 say thank you
2 say yes to an invitation
3 say no to an invitation
4 give a reason
5 talk about the next time they'll meet

d Correct the mistakes in each of the sentences. Use the emails in this lesson to help you.
1 You like to come to my birthday party?
2 Thanks that you invited me to your wedding.
3 It's afraid I can't go to the cinema with you.
4 I love to come, but I'm busy that weekend.
5 I'm looking forward to see you tomorrow.

4 WRITING

a Work in pairs. You are organising an activity at the weekend. Write an invitation to another pair of students. Include these points:

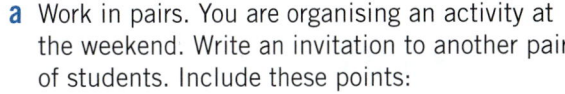
- ask them how they are
- invite them to come
- say where and when the event is
- tell them what they need to bring

b Swap invitations with another pair. Write a reply to the invitation. Include these points:

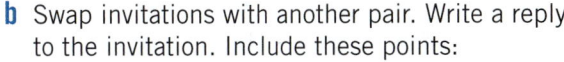
- say thank you
- decide if you can go (If you can't go, give a reason.)
- add a comment or a question

c Give your reply back to the other pair. Look at their invitations and replies. Have they included these points?

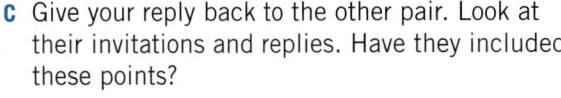
- said clearly where and when the event is
- used the correct language for the invitation
- used the correct language to reply to the invitation

45

UNIT 4
Review and extension

1 GRAMMAR

a Complete the sentences with the correct form of *going to* and the verbs in the box.

buy   go   travel   meet   not take   watch

1 I ___ a film at the cinema soon.
2 They ___ around South America this summer.
3 Síle and Sean ___ on holiday by the sea next summer.
4 I ___ an English exam this year.
5 She ___ something from the shops after work.
6 We ___ some friends for lunch tomorrow.

b Complete the conversation with the present continuous forms of the verbs.

A ¹___ (you / do) anything this Saturday?
B I'm ²___ (go) to my sister's in the evening. She ³___ (have) a party. I ⁴___ (not do) anything in the afternoon.
A Great! I ⁵___ (have) a barbecue. Do you want to come? Tina and Matt ⁶___ (come).
B Sounds good! Do you want me to bring anything?
A Well, I ⁷___ (make) vegetarian food. Is that OK?
B Yes, that's great.

c 💬 Practise the conversation in 1b.

d Complete the text messages with *will*, *won't* or *shall*.

> Hi! I'm almost at the cinema. ¹___ (I / get) the tickets when I arrive. ²___ (I / get) you something to eat or drink? Try to be on time …
>
> Hi. ³___ (I / have) a lemonade please. ⁴___ (I / eat) something later. ⁵___ (we / go) for coffee after the film? I promise ⁶___ (I / be) late!

2 VOCABULARY

a Where do these clothes and accessories go on the body? Write the correct numbers.

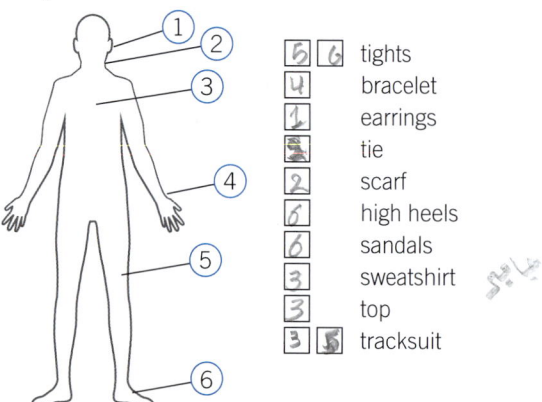

5/6	tights
4	bracelet
1	earrings
2	tie
2	scarf
6	high heels
6	sandals
3	sweatshirt
3	top
3/5	tracksuit

b 💬 Talk about the clothes and accessories you are wearing.

3 WORDPOWER *look*

a Match the words in bold (1–5) with definitions (a–e).

1 We're really **looking forward to** our holiday in Florida.
2 I'm **looking after** my friend's cat while he's on holiday.

3 I didn't know the address, so I **looked** it **up** online.
4 He doesn't **look** very well – maybe he's got a cold.

5 I was only in the city an hour, so I didn't have time to **look around**.

a ☐ visit a place and see the things in it
b ☐ appear, seem
c ☐ feel happy and excited about a future event
d ☐ try to find information in a book or on a computer
e ☐ give a person or animal what they need

b Choose the correct answers.

1 I really like looking *after / up* young children.
2 I'm really looking *after / forward to* the weekend.
3 I always look *up / out* a film online before I see it.
4 I spend too much time looking *at / to* social media sites.
5 I always look *for / to* special offers when I go shopping.
6 I *look / look like* tired when I don't get much sleep.
7 I love looking *around / up* clothes shops.

c 💬 Work in pairs. Which of the sentences in 3b are true for you?

⟳ REVIEW YOUR PROGRESS

How well did you do in this unit? Write 3, 2 or 1 for each objective.
3 = very well   2 = well   1 = not so well

I CAN …

Talk about your plans for celebrations	☐
Plan a day out in a city	☐
Make social arrangements	☐
Write and reply to an invitation	☐

CAN DO OBJECTIVES

- Talk about what people do at work
- Talk about your future career
- Make offers and suggestions
- Write a job application

UNIT 5
Work

GETTING STARTED

a ▶ 2.2 Look at the picture of people at work. What do you think their jobs are? Listen and check your ideas.

b 💬 What are the good things about their jobs? What are the bad things?

c 💬 Why is the man stretching his arms up? What do you think he's saying to his colleague?

d 💬 Work in pairs. Have a conversation using your ideas in c. Take turns being the man stretching his arms and his colleague.

47

5A I have to work long hours

Learn to talk about what people do at work
G must / have to / can
V Work

THE HAPPIEST JOBS

We spend most of our time at work. When we're not there, we're probably thinking about it. But what makes us happy at work? And which workers are the happiest? Here are twelve of the happiest and least happy jobs in the UK, according to the City & Guilds 'Career Happiness Index'.

% AGREEING THEY ARE HAPPY AT WORK		
1 _____	😊😊😊😊😊😊😊😊😊	87%
2 _____	😊😊😊😊😊😊😊😊	79%
plumbers	😊😊😊😊😊😊😊	76%
scientists	😊😊😊😊😊😊	69%
doctors and dentists	😊😊😊😊😊😊	65%
lawyers	😊😊😊😊😊😊	64%
3 _____	😊😊😊😊😊	62%
teachers	😊😊😊😊😊	59%
4 _____	😊😊😊😊😊	58%
electricians	😊😊😊😊😊	55%
IT workers	😊😊😊😊	48%
5 _____	😊😊😊😊	44%

1 VOCABULARY Work

a 💬 Look at the photographs. Which jobs can you see?

b 💬 Work in pairs. Make a list of as many jobs as you can. You have one minute.

c ▶ Now go to Vocabulary Focus 5A on p.136

2 READING

a 💬 Work in pairs. Read the first part of the article: *The Happiest Jobs*. Where do you think these jobs go in the list?

bankers   gardeners   hairdressers   nurses   accountants

b 💬 Check your ideas on p.127. Are you surprised? Why? / Why not?

c 💬 What do you think makes people happy at work? Make a list of ideas with a partner.

d Read the second half of the article. Was your list correct?

e 💬 Work in pairs. Answer the questions.
1 Do you know anyone who does any of the jobs in the article? How do they feel about their job?
2 Which job in the article is the most similar to your (future) job?
3 Did anything in the article surprise you? Was there any information that you already knew?
4 Do you think the results would be the same in your country? Why / Why not?

THE HAPPIEST WORKERS: WHY THEY'RE HAPPY

So what makes us happy at work? What you do in your job and where you do it is very important:
* 89% of gardeners feel their work is important and useful. Only 35% of bankers feel the same.
* 82% of gardeners said they use their skills every day, compared to only 35% of bankers.
* 89% of gardeners said they like their working environment, but only 24% of bankers said the same.

The people we work with matter:
* The most important thing of all is that other people value your work. 67% of all workers put this first.
* Most workers said that good relationships with colleagues are important. Scientists get on best with their colleagues (90%).

More money doesn't make us happier:
* 61% of workers said that it is very important for them to earn a good salary, but …
* Workers who earn over £60,000 a year are the unhappiest.
* Self-employed people earn less but are much happier at work (85%) than people who work for a company.

PLUMBERS
74% think their work is important and useful.
67% use their skills every day.

HAIRDRESSERS
Only 7% are unhappy in their jobs.
86% get on well with their colleagues.

GARDENERS
89% think their work is important and useful.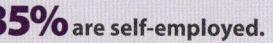
35% are self-employed.

48

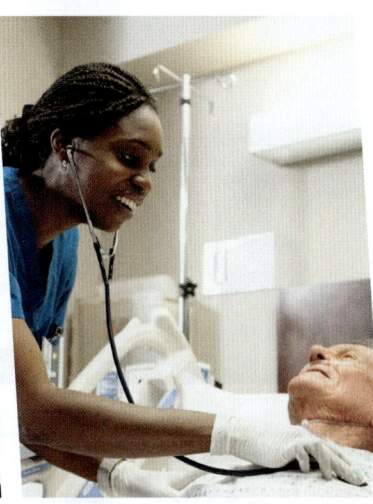

UNIT 5

4 GRAMMAR must / have to / can

a Look at the sentences. Match the underlined words with the meanings.

1 To become a nurse you have to do well at school.
2 You don't have to wear a suit or go to many meetings.
3 You can't relax because if something goes wrong, you lose money.

a _____ = this is not necessary
b _____ = this is not allowed or not possible
c _____ = this is necessary

b Compare the written rules from John and Alisha's workplaces with the things they said. Complete the rules below.

> Nurses must not lift patients without another nurse present.

> You can't lift a patient on your own.

> You always have to switch off the mains power.

> Electricians must switch off the mains power before they start work.

In written English, we use:
_____ to say that that something is necessary
_____ to say that something is not allowed or is not possible

c ▶ Now go to Grammar Focus 5A on p.150

d 💬 What do you have to do if you work in these places? What can't you do?

• office   • restaurant   • bank   • school

> In a school, you can't leave children on their own.

> Yes, and you have to wear a suit.

e Write rules for the people who work in each place in 4d. Use *must* and *must not*.

Teachers must not leave children on their own.
Teachers must wear a suit.

5 SPEAKING

a 💬 Choose five of the jobs from the list. Think of three advantages and three disadvantages for each job.

• scientist   • lawyer   • accountant   • electrician
• IT worker   • engineer   • nurse   • pilot
• police officer   • receptionist   • secretary

b 💬 Which job do you think is the hardest? Which job is the most interesting?

> Receptionists don't have to have a university degree. And they can find a job quite easily.

> But they have to work long hours. And they don't earn a good salary.

3 LISTENING

a 💬 What do you think these people like about their jobs?

1 Alisha, nurse
2 John, electrician
3 Miriam, banker

b ▶2.5 Listen to Alisha, John and Miriam and check your ideas in 3a.

c ▶2.5 Listen again and answer the questions about each person's job.
1 What qualifications, experience and other abilities are necessary for the job?
2 What is difficult about the job?

d 💬 Which of the three jobs would you prefer to do? Why? Would you be good at it?

49

5B I might get a job today!

Learn to talk about your future career
G will and might for predictions
V Jobs

1 SPEAKING

a What can you do if you need a job? Where can you go? Who can you speak to?

b Match the worries 1–3 with the situations in the pictures.
1 ☐ I'll say something stupid on my first day.
2 ☐ I won't find a job I'll enjoy.
3 ☐ They'll ask me really difficult questions.

a looking for a job

b having a job interview

c starting a new job

c Have you ever had any of the worries in 1b? Tell a partner.

2 LISTENING

a ▶2.9 Listen to three people talking about finding work. Where are they? Who is the most positive about finding work? Who is the least positive?

Sara

Marco

Kate

b ▶2.9 Read the predictions each speaker made. Listen again. What reasons do they give for each prediction?
Sara
1 It won't be easy to find a job I'll enjoy.
2 I don't think I'll get an interview.
Marco
3 I'm sure I'll make some really useful contacts.
4 I might get a job today!
Kate
5 I might not get my perfect job.
6 I'm sure I'll find some kind of work.

c Have you ever been to a careers fair? What was it like?

3 GRAMMAR
will and *might* for predictions

a Look at the sentences in 2b again. Then underline the correct word to complete the rule about *will* and *might*.

> We use *will* and *might* to make predictions about the future.
> *will* and *won't* are *more* / *less* sure than *might* and *might not*.

b ▶ Now go to Grammar Focus 5B on p.150

c Write a positive response to each worry in 1b. Then compare with other students. Whose responses are most positive?

I won't find a job → You might find something
I'll enjoy.   really interesting.

d ▶ **Communication 5B** If your partner has got a job: go to p.130.
If your partner does not have a job: go to p.128.

50

Planning a safe future career

4 VOCABULARY Jobs

a 💬 Find the jobs in the photos on the page.
- ☐ computer programmer
- ☐ carer
- ☐ shop assistant
- ☐ postman
- ☐ builder

Do you know anyone who does these jobs?

b ▶ Now go to Vocabulary Focus 5B on p.136

c ▶ 2.13 **Pronunciation** Listen to the words. How does the speaker say the consonant sound /ʃ/ in the part of the words in **bold**?

musi**c**ian   politi**c**ian   **sh**op assistant

d ▶ 2.14 Listen to the words. Which words have the /ʃ/ sound? <u>Underline</u> the letters.

qualification   question   information
machine   experience   change

e Practise saying the words in 4c and 4d.

5 READING

a 💬 Look at the jobs in the photos. Answer the questions with a partner.
1. Which jobs do you think might disappear in the future?
2. Which jobs do you think there will be more of in the future?

b Now read the article and check your ideas in 5a.

c Read the article again. What will happen because of these things?
- online shopping
- sending emails
- digital photos
- 3D printers
- environmental problems
- living longer
- studying online

6 SPEAKING

a 💬 Work in small groups. Look at the predictions. Do you think these things will happen in your lifetime? Why / Why not?
1. 3D printers will make parts of buildings or whole buildings.
2. People won't print photos any more.
3. There won't be many shops.
4. There won't be any huge offices. People will generally work at home.
5. Companies will pay the bosses less and other staff more.
6. A normal working week will have four days, not five.

b Work alone. Write three new predictions.

c 💬 Read your predictions to your group. Do they agree?

Choose your future career carefully – experts are predicting big changes in the jobs we'll do in the next ten or twenty years. Some jobs might disappear, but others will become more important.

The Internet will have a big effect. People already choose to do a lot of their shopping online, so there won't be as many shops, and there won't be many jobs for shop assistants. Some postmen and other post office staff might lose their jobs, because people will send everything by email.

Another job that might disappear because of technology is photo processors – the people who print photos. This is because most of us keep our photos on our computers now and never print them. Also, there might not be as many jobs for builders as there are today. 3D printers will soon make parts of buildings or even whole buildings in just a few hours.

So which jobs are safe?

- **Computer programmers** – a hundred years ago there were none, but now there are lots of them and there will be even more in future because almost all jobs will need computers.
- **Environment protection officer** – there will be a lot of new 'green' jobs as environmental problems get more serious.
- **Carers** – people will live longer and we'll need carers to look after us in old age.
- **Online education manager** – many students will take online courses. There will be jobs for people to create and organise the courses.

And of course, we will still need **actors** and **musicians** to entertain us, **lawyers** to argue and **politicians** to make the big decisions.

5C Everyday English
I'll finish things here, if you want

Learn to make offers and suggestions
- **P** Sentence stress: vowel sounds
- **S** Reassurance

1 LISTENING

a 💬 When was the last time someone asked you for help? Who was it? What did he / she ask?

b 💬 Look at the picture of Rachel and read the text message. How is she feeling? Who is the text from? What's the problem?

c ▶ 2.15 Watch or listen to Part 1. Answer the questions.
1 What does Tina think Rachel should do for Annie?
2 What does Tina offer to do?
3 Why is Rachel worried about leaving early?
4 How are they going to deal with the problem?

d 💬 What would you do in Rachel's situation? Would you call Annie or go and see her? Why?

2 CONVERSATION SKILLS Reassurance

a ▶ 2.15 Watch or listen again. Match the sentences with the responses.
1 ☐ But I can't leave you here on your own.
2 ☐ We've still got so much to do.
3 ☐ It means you won't be able to leave early today.
4 ☐ OK, well if you're sure.

a **Never mind**.
b Of course. **It's no problem**.
c I'll be fine! **Don't worry about it**.
d Oh, **it doesn't matter**.

b ▶ 2.16 Why do you think Tina uses the expressions in **bold** in a–d? Listen and repeat the phrases.

c 💬 In pairs, look at situations 1–6. Take turns to apologise for the problems. Respond with expressions a–d in 2a.
1 You can't help your partner this weekend.
2 You lost your partner's book.
3 You have to cancel the dinner party.
4 You don't have the money you owe your partner.
5 You can't come to the cinema tonight.
6 You're going to be late for the party.

> I'm really sorry, but I can't help you this weekend. I have to work.

> Oh, it doesn't matter.

3 LISTENING

▶ 2.17 Watch or listen to Part 2. Which jobs will Tina do before she goes home?
1 ☐ finish off the flowers
2 ☐ start the order for Mrs Thompson
3 ☐ start the order for the birthday party
4 ☐ put the alarm on
5 ☐ take out the rubbish
6 ☐ take the order for the wedding

4 USEFUL LANGUAGE
Offers and suggestions

a ▶2.18 Listen and complete the sentences.
1. ☐ _____ finish things here, if you want.
2. ☐ Why _____ you tell me what we still need to do?
3. ☐ _____ I finish off those flowers?
4. ☐ Would you _____ me to prepare some of the orders for tomorrow?
5. ☐ You _____ start with that order for Mrs Thompson.
6. ☐ Maybe you _____ start on the order for that big birthday party.
7. ☐ Do you want _____ to take out the rubbish when I leave?
8. ☐ How _____ taking her some flowers?
9. ☐ Why _____ I deal with this?

b Look at the sentences in 4a again. Mark them O (offer) and S (suggestion).

c Work in pairs. What offers and suggestions could you make in situations 1–4? Use the phrases and your own ideas.

I'll …   Why don't I / you … ?   Shall I … ?
Would you like me to … ?   Maybe you should …
How about … ?   Do you want me to … ?

1. It's raining. Your friend has to walk to the station, but doesn't have an umbrella.
2. Your colleague has to write a report for her boss before the end of the day. There's not enough time.
3. Your friend wants to go for a meal. You don't like the restaurant he suggests.
4. You see a tourist. She's lost her bag and doesn't have any money.

Why don't I drive you to the station?

How about getting a taxi?

5 PRONUNCIATION
Sentence stress: vowel sounds

a ▶2.19 Listen to the phrases from 4a. Are the highlighted modal verbs stressed?
1. **Shall** I finish off those flowers?
2. **Would** you like me to prepare some of the orders for tomorrow?
3. You **could** start with that order for Mrs Thompson.
4. Maybe you **should** start on the order for that big birthday party.

b ▶2.19 Listen again. Which vowel sound do you hear in each of the modal verbs?

c Practise saying the sentences in 5a.

6 SPEAKING

a Work in groups of four. Choose one of the two events to organise.

A work meeting

- book meeting room
- arrange hotel for guest from advertising company
- book taxis for colleagues from other office
-
-
-

A surprise birthday party for a friend

- buy food and drink
- make and send invitations
- book somewhere for the party
-
-
-

b Work with a partner in your group. Look at the list of things to do for the event you chose. Add three more things.

c Work in your group again. Now you have to organise the event. Make offers and suggestions to decide which person in your group will do which job.

Shall I book a meeting room?

OK, why don't you call a hotel?

Would you like me to buy the food?

Sure. How about going to the supermarket?

Unit Progress Test

CHECK YOUR PROGRESS

You can now do the Unit Progress Test.

5D Skills for Writing
I am writing to apply for a job

Learn to write a job application

W Organising an email

a

We're looking for keen young people to work in our cafés. No experience necessary – we'll give you the training you need to become a barista!

Contact us at www.cubacoffee.com and send us your CV.

b Q.net ✓ Situation Vacant

Students required to work for a market research company. Interview people in the street or on the phone in our offices. Good pay – work when you want to.

Visit our website at www.customer-Q.net

c electrostores

Sales assistants wanted to sell mobile phones in our superstores. Earn 10% on every phone you sell. Find us at www.electrostores.com/mobiles

Free training programme.

d Saveco

Weekend and summer jobs for students

Join our team and earn money. General assistants required for checkout and meat and fish counters. Good pay and conditions.

Contact: reply@saveco.com

1 SPEAKING AND LISTENING

a 💬 Have you ever had a summer job or a part-time job? What was it? Did you enjoy it?

b 💬 Read the job adverts. Which jobs in the adverts could these sentences describe?
1 ☐ You have to start early in the morning.
2 ☐ You need to be good with money.
3 ☐ You need to like working fast.
4 ☐ It's nice because you can talk to people.
5 ☐ You have to be good at explaining things.
6 ☐ You can earn extra money from tips.

c 💬 Work in pairs. Answer the questions about the jobs in the adverts.
1 Which job would you most like to do? Why?
2 Which job would you least like to do? Why?
3 Which job would you do best? Why?

d ▶ 2.20 Listen to two students, Penny and John, and answer the questions.
1 Which jobs in the adverts are they talking about?
2 Do they like the jobs? Why / Why not?

e ▶ 2.20 Listen again and choose the correct answers.
1 John *has / hasn't* worked in the café before.
2 John *likes / doesn't like* working quickly.
3 John *sometimes / always* makes £20 in tips.
4 Penny *has / hasn't* worked in a café before.
5 Penny *is / isn't* going to apply for the job.

2 READING

Read Penny's job application. Are sentences 1–4 true (*T*) or false (*F*)? Correct the false sentences.
1 ☐ She tells them she has worked in cafés before.
2 ☐ She saw the ad in the newspaper.
3 ☐ She can't work this summer, because she's studying.
4 ☐ She wants to know how much she will earn.

---

① Dear Sir/Madam,

② I am writing to apply for the job of barista at the Cuba Coffee Company, which you advertised on your website.

③ I am a student at the University of Manchester and I am available to work in August and September.

④ A job with you will be an exciting opportunity for me to learn new skills and to work in a new environment. I have a lot of experience of working in a team and helping customers at *Saveco* supermarket. My experience of working in a fast, busy supermarket will be very useful for this job.

⑤ I attach a copy of my CV with details of my past employment.

⑥ Could you please send me information about the salary and working hours, and also more details about your training programme?

⑦ I look forward to hearing from you.

Yours faithfully,

Penny Longwell

54

3 WRITING SKILLS Organising an email

a Penny's email in 2 has seven parts. What does each part of the letter do?

- [ ] says why she's writing
- [ ] asks for more information about the job
- [ ] describes documents she's sending with the email
- [ ] opens the email
- [ ] closes the email
- [ ] says why she wants the job and describes her experience
- [ ] says what she's doing now and when she can work

b Look at sentences 1–5. Which ones are about … ?

- what you are doing now
- past jobs
- skills

1 I am good at working in a team.
2 I have experience of working in a restaurant.
3 I am currently working as a sales assistant in a bookshop.
4 I am studying engineering in Madrid.
5 I speak fluent English.

c What are the missing prepositions? Complete the sentences.

1 I am writing to apply _____ the job _____ barista.
2 I am a student _____ the University of Manchester.
3 I have a lot _____ experience _____ working _____ a team.
4 I look forward _____ hearing from you.

d Put the parts of the email below in the correct order.

- I attach a copy of my CV.
- I look forward to hearing from you. Yours faithfully,
- I am writing to apply for the job of sales assistant.
- Dear Sir/Madam,
- I would like to work for your company, because it would be a good opportunity for me to improve my communication skills. I have three years' experience of sales.
- Could you send me more information about the working hours?
- I am currently working as a sales assistant in a clothes shop.

4 WRITING A job application

a Read the adverts on *Jobsearch.com*. Choose one and write an email applying for the job. Include these parts:

- open the email
- say why you are writing
- say what you are doing now
- say why you want the job
- describe documents you are sending
- ask for more information
- close the email

b Work in groups. Read the applications together. Which student would you give each job to? Why?

Jobsearch.com

Home   New Jobs   Advice

Use your English … and your local knowledge!
Get a holiday job as a guide for English-speaking tourists to your town.
You will need:
- *a good level of English*
- *knowledge of your local town or area*

VIEW JOB

Work with children and have a holiday
We're looking for people to work on an international holiday camp for children aged 10–15. You will help organise activities and trips, and speak English with the children. We prefer someone with experience of working with children.

VIEW JOB

Evening jobs with Megapizza
We need people to serve and deliver pizzas in the evenings and at weekends.
Good pay and conditions. Must have driving licence.
Contact: *jobs@megapizza.com*.

VIEW JOB

UNIT 5
Review and extension

1 GRAMMAR

a Choose the correct answers.
1 Employees must not use their computers to send personal emails.
   'We _____ use our computers to send personal emails.'
   (a) have to   (b) don't have to   (c) can't
2 Employees can leave the building at lunch time.
   'We _____ stay in the building at lunch.'
   (a) must   (b) don't have to   (c) can't
3 Employees _____ use social media.
   'We can't use social media at work.'
   (a) must not   (b) must   (c) don't have to
4 Employees _____ make local phone calls on company phones.
   'We don't have to use our mobiles to make local calls.'
   (a) can   (b) can't   (c) must
5 Employees _____ wear a shirt and tie.
   'We have to wear a shirt and tie.'
   (a) can   (b) must not   (c) must

b Match sentences (1–5) with meanings (a–c).
1 ☐ It won't be difficult for me to find a job.
2 ☐ I think I'll finish university next year.
3 ☐ I might work for a bank one day.
4 ☐ I'll find a good job in the USA.
5 ☐ I might not find a job I like in my home town.

a completely sure   b fairly sure   c not sure

c 💬 Which of the sentences in 1b are true for you?

2 VOCABULARY

a Choose the best jobs for each person (1–7).

| accountant | carer | hairdresser | IT worker |
| journalist | politician | vet |

1 I really like working with animals. _____
2 I enjoy helping older people. _____
3 I want to tell people what's happening in the world. _____
4 I'm good with numbers. _____
5 I like meeting people and helping them look good. _____
6 I want to make my country a better place. _____
7 I enjoy working with computers. _____

b 💬 Which jobs would you like and not like in 2a?

c Match the sentence halves.
1 ☐ In my job, I have to work
2 ☐ My job's interesting, because I have to make
3 ☐ I don't have a boss, because I'm
4 ☐ I enjoy being in my office. We're lucky that we have
5 ☐ I'm tired at the end of the day, because I deal with

a self-employed.
b very long hours.
c a nice working environment.
d important decisions every day.
e lots of serious problems.

3 WORDPOWER *job* and *work*

a Look at the sentences. Which word (*job* or *work*) is countable? Which is uncountable?
1 I've got a really interesting **job**.
2 I'm looking for **work** at the moment.

b Match the uses of *work* and *job* (1–4) with the meanings (a–d).
1 ☐ 90% of gardeners feel their **work** is important and useful.
2 ☐ We spend most of our time at **work**.
3 ☐ I've got a lot of **jobs** to do at home this weekend.
4 ☐ I enjoy my course, but it's hard **work**.

a when you use lots of energy to do something
b the activity or activities you do for your job
c activities you have to do, often without getting money
d the place where you work

c Match sentences (1–3) with replies (a–c).
1 ☐ Why isn't my email **working** on this computer?
2 ☐ Is the medicine from the doctor **working**?
3 ☐ I can't **work** this **out**. Do you know the answer?

a No, it's a very difficult question.
b I don't know. Maybe there's a problem with the Internet.
c Definitely. I feel much better.

d Complete the sentences with *work* or *job*.
1 I'm painting my apartment at the moment. It's a lot of hard _____.
2 I'm starting a new _____ soon.
3 My mobile doesn't _____ when I'm inside this building.
4 I've got an important _____ to do at home this weekend.
5 I leave _____ early on Fridays.
6 The education system in my country doesn't _____ well.
7 I know a lot of people who are trying to find _____.
8 I can't _____ out how to download this application form.

e Complete these sentences with your own ideas.
1 I can't work out …
2 I would like to get a job …
3 Two jobs I need to do this week are …
4 … makes me happy at work.
5 I need do some hard work …
6 … doesn't work very well.

f 💬 Compare your sentences in 3e with another student.

🔄 REVIEW YOUR PROGRESS

How well did you do in this unit? Write 3, 2 or 1 for each objective.
3 = very well   2 = well   1 = not so well

I CAN …

Talk about what people do at work	☐
Talk about your future career	☐
Make offers and suggestions	☐
Write a job application	☐

CAN DO OBJECTIVES

- Give advice on common problems
- Describe extreme experiences
- Ask for and give advice
- Write an email giving advice

UNIT 6
Problems and Advice

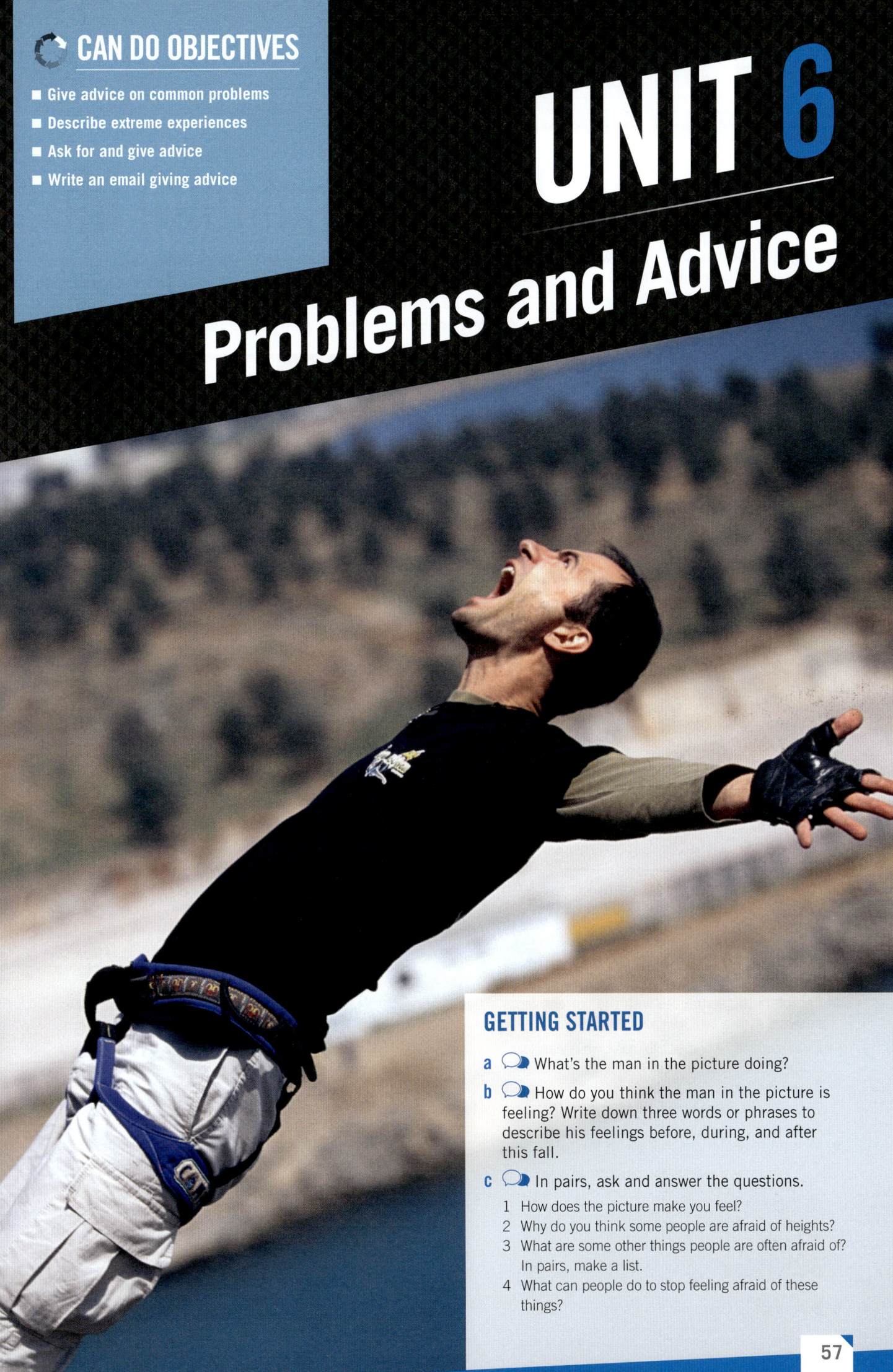

GETTING STARTED

a 💬 What's the man in the picture doing?

b 💬 How do you think the man in the picture is feeling? Write down three words or phrases to describe his feelings before, during, and after this fall.

c 💬 In pairs, ask and answer the questions.
1. How does the picture make you feel?
2. Why do you think some people are afraid of heights?
3. What are some other things people are often afraid of? In pairs, make a list.
4. What can people do to stop feeling afraid of these things?

6A You should have a break

Learn to give advice on common problems
- G Imperative; should
- V Verbs with dependent prepositions

1 READING

a 💬 Look at the problems in the pictures. Does anyone you know have any of these problems? How could you solve them? Tell a partner.

b Read the advice. Which four problems in the pictures is it for? Complete the headings 1–4.

c Read the advice again. What is the advice about these things? Make notes.

1. • music
   • 15 minutes
2. • rules
   • a pile
3. • breaks
   • rewards
4. • screens
   • milk

d 💬 Cover the article. Use your notes. Try to remember the advice in the article.

e 💬 Do you think the advice in each paragraph is useful? Why / Why not?

How to deal with life's

You don't have any money, you never finish anything you start, your house is dirty, you can't find a good job and your whole life is terrible. Well, maybe it isn't that bad! If you'd like to improve things, we can help. Here are our top ways to deal with some of life's little problems.

I can't concentrate on my work

I'm addicted to my mobile

My home is a mess

I don't sleep well

I have too much work to do

I don't have enough money

I'm always late

I feel tired all the time

2 GRAMMAR Imperative; should

a Complete the sentences with the correct verbs. Check your answers in the article.
1. Turn on the TV or _____ to music while you clean.
2. You should _____ to drink less coffee and smoke less, too.
3. You shouldn't _____ for hours without a break.
4. Don't _____ devices with bright screens before you go to sleep.

b Match the sentences in 2a with the rules.

> To give advice, we use:
> ☐ infinitive
> ☐ don't + infinitive
> ☐ subject + should + infinitive
> ☐ subject + shouldn't + infinitive

c ▶ Now go to Grammar Focus 6A on p.152.

d ▶2.23 **Pronunciation** Listen to the sentence. Is the vowel sound long or short in the words shouldn't and use?

You sh**ou**ldn't **u**se your mobile phone before you go to sleep.

e ▶2.24 Listen to the sentences. Do the letters in **bold** have the long vowel /uː/ or the short vowel /ʊ/?
1. You sh**ou**ldn't **u**se your comp**u**ter all day.
2. L**oo**k for n**ew** ways of d**oi**ng exercise.
3. Find a g**oo**d time of day to study.
4. Ch**oo**se the healthiest f**oo**d.
5. Read a b**oo**k before you go to sleep.

f Practise saying the sentences in 2e.

little problems

1

Learn to enjoy cleaning and tidying. People who enjoy this usually have clean homes. Turn on the TV or listen to music while you clean. Start by cleaning every day, but only for fifteen minutes. When the 15 minutes are finished, you should stop. Don't worry if things aren't perfectly clean. Do a little bit of cleaning every day and in a week your place will look great.

2

It's important to give yourself rules. When you go out with friends, decide how many times you will look at your phone – maybe only two or three times in an evening. Ask your friends about how they feel. If they have the same problem as you, put all of your phones together, in a pile and out of the way. That way, no one can look at their phone and you can all enjoy each other's company.

3

The machine we use so much for work – our computer – is the same machine we often use to have fun. So control how you use your computer. If your problem is that you check your email every five minutes, you can get programs that stop the Internet from working for a period of time you choose. Use this time to focus on your work. But you shouldn't work for hours without a break. Work for 25 minutes, and then have a five-minute rest. Rewards are really important, too. Have a biscuit or get some fresh air every hour or so.

4

First think about your body. Exercising regularly will help you to fall asleep more easily. You should try to drink less coffee and smoke less, too. These bad habits keep you awake. Don't use devices with bright screens, for example, your mobile phone, before you go to sleep. They make your brain think that it is daytime, instead of night. Read a book and drink a cup of warm milk or herbal tea in the evening. Then you'll feel ready for sleep.

UNIT 6

3 VOCABULARY
Verbs with dependent prepositions

a Complete the sentences with the correct prepositions from the box.

at   about (x2)   with   to   on

1 What is a problem you have to deal _____ every day?
2 Do you listen _____ music while you clean?
3 How often do you look _____ your phone?
4 What stops you concentrating _____ your work?
5 Do you think _____ your work at weekends?
6 Who can you ask _____ problems at school or work?

b Work in pairs. Ask and answer the questions in 3a.

c Match the sentence halves to make advice for two problems.

1 ☐ Don't **borrow** money
2 ☐ Only **spend** money
3 ☐ Don't **pay**
4 ☐ You should **wait**
5 ☐ You should **ask**
6 ☐ **Talk**
7 ☐ You should **think**
8 ☐ Eat a good breakfast so you **arrive**

a **for** the sales to buy expensive things.
b **for** friends' meals when you go out.
c **on** things you really need.
d **from** friends because it creates problems.
e **of** ways to save energy.
f **for** a few days off.
g **at** work or school full of energy.
h **to** a doctor about how you feel.

d ▶2.25 Listen and check your answers in 3c. Which two problems is the advice for?

e Cover one half of the sentences in 3c. Try to remember the advice.

4 SPEAKING

a ▶ Communication 6A Student A: go to p.130. Student B: go to p.129.

b Work in pairs. Choose one of the problems and write some advice.

- I feel really stressed before exams.
- I'm not creative enough at work.
- I don't laugh very often.
- I never finish anything I start.
- I always lose important things.

c Work in small groups. Present the problems and your advice. Whose advice is the most useful for you?

6B I was very frightened

Learn to describe extreme experiences
G Uses of to + infinitive
V -ed / -ing adjectives

1 VOCABULARY -ed / -ing adjectives

a 💬 Look at the pictures on this page. How do you think the people are feeling? Make a list of words.

b Read the sentences and answer the questions.

Johan's day at the beach was very <u>relaxing</u>.
After a day at the beach, Johan was completely <u>relaxed</u>.

a Which adjective describes how he feels?
b Which adjective describes the thing that makes him feel like that?

c ▶ Now go to Vocabulary Focus 6B on p.137

2 READING AND LISTENING

a 💬 Have you tried scuba diving? Would you like to? How do you think you would feel if you saw a shark?

b 💬 Match the words with a–f in the pictures. Use the words to describe the scene.

☐ scuba diver ☐ shark ☐ reef
☐ the surface ☐ breathe (v.) ☐ air

c Read *Sharks saved my life*. Which sentence is true about Caroline's experience in Egypt?

1 She went scuba diving to deal with her fear of sharks.
2 She was afraid, because she went scuba diving in very deep water.
3 She got lost when she was scuba diving.

d Read the article again. Answer the questions with a partner.

1 Why did Caroline go to Egypt?
2 Why did she ask the instructor how deep the water was?
3 How did she feel when they got to the reef? Why?
4 Why didn't Caroline to go back up to the surface of the water fast?

e 💬 What do you think happened next? How do you think sharks saved Caroline's life?

f ▶2.28 Listen to the rest of the story and check your ideas in 2e.

g ▶2.28 Listen again and answer the questions.

1 What happened after Caroline saw the sharks?
2 How did Caroline feel when she was back on the fishing boat?
3 How has the experience changed Caroline?

h 💬 Ask and answer the questions.

1 Were you surprised by anything in the story?
2 Do you think you would feel the same way as Caroline if this happened to you?

SHARKS
SAVED MY LIFE

I started scuba diving because I was interested in sharks. I learnt how to dive in England, but English waters were very disappointing. So I decided to try the Red Sea in Egypt.

The diving there was much more interesting. I saw so many beautiful fish, including sharks. After a few days, my instructor suggested a trip to the Shaab Shagra reef to swim with the sharks there.

We went out in an old fishing boat and I asked him, 'How deep is the water?' 'Not deep. 30 metres,' he said. I thought, 'Good, I can do that but I can't go below 30 metres.' I didn't have any experience of deep diving, and I knew that below 30 metres people often feel strange.

Some people suddenly feel very happy. Other people get confused, and they don't know which way is up or down.

I jumped in and followed my instructor. When we got down to the reef I looked at my diving watch to see how deep we were. I was shocked to see we were at 40 metres! I was scared and I was breathing very quickly. I thought to myself, 'Don't use all your air. Breathe slowly.' But I was really frightened and I couldn't slow my breathing down.

I was really worried about my air. How much did I need? Did I have enough? I remember looking up at the light. I felt terrified, and I just wanted to go back up to the surface fast. But I knew that if you go up too fast you can get 'the bends' and die in terrible pain. I was thinking, 'Don't go up. You'll die.' But my heart was saying, 'Go up! Go up!' I looked for my instructor. But I couldn't get his attention.

60

UNIT 6

3 GRAMMAR Uses of to + infinitive

a Look at the sentences. Complete the gaps with the words in the box.

| to see   to do   to be   to get |

1 I didn't really know what _____.
2 I just wanted _____ out of the water.
3 I was happy _____ alive.
4 I looked at my diving watch _____ how deep we were.

b ▶ 2.29 Listen and check.

c Match the sentences in 3a with the rules.

We use *to* + infinitive:
☐ to give a reason   ☐ after adjectives
☐ after certain verbs   ☐ after question words

d ▶ 2.29 **Pronunciation** Listen to the sentences from 3a again. Which part of the infinitive is stressed – *to* or the verb?

e Look at the article in 2c again. Underline another example for each use of the infinitive in 3c.

f ▶ Now go to Grammar Focus 6B on p.152

g Choose one topic to talk about in each pair of topics 1–4 below. Think about what you will say.
1 • an interesting place you've visited. Why did you go there? (to …)
  • an important course you've done. Why did you do it? (to …)
2 • a time when you decided to do something, but then changed your mind. What was it?
  • a time when you tried to do something difficult. What happened?
3 • a time when you didn't know what to do or where to go. What did you do?
  • a problem that you didn't know how to deal with. What happened?
4 • someone you were surprised to see somewhere. Who was it? Where did you see the person?
  • some information you were shocked to hear. What was it?

h 💬 Work in pairs. Talk about your ideas in 3g.

4 LISTENING

a 💬 You are going to hear about another experience. Look at the words in the box. What do you think happened?

| parachute   6,000 metres   wind (n.)   get stuck
hang   free (v.)   pull along   lucky |

b ▶ 2.31 Listen to the interview and check your ideas in 4a.

c ▶ 2.31 Look at the interviewer's questions below. Listen again and make notes on Aaron's answers.
1 What happened to you?
2 How did it happen?
3 What went wrong?
4 How did you feel?
5 Did the others help you?
6 Did that experience stop you from jumping?

d 💬 Tell Aaron's story with partner. Use your notes to help you.

5 SPEAKING

a 💬 Do you know about a person who has had an experience like the situations in this lesson? Try to think of a time when someone:
• had a dangerous or frightening experience
• had a lucky experience
• learned something from a difficult situation
• changed a lot because of an experience
• had an experience that made them very happy.

b Prepare some notes about one experience you talked about in 5a. Use the questions to help you.
• What was the person's situation at the time?
• What exactly was the experience?
• How did the person feel?
• What did other people do?
• How did the experience change the person?

c 💬 Work in new pairs. Tell your partner about the experience. Choose the best story to tell to the whole class.

6C Everyday English
What do you think I should do?

Learn to ask for and give advice
- **P** Main stress
- **S** Showing sympathy

1 LISTENING

a When you have a problem, who do you prefer to talk to about it?

b Look at the picture. Annie is telling Rachel about some bad news. What do you think the news might be?

c ▶ 2.32 Watch or listen to Part 1 and check your ideas.

2 CONVERSATION SKILLS
Showing sympathy

a ▶ 2.32 Which of the phrases did Rachel use to show she feels sorry for Annie? Watch or listen again and check.

1. How awful.
2. That's terrible.
3. What a pity.
4. I'm really sorry to hear that.
5. That's a shame.

b Look at the two phrases in 2a that Rachel didn't use. Would you use them in a similar situation or in a less serious situation?

c ▶ 2.33 Listen and repeat the phrases in 2a.

d Work in pairs. Take turns to give bad news. Respond with the best phrases from 2a.
- your boyfriend / girlfriend forgot your birthday
- you broke your leg playing football
- you missed your train and waited two hours for the next one
- you spent hours preparing dinner and then burnt the food
- someone stole your phone and money when you were on holiday

3 LISTENING

a ▶ 2.34 Watch or listen to Part 2. What advice does Rachel give about … ?
1. Annie's boss
2. Annie's colleagues
3. Mark
4. changing jobs

b ▶ 2.34 Watch or listen again. Which advice in 3a does Annie disagree with? Why?

c Which of Rachel's advice do you think is most useful? What else could Annie do?

4 PRONUNCIATION Main stress

a ▶ 2.35 Listen to the sentences. Underline the word in each sentence that Rachel stresses the most.
1. Did you ask when you're going to lose your job?
2. Maybe there'll be other jobs there.
3. You work in marketing, right?
4. Mark works in marketing, too.
5. Changing jobs could be a good thing.

b Why does Rachel stress the words you underlined in 4a? Choose the best answer.
1. to show more sympathy
2. none of the other words are important
3. the underlined words are the most important

c ▶ 2.35 Listen to 4a 1–5 again and repeat.

d Practise the dialogues with a partner. Stress the underlined words.
1. **A** We're meeting at 4 pm.
   B I know. But I don't know <u>where</u>!
2. **A** I'm really busy at work at the moment.
   B You work in a <u>bank</u>, right?
3. **A** I used to work for IBM.
   B Really? <u>I</u> used to work for IBM, too!
4. **A** I don't think it's a good time to change jobs.
   B I'm not sure. I think there are <u>lots</u> of interesting jobs out there.

62

UNIT 6

5 USEFUL LANGUAGE
Asking for and giving advice

a ▶ 2.36 Listen and complete the phrases.

Asking for advice
1 _____ do you think I should do?
2 Do you _____ I should speak to him about it?

Giving advice
3 _____ get all the details first.
4 I think you _____ speak to your boss again.
5 I think it's a _____ _____ to ask.
6 I _____ worry too much.

b Look at Annie's responses to Rachel's advice. Which phrases show that Annie doesn't agree with the advice?
1 I don't think that's a good idea.
2 I suppose so.
3 I don't think I should do that.
4 You're right.

c ▶ 2.37 Listen and repeat the phrases in 5a and 5b.

d Complete the dialogue. Then practise the dialogue with a partner.
A I just heard I didn't get that job. I'm really disappointed. What do you ¹_____ I should do?
B I'm really sorry to ²_____ that. But I wouldn't ³_____ too much – you'll find something soon.
A I ⁴_____ so. But I'm surprised. I thought the interview went very well.
B Well then, I think you ⁵_____ write to the company. ⁶_____ them for some information about your interview.
A I don't think ⁷_____'s a good idea. They won't want to give me information like that.
B I think it's a good ⁸_____ to ask. I've done that before and the information can be really useful.
A You're ⁹_____. I'll send them an email tomorrow.

6 LISTENING

a ▶ 2.38 Annie is worried about Leo. Watch or listen to Part 3 and answer the questions.
1 Why is Annie worried about Leo?
2 What explanation does Rachel give?

b 💬 Ask and answer the questions.
1 What other reasons could there be for Leo's behaviour?
2 Do you think Annie is right to worry?

7 SPEAKING

a You are going to tell your partner about something bad that happened to you. Read the cards 1–4 and choose a problem. Think about what you want to say.

1 Someone stole your bag in a café.
- What was in the bag?
- What were you doing when the person stole it?
- Who do you think stole it?
- How did you feel?
- What problems will you now have without your bag?

2 You failed an important exam.
- What was the exam?
- Why was it important?
- Did you think you would pass?
- Who else will be upset that you failed?

3 You had an argument with your best friend.
- Do you normally argue with your best friend?
- What was the argument about?
- How did it start?
- Do you want to contact your friend again?

4 Your boss said your work wasn't good enough.
- What work was it?
- What did your boss say exactly?
- How did you feel?
- Do you think this will create problems for you in the future?

b 💬 Student A, tell your partner about what happened. Student B, show sympathy and give Student A some advice.

c 💬 Now swap roles.

d 💬 Did your partner show sympathy? Was their advice helpful?

Unit Progress Test

CHECK YOUR PROGRESS

You can now do the Unit Progress Test.

63

6D Skills for Writing
I often worry about tests and exams

Learn to write a message giving advice

W Linking: ordering ideas and giving examples

1 LISTENING AND SPEAKING

a Are these situations connected to work or study? Write work (*W*), study (*S*) or both (*B*).

1. ☐ doing exams or tests
2. ☐ doing a presentation
3. ☐ managing other people
4. ☐ making business decisions
5. ☐ learning to communicate in a foreign language
6. ☐ reading all the books on a booklist

b 💬 What problems do people sometimes have in the situations in 1a?

c ▶ 2.39 Listen to Chloè, Bob and Marisa talking about problems with work and study. Complete the first row of the table.

	Chloe	Bob	Marisa
What's the main problem?			
What are the details of the problem?			
How does she/he feel?			
What advice has she/he had from friends or family?			

d ▶ 2.39 Listen again and complete the table.

e 💬 What advice would you give to Chloe, Bob and Marisa?

2 READING

a Eliza teaches English. She has a wiki for her class where students can write and ask for advice. Read Sevim's message. What does Sevim want help with?

b Read Eliza's reply. How many suggestions does Eliza make?

c Read the text again. Are sentences 1–5 true (*T*) or false (*F*)? Correct the false sentences.

1. ☐ Eliza always felt relaxed about speaking Turkish.
2. ☐ Eliza thinks language learners should try not to make mistakes.
3. ☐ Eliza says Sevim should use English with the students in her class.
4. ☐ Sevim can pay extra to go to a chat group at the study centre.
5. ☐ Eliza thinks you can practise speaking on the Internet.

Sevim Monday 12.21pm

Dear Eliza

I think my reading and listening are alright for my level, but I'm worried about my speaking. I don't feel very relaxed when I speak English and I want to improve. Do you have any ideas?

Thank you

Sevim

UNIT 6

3 WRITING SKILLS Linking: ordering ideas and giving examples

a Eliza uses words and phrases to order information in her reply. Notice the <u>underlined</u> example.

<u>First of all</u>, don't worry about making mistakes.

<u>Underline</u> three more words in the message that order Eliza's ideas.

b Read the advice on studying vocabulary for an exam. Add words and phrases where you see ⌃ to order the information.

> ⌃ you can study vocabulary lists at the back of the course book. There are also some practice exercises there to help you. ⌃ you should test yourself on the words you have studied. For example, you can try writing down all the words you can remember about a particular topic. ⌃ you can work with another student and test each other. If you both speak the same language, you can translate words from your language into English. ⌃ it's a good idea to try and think about the words you've learned and use them in a conversation the same day. This is a very active way of studying vocabulary.

c Read the text in 2b again. Notice the highlighted expressions Eliza uses to give examples. Cover the text and complete the sentences.
  1 _____, it's a good idea to use only English in class …
  2 You can join a conversation group, _____ the chat groups in the study centre.
  3 _____, there are lots of websites where you can find speaking partners from all around the world.

d Match the sentence halves.
  1 ☐ You can download apps to help you study. For   a as DVDs, podcasts and online videos.
  2 ☐ There are lots of ways to practise listening, such   b instance, there are lots of books and magazines in the study centre.
  3 ☐ It's easy to get extra reading practice. For   c example, I use the *Cambridge Advanced Learner's Dictionary* on my phone.

 **Eliza**   Monday 14.08pm

Hi Sevim,

Thanks for your message and I'm glad that you wrote to me for ideas.

I remember when I was learning Turkish, I felt embarrassed about speaking. I could remember lots of words and I knew grammar rules, but speaking was difficult. I now feel a lot more relaxed about speaking, so here are some ideas that I've taken from my own experience.

First of all, don't worry about making mistakes. Other people will still understand you and they probably won't notice your mistakes. Secondly, remember that the only way to learn to speak a second language is by speaking. Use every chance you get to speak. ==For example==, it's a good idea to use only English in class and not speak to other students in Turkish. You should also try practising new vocabulary and grammar we learn in class by repeating it at home.

Next, you should think about extra speaking practice outside the classroom. You can join a conversation group, ==such as== the chat groups in the study centre. They are free to join. Finally, you can also practise speaking online. ==For instance==, there are lots of websites where you can find speaking partners from all around the world.

I hope this helps you and please feel free to talk to me after class next week.

Best wishes,
Eliza

4 WRITING

a Work in pairs. Read the ideas for Sevim about how to improve her writing. Add three more ideas to the list.

  • plan your ideas before you write
  • ask another student to check your grammar
  •
  •
  •

b Work in pairs. Write a message giving advice to Sevim. Make sure you order your ideas clearly and give examples.

c Work in groups of four. Read the other pair's message to Sevim. Does it contain similar ideas to your message? Are the ideas ordered clearly? Are there examples?

65

UNIT 6
Review and extension

1 GRAMMAR

a Complete the exchanges with *should* or *shouldn't*.

1. **A** I can't sleep.
   B You _____ drink coffee in the afternoon.
2. **A** My desk is messy.
   B I think you _____ tidy it at the end of every day.
3. **A** I'm addicted to TV.
   B You _____ watch more than two hours a day.
4. **A** I don't have time to keep fit.
   B You _____ try to walk for ten minutes every day.
5. **A** I don't have much money.
   B I don't think you _____ buy so many clothes.
6. **A** I don't know many people where I live.
   B I think you _____ join a club or a sports team.

b Change the advice in 1a into imperatives.

1. *Don't drink coffee in the afternoon.*

c Complete the sentences with the correct forms of the verbs in the box.

| do   drive   find   go   learn   meet |

1. Do you think people in your country should _____ more exercise?
2. Is it difficult _____ parking where you live?
3. Do you need _____ to the shops today?
4. Do you think everyone should _____ a foreign language?
5. Is it easy _____ new people where you live?
6. Do you know how _____?

d 💬 Ask and answer the questions in 1c.

2 VOCABULARY

a Complete the sentences with the correct forms of the verbs in the box.

| arrive   ask   borrow   concentrate   deal   spend |

1. Sometimes I find it hard to _____ on my work.
2. What time did you _____ at the airport?
3. She _____ the waiter for the bill.
4. We _____ a car from a friend for the day.
5. They _____ too much money on food last month.
6. I _____ with a lot of different people in my job.

b Choose the correct answers.

1. I felt so *relaxed / relaxing* during my holiday.
2. The news was really *shocked / shocking*.
3. I needed to rest after my *tired / tiring* day.
4. I had a really *amazing / amazed* time in the city.
5. It's very *annoyed / annoying* when you have to queue.
6. I was *embarrassed / embarrassing* when I fell over.

c 💬 Talk about when the situations in 2b have been true for you.

3 WORDPOWER verb + *to*

a Match sentences (1–2) with the replies (a–b).

1. My chair at work isn't very comfortable.
2. I can't afford to go to the cinema tonight.

a ☐ I think you should stop **lending** money **to** your friends.
b ☐ I think you should **explain** the problem **to** your boss.

b Which verb + *to* combination in **bold** in 3a is a way of giving? Which is a way of communicating?

c Look at the sentences. Add the verb + *to* combinations to the table.

1. You have to **pay** a lot of money **to** the government when you start a new business.
2. She **wrote to** the newspaper to tell them what happened.
3. I **sold** my car **to** my brother-in-law.
4. I always **read to** my children before they go to sleep.
5. She **described** the building **to** her friend, but he couldn't find it.
6. She **brought** flowers **to** her mother to say sorry.

Communicating	Giving
explain to	lend to

d Where does *to* come in the sentences? Tick the correct answer.

1. ☐ before the object of the verb
2. ☐ after the direct object and before the indirect object

e Put *to* in the correct places in the sentences.

1. They sold their house some friends from another country.
2. When Steve described his holiday his friends, they were amazed.
3. Please bring something to drink the party.
4. I read the joke my friend, because it was funny.
5. Tara lent an umbrella her neighbour, because it was raining.
6. Did you write the letter the bank like I told you?
7. I explained the problem the company, but they didn't help me.
8. I paid the money for my course the school last week.

f Write five sentences about your life using the verbs + *to* from the table in 3c.

🔄 REVIEW YOUR PROGRESS

How well did you do in this unit? Write 3, 2 or 1 for each objective.
3 = very well   2 = well   1 = not so well

I CAN ...

Give advice on common problems	☐
Describe extreme experiences	☐
Ask for and give advice	☐
Write an email giving advice	☐

Communication Plus

3C Student C

a You are a shop assistant. Look at the photos of your products and read the descriptions.

Hot lips telephone £15.50
– Fun gift: people who love to talk
– Looks great in any home
– Ringtone: choose, five fun sounds

Modern spice rack £39.99
– Perfect gift: cooks, food lovers
– 20 jars, quality herbs and spices
– Fix to wall / free standing

Football mug £4.99
– Great gift: football fans
– Fill with favourite hot drink
– Dishwasher safe

Scented candles £9.99
– Colourful gift for the home
– Three scents: vanilla, rose, pine
– Create a romantic atmosphere

Classic clock £20.00
– Stylish gift: man or woman
– Traditional design
– Batteries included

Animal slippers £15.99 one pair
SPECIAL OFFER £25.99 both designs
– Fun gift: man, woman, couple
– Fox / Rabbit design

b Students A and B are customers in your shop. Listen to their questions and describe some of your products. Ask your customers to pay for the product when they have chosen.

c ▶ Now swap roles. Go to p.130

5A
1 gardeners, 2 hairdressers, 3 nurses, 4 accountants, 5 bankers

2B Student A

a Read the text and answer the questions.
1 Where were they going?
2 How were they travelling?
3 What was the problem?
4 Who helped solve the problem? How?
5 What happened in the end?

Did you mean Capri?
Swedish tourists miss their destination by 600 km

Two Swedish tourists on holiday in Italy got a surprise after a spelling mistake on their GPS took them 600 kilometres from their destination.

The Swedish couple were travelling around Italy, and wanted to go to Capri. Capri is an island in the south of the country, famous for its beautiful coastline and a popular tourist destination. The couple put their destination into their car's GPS, but they made a spelling mistake. They accidentally typed CARPI instead of CAPRI. There is a real place called Carpi in Italy, but it is a small town in the north of the country.

The couple followed the GPS directions. Although they were travelling to an island, it didn't worry them that they didn't cross a bridge, take a boat or see the sea. When they arrived in Carpi, they went to the tourist office. They asked for directions to the Blue Grotto, a famous sea cave in Capri. But, of course, the tourist official couldn't understand. He thought they wanted to go to a restaurant called the Blue Grotto.

When the official realised that the couple thought they were in Capri, he explained their mistake. The couple got back into their car and started driving south. The official said, 'They were surprised, but not angry.'

b ▶ Now go back to p.21

4B Student A

a Read the sentences to Student B. Listen to their reply.
1 My flight arrives at 5 pm.
2 I'd like to buy some clothes.
3 I don't understand the menu.
4 I don't like crowds.
5 I'd love to see some art.

b Listen to Student B's sentences. Choose the best reply.
I'll take you to the airport soon.
Shall we visit the castle?
Shall I come and pick you up?
I'll take you to a nice park.
I'll find a good place to eat nearby.

c ▶ Now go back to p.41

2C Student B

a Read card 1. Think about what Student A will ask you.

> You are a platform attendant at a UK train station.
> - first train to Manchester at 7.10 am
> - trains every hour
> - prices: adult £32, student £22
> - passengers can only use their tickets on the train they book
> - no lockers in UK stations
> - the waiting room is by the station entrance

b Start the conversation with Student A. Say 'How can I help you?'

c Now look at card 2. Listen to Student A and reply. Find out the information you need.

> 2 You want to visit Warwick Castle.
> - where / castle?
> - ⊕ open?
> - £ adult and child tickets?
> - where / buy tickets?
> - how often / tours?
> - take a picnic?

2B Student B

a Read the text and answer the questions.
1 Where were they going?
2 How were they travelling?
3 What was the problem?
4 Who helped solve the problem? How?
5 What happened in the end?

Coach passengers asked to get out and push

A group of coach passengers got some unexpected exercise when their coach broke down and the driver asked them to get out and push. The driver asked his 25 passengers for help after the 11.15 am coach from Heathrow airport to Norwich broke down while it was turning a corner.

A 77-year-old passenger, who was travelling back from a holiday in Italy with his wife, said, 'We heard an awful noise … and the driver could not get the coach to move.' The coach was stopping other cars from using the road, so ten passengers got out and tried to push the coach, which weighed 14 tonnes*. The passenger said, 'It was an amazing sight … Luckily, there were lots of strong young men on board – but a couple of women joined in as well.'

A car stopped to help and pulled the coach along with a rope while the people pushed it 200 metres to the bus station. The passengers then waited over an hour with their luggage for another coach to arrive, so they could complete their journey.

The coach company says the coach driver was wrong to ask his passengers to help and that they will give him training immediately.

* 14 tonnes = 14,000 kg

b ▶ Now go back to p.21

5B If your partner *hasn't* got a job …

a Ask your partner about the job he/she would like to do in the future.
Do you think … ?
- it'll be easy to find work
- you'll earn a good salary when you start
- you'll need to speak English at work
- there'll be a lot of other people who want this job
- you'll work for a company or be self-employed
- you'll move to another place for work
- you'll use your qualifications

b Then swap roles and answer your partner's questions. Give more information if you can.

c ▶ Now go back to p.51

Communication Plus

4C Student B

a Student A is going to invite you to dinner. Complete your diary with plans for three days.

> Wednesday: *making diner*
> Thursday: *shopping*
> Friday: *go paerk*
> Saturday:
> Sunday:

b Answer Student A's call. Arrange an evening for dinner. Offer to bring something.

6A Student B

a Read the advice for people who are always late.

> No one wants to be the person who always arrives last. Here's some advice to help you get there on time, whatever the occasion.
>
>
> I'm always late
>
> **Make a list of everything you need to do** the day before an important event. Do you need to wear smart clothes? Buy a gift? Find out train times? Then do all the jobs on your list and you'll be ready to go the next day.
>
> **Do only the things you need to do.** Use your time carefully before an appointment. Don't try to be perfect. Think about each action. Do you really need to print that document? If it's not necessary, don't do it.
>
> **Think about how other people feel.** Being late tells other people, 'My time is more important than yours.' People who are often late don't usually understand how rude it is. Remember this and you will have another reason to arrive on time.

b Listen to Student A's advice about the same problem.

c Cover the text. Tell Student A about the advice you read.

d Answer the questions with Student A.
   1 Which of the six pieces of advice is the most useful?
   2 Do you know anyone who needs this advice?

e ▶ Now go back to p.59

4B Student B

a Listen to Student A's sentences. Choose the correct reply.
   • Shall I read it for you in English?
   • Shall we go to a gallery?
   • OK – so we won't go to the market.
   • I'll meet you at the airport.
   • Shall we go to a shopping centre?

b Read the sentences to Student A. Listen to their reply.
   1 My hotel doesn't have a restaurant.
   2 I'd like to go for a walk.
   3 My flight leaves in three hours.
   4 I'm interested in history.
   5 There's a long queue for taxis.

▶ Now go back to p.41

1C Student B

a Read card 1. Think about what you want to say.

b Listen to Student A and reply. Use your own name.

> **1** You are walking down the street and you see your friend.
> • say hello
> • listen to your friend's news and respond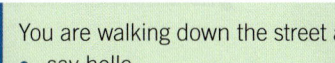
> • give your news:
>   ▸ you moved to a new flat last week
>   ▸ *your own idea*
> • say goodbye

c Now look at card 2. Start the conversation with Student A. Use your own name.

> **2** You meet a new colleague for the first time.
> • say who you are
> • listen to what they say and respond
> • give some information:
>   ▸ you work in IT
>   ▸ *your own idea*
> • say goodbye

3C Students A and B

a You want to buy a present for a friend. Choose someone you both know.

b Student C is a shop assistant. Ask about the products in the shop. Choose the best product for your friend and buy it.

c Now swap roles. Student B: You are the shop assistant – go to p.127. Student A: Stay on this page.

3B RESULTS

Mostly 'a': You are a big spender. You spend a lot of money without thinking. Maybe you need to start to plan your spending a bit better.

Mostly 'b': You are a smart spender. You spend money, but you are clever when you do it. You find all the special offers. But don't buy things that you don't need!

Mostly 'c': You are a non spender. You don't like spending and you only do it when you really have to.

▶ Now go back to p.30

5B If your partner *has* got a job …

a Ask your partner about their future in their job.
Do you think … ?
- you'll work longer hours
- you'll earn more money
- you'll need new skills
- you'll go to more meetings
- you'll travel abroad for work
- you'll need to speak English at work
- you'll become a boss

b Then swap roles and answer your partner's questions. Give more information if you can.

c ▶ Now go back to p.51

6A Student A

a Read the advice for people who are always late.

I'm always late

No one wants to be the person who always arrives last. Here's some advice to help you get there on time, whatever the occasion.

Imagine the worst. Don't think that everything will go perfectly and you will arrive at a place in the shortest time possible. Leave earlier than you need to. Then, when you can't find a parking place, or there's a long queue, it won't make you late.

Tell people how much time you have. When someone starts talking to you, and you don't have much time, say 'I only have five minutes.' Then, after five minutes, make sure you leave. Say 'I'm sorry but I have to go.' Nobody will think you are rude.

Find things to do while you wait. Some people are always late, because they hate waiting for other people. If this is you, you should take something with you to do while you are waiting. Don't try to do 'just one more thing' before you leave for an appointment.

b Cover the text. Tell Student B about the advice.

c Listen to Student B's advice for the same problem.

d Answer the questions with Student B.
1 Which of the six pieces of advice is the most useful?
2 Do you know anyone who needs this advice?

e ▶ Now go back to p.59

Vocabulary Focus

1A Common adjectives

a ▶ 1.4 Listen to the conversations and look at the pictures. Underline the adjectives.

b Look at these adjectives and answer the questions. Use the conversations in **a** to help you.

delicious /dɪlɪʃəs/   ugly /ʌgli/   serious /sɪəriəs/
rude /ruːd/   alright /ɔːlraɪt/   silly /sɪli/
boring /bɔːrɪŋ/   strange /streɪndʒ/

Which adjective means … ?
1 OK _alright_
2 not normal _strange_
3 not beautiful _ugly_
4 not polite _rude_
5 the food is good _delicious_
6 stupid _silly_
7 bad (for a problem) _serious_
8 not interesting _boring_

c Now look at these adjectives.

gorgeous /gɔːdʒəs/   horrible /hɒrɪbəl/   lovely /lʌvli/
amazing /əmeɪzɪŋ/   awful /ɔːfəl/   perfect /pɜːfekt/

Which adjective means … ?
- very nice/good _amazing gorgeous lovely perfect_
- very bad _awful horrible_

d ▶ 1.5 Listen to the adjectives in **b** and **c**. How many syllables are there in each word? Underline the stressed syllable in each word.

e Practise the conversations with a partner.

f ▶ Now go back to p.8

2A Tourism

a ▶ 1.29 Match the holiday items with the pictures. Listen and check. Repeat the words.

8 backpack /ˈbækpæk/
6 foreign currency /ˌfɒrən ˈkʌrənsi/
1 guidebook /ˈɡaɪdbʊk/
2 map /mæp/
5 passport /ˈpɑːspɔːt/
3 suitcase /ˈsuːtkeɪs/
4 sunglasses /ˈsʌŋɡlɑːsɪz/
7 suntan lotion /ˈsʌntæn ˌləʊʃən/

b 💬 Which of the items in **a** do you always take on holiday?

c ▶ 1.30 Complete the travel phrases with the words in the box. Listen and check.

holiday   sightseeing /ˈsaɪtsiːɪŋ/   visa /ˈviːzə/
campsite /ˈkæmpsaɪt/   souvenirs /ˌsuːvənˈɪəz/
money   accommodation /əˌkɒməˈdeɪʃən/
hotel   hostel /ˈhɒstəl/   adventure /ədˈventʃə/
luggage /ˈlʌɡɪdʒ/

1 We **went away on** _holiday_ for three weeks.
2 We needed to **get a** _visa_ from the embassy, before we travelled.
3 We also **exchanged** some _money_ at the bank.
4 We **booked** all of our _accommodation_ online.
5 When we arrived, we **checked into** our luxury _hotel_ and **unpacked** our _luggage_.
6 We **did** some _sight_. The castles and gardens were gorgeous!
7 We **bought** _souvenirs_ for our friends and family.
8 The second week, we **checked out of** our hotel and **stayed in** a _hostel_. It was cheap and friendly!
9 The third week we **stayed on** a _campsite_ by the beach.
10 We **had** a great _adventure_ and we didn't want to come home.

d 💬 Work in pairs. Think of your last holiday. Which of the things in **c** did you do? Tell your partner.

e ▶ Now go back to p.19

133

2B Travel collocations

a ▶1.31 Listen to sentences 1–9 and look at the journey on the map. Match the words in **bold** with their definitions a–i.
1. ☐ We **travelled around** Europe last year.
2. ☐ We **set off** in June.
3. ☐ We **took off** late but …
4. ☐ … we **landed** on time in Berlin.
5. ☐ We **hitchhiked** across Germany.
6. ☐ A kind man **gave us a lift** to Frankfurt.
7. ☐ We **boarded a train** to Paris.
8. ☐ We **changed** at Strasbourg.
9. ☐ We **got to** Paris at seven thirty.

a get on a bus/train/plane
b get off one train and get on a different train
c drive another person to their destination
d leave an airport by plane
e stand by the road and ask for free rides
f arrive at a place
g arrive at an airport by plane
h visit many different places in a large area
i start a journey

b 💬 Cover the sentences 1–9 and use the map to retell the story in **a**.

c Match the travel problems with the pictures.
1. ☐ They **missed** their train.
2. ☐ My car **broke down** on the motorway.
3. ☐ There was a lot of **turbulence** /ˈtɜːbjʊləns/ during the flight.
4. ☐ I **had a crash** on the drive to work.
5. ☐ The **traffic jam** went on for miles down the road.
6. ☐ There was **something wrong with** the plane.
7. ☐ There was a **strike** so there were no buses.
8. ☐ We **got lost** in the city centre.
9. ☐ There was a **long queue** /kjuː/ at the ticket office.
10. ☐ There was a **delay** at the station.

d ▶1.32 Listen and check. Then listen and repeat.

e 💬 Cover the sentences in **c** and try to remember them. Use the pictures to help you.

f 💬 Ask and answer the questions.
1. Which of the problems in the pictures have you had on journeys this year?
2. Is there a country you'd like to travel around?
3. When was the last time someone gave you a lift?
4. How do you feel when a plane takes off and lands?
5. Do you know anyone who hitchhikes? Do you think it's a good idea?

g ▶ Now go back to p.20

134

3B Money

a ▶1.50 Match each sentence with a picture to tell two stories. Listen and check.

- 5 / 4 Carol now **owed** Fay £700. So she **got a loan** for £1000 from the bank.
- 6 / Fay offered to **lend** her some money, so she **borrowed** £100.
- 3 Carol saw some shoes she loved, but she didn't have any **cash**.
- 2 One day Carol and Fay went shopping in **the sales**.
- 6 She **paid back** the £700 pounds (and spent the rest on shoes!)
- 1 Carol had a problem. She **spent** a lot of money on shoes.

- 5 / 8 When Brian got home he found a **special offer** online.
- 1 Brian was **saving up for** a camera.
- 2 He saw a great camera but it **cost** £499.
- 4 He asked the shop assistant for a **discount** but she said no.
- 6 So he got the camera for £399! He was very happy!
- 3 Brian **couldn't afford** it. He only had £400 in his **bank account**.

b Cover the sentences and use the words in the box to tell the stories.

| **Carol** spend money on   the sales   cash   lend |
| borrow /ˈbɒrəʊ/   owe /əʊ/   get a loan /ləʊn/   pay back |

| **Brian** save up for   cost   afford /əˈfɔːd/ |
| bank account /əˈkaʊnt/   discount /ˈdɪskaʊnt/ |
| special offer |

c ▶ Now go back to p.30

4A Clothes and appearance

a Read the lists of words. Which words do you already know?

Small clothes: socks, shorts, underwear /ˈʌndəweə/, tights /taɪts/

Accessories: necklace, sunglasses, belt, scarf, handbag, bracelet /ˈbreɪslət/, earrings /ˈɪərɪŋz/, tie /taɪ/, gloves /glʌvz/

Footwear: trainers, boots, flat shoes, high heels, sandals /ˈsændəlz/

Clothing: jumper, suit, raincoat, top, tracksuit /ˈtræksuːt/, sweatshirt /ˈswetʃɜːt/

c ▶1.63 Listen and check your answers in **b**. Repeat the words.

d Cover the words. Can you remember the names of all the things in the pictures?

e Match the sentence halves.
1. ☐ I need a haircut so I'm **go**ing
2. ☐ I'm going to go shopping and **get**
3. ☐ I want to **look**
4. ☐ He should **have**
5. ☐ It's an expensive restaurant so please **wear**
6. ☐ She has very long nails so she often **go**es

a **a new outfit** for the party.
b **something nice**.
c **to the hairdresser's** this afternoon.
d **a shave** before he grows a beard.
e **my best** because all my family is coming.
f **to the beautician's**.

f ▶1.64 Listen and check your answers to **e**.

g Work in pairs. Ask and answer the questions.
- When was the last time you wanted to look your best?
- What did you wear? Did you get a new outfit?
- Did you have a shave / go to the hairdresser's / the beautician's?

h ▶ Now go back to p.38

b Write the correct word from **a** next to each picture.

① ② ③ ④

⑤ ⑥ ⑦ ⑧

⑨ ⑩ ⑪ ⑫

135

5A Work

a ▶2.3 Match the jobs with the pictures. Listen and check.
1. ☐ gardener /ˈɡɑːdnə/
2. ☐ hairdresser /ˈheədresə/
3. ☐ plumber /ˈplʌmə/
4. ☐ scientist /ˈsaɪəntɪst/
5. ☐ lawyer /ˈlɔɪə/
6. ☐ accountant /əˈkaʊntənt/
7. ☐ electrician /ɪlekˈtrɪʃən/
8. ☐ banker /ˈbæŋkə/
9. ☐ IT worker

b ▶2.3 Listen to the words in **a**. Which syllables are stressed? Add **1–8** to the table.

X x	X x x	x X x	x x X x
gardener			

c ▶2.4 Choose the correct verbs to complete the sentences. Then listen and check. Repeat the sentences.

'm   deal   with   earn   ~~have~~   make   need   work

1. They __have__ — a nice working environment. /ɪnˈvaɪrənmənt/
   — a lot of skills.
2. I _____ — long hours.
   — weekends.
   — in a team.
3. You _____ — several years of training.
   — good qualifications. /kwɒlɪfɪˈkeɪʃənz/
   — a university degree. /juːnɪˈvɜːsɪti dɪɡriː/
4. I _____ — serious problems.
   — people every day.
5. I _____ — a good salary. /ˈsæləri/
6. I _____ — self-employed. /ɪmˈplɔɪd/
7. I _____ — important decisions. /dɪˈsɪʒənz/

d 💬 Name one job for each description in **c**.

> Plumbers have a lot of skills.

We normally say *I work in IT* not *I'm an IT worker*.

e ▶ Now go back to p.48

5B Jobs

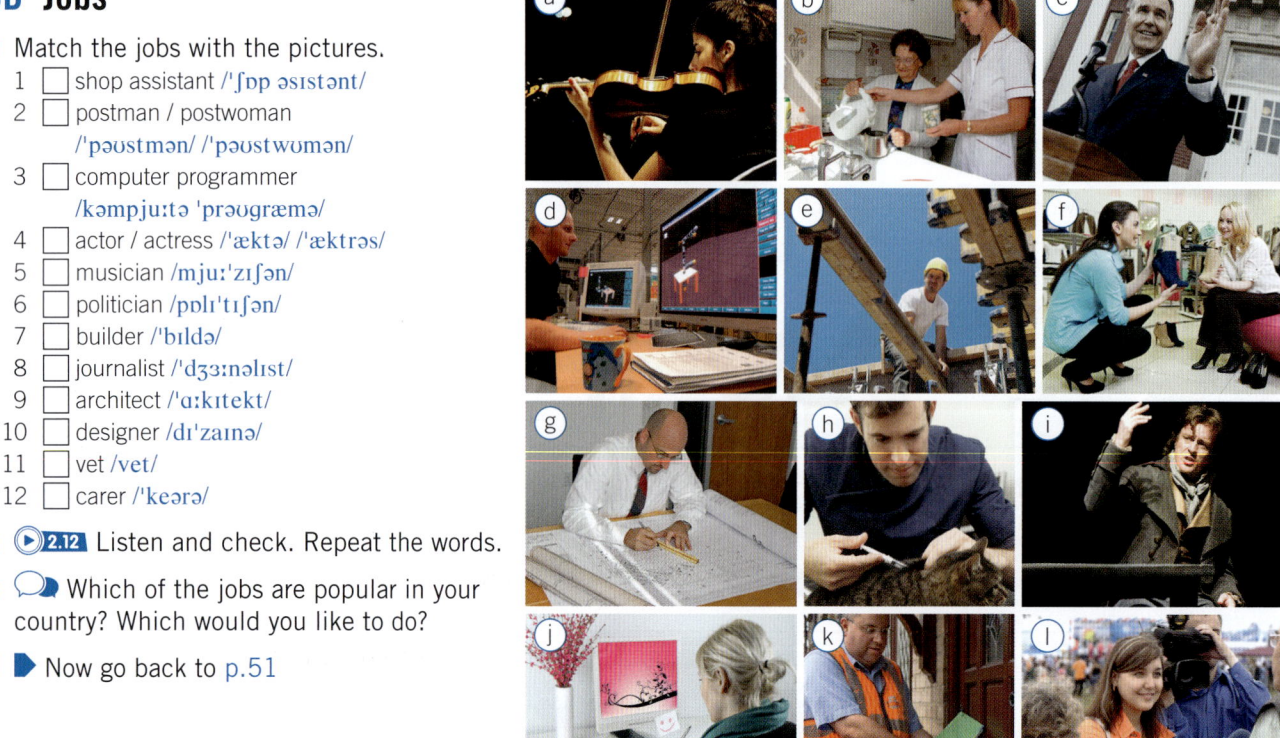

a Match the jobs with the pictures.
1. ☐ shop assistant /ˈʃɒp əsɪstənt/
2. ☐ postman / postwoman /ˈpəʊstmən/ /ˈpəʊstwʊmən/
3. ☐ computer programmer /kəmpjuːtə ˈprəʊɡræmə/
4. ☐ actor / actress /ˈæktə/ /ˈæktrəs/
5. ☐ musician /mjuːˈzɪʃən/
6. ☐ politician /pɒlɪˈtɪʃən/
7. ☐ builder /ˈbɪldə/
8. ☐ journalist /ˈdʒɜːnəlɪst/
9. ☐ architect /ˈɑːkɪtekt/
10. ☐ designer /dɪˈzaɪnə/
11. ☐ vet /vet/
12. ☐ carer /ˈkeərə/

b ▶2.12 Listen and check. Repeat the words.

c 💬 Which of the jobs are popular in your country? Which would you like to do?

d ▶ Now go back to p.51

136

Vocabulary Focus

6B -ed and -ing adjectives

a ▶ 2.26 Look at the pictures. Complete the sentences with the pairs of words. Listen and check.

annoying / annoyed
1 a Magda was _____ by the music from the neighbour's flat.
   b The music from the neighbour's flat was really _____ .

disappointing / disappointed
2 a Will's birthday present was very _____ .
   b Will was very _____ by his present.

confusing / confused
3 a Andreas was very _____ by the road signs.
   b The road signs were really _____ .

tiring / tired
4 a Sara was _____ after a long day at work.
   b Sara had a really _____ day at work.

frightening / frightened
5 a Mehmet thought the animals were _____ .
   b Mehmet was _____ of the animals.

amazing / amazed
6 a The fireworks looked _____ .
   b Everyone was _____ by the fireworks.

embarrassing / embarrassed
7 a Liza was _____ by her boyfriend's dancing.
   b Liza's boyfriend's dancing was _____ .

surprising / surprised
8 a Anita was _____ to get the news from her sister.
   b Anita got some _____ news from her sister.

shocking / shocked
9 a The price of the meal was _____ .
   b They were _____ when they got the bill for the meal.

b ▶ 2.27 Listen to the -ed adjectives. How many syllables are there? Then listen again and repeat.

amazed /əˈmeɪzd/
excited /ɪkˈsaɪtɪd/
annoyed /əˈnɔɪd/
confused /kənˈfjuːzd/
disappointed /dɪsəˈpɔɪntɪd/
embarrassed /ɪmˈbærəst/
frightened /ˈfraɪtənd/
interested /ˈɪntrəstɪd/
shocked /ʃɒkt/
surprised /səˈpraɪzd/
tired /taɪəd/

c 💬 Talk to a partner. Which word(s) could describe your feelings in these situations?
1 You can't understand the instructions for your new phone.
2 You are walking alone in a forest at night.
3 You hear some very bad news that you can't believe is true.
4 You have just broken a box of eggs in the supermarket.
5 Your boss has forgotten to tell you where the meeting is.
6 You have just run 10 km.
7 The weather on holiday was terrible every day.
8 You suddenly get a big pay rise.

d Write a sentence about each situation in **c** using an -ed or an -ing adjective.
My new phone is very confusing.

e 💬 Compare your sentences with a partner. Are they similar?

f ▶ Now go back to p.60

Grammar Focus

1A Question forms

Questions with *be*

In questions with *be*, the verb *be* goes before the subject. We don't add an auxiliary verb.

▶ 1.6

Question word	be	Subject	
How	**'s**	the food?	–
What	**was**	the party	like yesterday?
–	**Are**	you	a teacher?
–	**Were**	they	late?

> **Tip** When we want to ask for a description or an opinion we can use:
> **be like**   **How ...** with the verb **be**
> A What **was** the film **like**?   A **How was** your holiday?
> B It was alright.   B Fantastic!

Questions with other main verbs

In questions with other verbs, we add an auxiliary verb to form questions. The auxiliary verb goes before the subject.

▶ 1.7

Question word	Auxiliary verb	Subject	Main verb	
Where	**do**	you	live?	–
What time	**did**	they	arrive	at the party?
–	**Does**	the film	have	a happy ending?
–	**Did**	you	make	the food?

In questions with *do* or *did*, the main verb is in the infinitive:
Does she **live** here? NOT ~~Does she lives here?~~
Did you **come** by taxi? NOT ~~Did you came by taxi?~~
Modal verbs like *can* are also auxiliary verbs:
What **can** you see?

Wh- questions start with a question word: *Who, What, Where, When, Why, Which, Whose, How; How much, How many, What time, What colour, What kind of car*, etc.

1B Present simple and present continuous

Present simple

We use the present simple to describe:
- routines and habits
  *I **send** a lot of emails.*
- situations which are generally true or stay the same for a long time:
  *He **doesn't work** very hard.*

We use adverbs of frequency with the present simple:
*I **always** / **sometimes** / **rarely** / **never** write letters.*
*I write letters **once** / **ten times** a **week** / **year**.*

The verb *be* doesn't have the same form as other verbs:
*I **am** a student.   They **are** not here.*
*Is she always friendly? Yes, she **is**.*

Present continuous

We use the present continuous to describe:
- actions right now, at the moment of speaking:
  *He**'s not cooking** dinner, he**'s watching** TV.*
- temporary actions around the present time:
  *They**'re travelling** around Asia this year.*

We often use these time expressions with the present continuous:
*I'm working at a supermarket **right now** / **these days** / **at the moment** / **today** / **this summer**, etc.*

SPELLING: verb + -ing

Most verbs	+ -ing
sleep watch say	sleeping watching saying
Stressed vowel + one consonant (not w, x, y)	**2× consonant + -ing**
stop run get	stopping running getting
Consonant + -e	**– -e and + -ing**
live make have	living making having

▶ 1.13

	I / You / We / They	He / She / It
+	We **live** next door.	He **lives** here.
–	I **don't work** here.	She **doesn't work** here.
Y/N?	**Do** your friends **write** emails? Yes, they **do**. / No, they **don't**.	**Does** your sister **write** a blog? Yes, she **does**. / No, she **doesn't**.

> **Tip** Some verbs, which describe feelings and states, are not usually used in continuous tenses:
> be like   love   hate   prefer   know   understand   remember   forget   want   own   need
> *I **need** a new computer.* NOT ~~I'm needing a new computer.~~
> *He **doesn't understand** you.* NOT ~~He isn't understanding you.~~

▶ 1.14

	I	He / She / It	You / We / They
+	I**'m watching** TV.	She**'s helping**.	We**'re working** hard.
–	I**'m not feeling** well.	It**'s not raining**.	They**'re not sleeping**.
Y/N?	**Am** I **looking** alright? Yes, I **am**. / No, I**'m not**.	**Is** he **working** late? Yes, he **is**. / No he **isn't**.	**Are** they **enjoying** the party? Yes, they **are**. / No, they **aren't**.

> **Tip** *is not* and *are not* can be contracted two different ways:
> is not = isn't = 's not
> are not = aren't = 're not

142

Grammar Focus

1A Question forms

a Underline the main verb in each question.
1. Where do you <u>live</u>?
2. How are you today?
3. Did you see the football match yesterday?
4. Who do you know at this party?
5. What did you do at the weekend?
6. What kind of food do you like?
7. What's the food like?
8. Can I sit here?

b Look at the questions in **a** again. Tick (✓) the questions which have an auxiliary verb.

c Add the word at the end of the line to form a correct question. Sometimes you also need to change the punctuation.

1. What kind of books you usually read?   *do*
   <u>What kind of books do you usually read?</u>
2. You watch the Olympics on TV?   *did*
   Did you watch the Olympics on TV?
3. What the food like in India?   *was*
   _____
4. You go to the gym?   *do*
   _____
5. How much she earn?   *does*
   _____
6. It cold today?   *is*
   _____
7. Where they go on holiday?   *did*
   _____
8. I late?   *am*
   _____

d Correct the mistake in each question.
1. **A** Why do want you to go home?
   B Because I'm tired.
2. **A** What did you meet at the party?
   B Rashid and Fran.
3. **A** How much your car was?
   B I paid £500.
4. **A** Which did you see film?
   B The new James Bond film.
5. **A** Who key is this?
   B Mine.
6. **A** How many people you did invite?
   B About 20.
7. **A** Was the film like?
   B It was pretty good.
8. **A** What kind music do you like?
   B I like dance music.

e ▶ Now go to back to p.9

1B Present simple and present continuous

a Choose the best ending for each sentence from each pair. Write the number in the box.

1. a ☐ I work in a bank …
   b ☐ I'm working in a café …
   1 but I don't enjoy it.
   2 but it's only a summer job.

2. a ☐ She drives to work every day …
   b ☐ She's driving right now …
   1 so she can't answer the phone.
   2 so she spends a lot on petrol.

3. a ☐ I write to my parents …
   b ☐ I'm writing to my parents …
   1 because their phone's broken.
   2 once a month.

4. a ☐ We're not eating there …
   b ☐ We don't eat there …
   1 today because it's full.
   2 because the food is awful.

b Choose the correct answer.
1. *I eat / I'm eating* my lunch at the moment. Can you wait?
2. Look at that man! He *doesn't wear / isn't wearing* any shoes.
3. *She normally goes / She's normally going* to the cinema on Tuesday nights.
4. *I study / I'm studying* hard, because I've got an exam next week.
5. Some of my friends *look / are looking* at their phones every five minutes.
6. My grandparents *hardly ever visit / are hardly ever visiting* us because they live in Australia.
7. We want to finish the project tonight, so *we work / we're working* late.
8. *Is your brother liking / Does your brother like* computer games?

c Complete the conversation with the present simple or present continuous.

A What [1] <u>are you doing</u> (you / do)?
B [2] _____ (I / check) Facebook.
A Really? But you checked it about 20 minutes ago. How often [3] _____ (you / check) your account?
B Well, [4] _____ (I / usually check) my account once a day. But today's different. [5] _____ (my sister / travel) around Africa at the moment, and I'm worried about her.
[6] _____ (she / usually send) me a message on Facebook two or three times a day, but the last time she wrote was a week ago.
A Maybe [7] _____ (she / travel) right now, and she can't use the Internet.
[8] _____ (she / go) on safari?
B No, I don't think so. [9] _____ (she / not like) the countryside. [10] _____ (she / prefer) cities. Oh … look! Here's a message from her. You were right! [11] _____ (she / drive) through the Masai Mara National Park at the moment.
A Where's that?
B [12] _____ (it / be) in Kenya.
[13] _____ (there / be) lots of wild animals there.
A Cool … that's amazing. So why [14] _____ (she / spend) her time on Facebook?

d ▶ Now go to back to p.11

143

2A Past simple

We use the past simple to talk about completed actions and situations in the past.
I **went** to Greece last summer. It **was** amazing.
I **didn't want** to leave.
Where **did** you **stay**?

The form of the past simple is the same for all persons.

▶ 1.25 In positive statements, regular verbs have *ed* endings:
I **decided** yesterday.
We **played** volleyball on the beach.

However, many common verbs are irregular:
go > I **went** there last year.
have > We **had** a lot of fun.
see > She **saw** the Taj Mahal.

There is a list of irregular verbs on p.176

To form negative statements and questions, we use the auxiliary verb *did*.

	I / You / We / They / He / She / It
–	I **didn't go** there.
Y/N?	**Did** you **have** fun? Yes, I **did**. / No, I **didn't**.

▶ 1.26 *be* doesn't have the same form as other verbs:

	I / He / She / It	You / We / They
+	The weather **was** great.	The shops **were** near the beach.
–	I **wasn't** very happy.	We **weren't** tired.
Y/N?	**Was** your tour guide good? Yes, she **was**. / No, she **wasn't**.	**Were** you late for your flight? Yes, we **were**. / No, we **weren't**.

We often use these time expressions with the past simple:
I drove to London   **last** week / year.
　　　　　　　　　two days **ago**.
　　　　　　　　　when I was a child.

They come at the beginning or the end of a sentence:
When I finished school, I went to university.
I went to Greece **two years ago**.

SPELLING: verb + -ed

Most verbs	+ -ed
play watch show	play**ed** watch**ed** show**ed**
Ending in -e	+ -d
liv**e** phon**e** agre**e** lov**e**	liv**ed** phon**ed** agre**ed** lov**ed**
Stressed vowel + consonant (not *w, x, y*)	2× consonant and + -ed
s**to**p pl**a**n pref**e**r	stop**ped** plan**ned** prefer**red**
Consonant -y	– -y, + -ied
marry study try	marr**ied** stud**ied** tr**ied** worr**ied**

I didn't want to go water skiing but when I tried it, it was brilliant

2B Past continuous

We use the past continuous to describe something in progress at a particular time in the past.
In 2010, I **was living** in Poland.
At 11 o'clock, he **was waiting** by the fountain.
When they arrived, I **was cooking** dinner.

Use the past continuous with the past simple:

- to describe long and short actions together:
  I **was reading** my book when the plane took off.

- to describe a longer action that stopped suddenly because something else happened:
  When I **was driving** to work, my car broke down.

We can use *when* to join the two parts of a sentence:
When my car broke down, I was driving to work.
My car broke down **when** I was driving to work.

💡 Tip
We often use the past continuous to describe the situation at the beginning of a story.
In 2010, we **were travelling** across Russia.
John **was driving** too fast down the motorway.

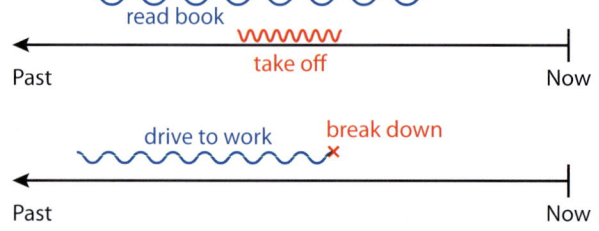

▶ 1.35

	I / He / She / It	You / We / They
+	I **was driving** to work.	You **were standing** on the platform.
–	He **wasn't** listening.	We **weren't** watching.
Y/N?	**Was** she **waiting** for you? Yes, she **was**. / No, she **wasn't**.	**Were** they **travelling** by train? Yes, they **were**. / No, they **weren't**.

Grammar Focus

2A Past simple

a Write the past simple form of the verbs. Some of them are irregular.

1. ask — asked
2. buy — bought
3. dance — danced
4. enjoy — enjoyed
5. find — found
6. forget — forgot
7. know — knew
8. learn — learned
9. hurry — hurried
10. meet — met
11. offer — offered
12. prefer — preferred
13. relax — relaxed
14. say — said
15. wear — wore

b Last week, Elliot's holiday was very good. Victoria's was very bad. Complete each sentence with the positive or negative form of the verb at the beginning of the line.

ELLIOT — My fantastic holiday

- be — 1 My plane wasn't late.
- arrive — 2 My bags arrived at the airport.
- be — 3 The people at the hotel were very nice.
- eat — 4 I ate the local food. It was great!
- rain — 5 It didn't rain.
- spend — 6 I didn't spend a lot of money. It was so cheap!
- speak — 7 I spoke to a lot of people.
- have — 8 I had a good time.

VICTORIA — My terrible holiday

- My plane was late.
- My bags didn't arrive at the airport.
- The people at the hotel weren't very nice.
- I didn't eat the local food. It was awful.
- It rained every day.
- I spent a lot of money. It was so expensive!
- I didn't speak to anybody.
- I didn't have a good time.

c Elliot asked Victoria about her holiday. Write Elliot's questions in the past simple.

1. E why / your plane / be late
   Why was your plane late?
   V I think there was a problem with the engine.
2. E when / your bags / arrive
   When did your bags arrive?
   V On the last day of my holiday.
3. E what / you / wear?
   What _____?
   V I bought some new clothes.
4. E the people / be friendly
   Were the people friendly?
   V No, they were rude.
5. E what / weather / be like
   What was the weather ?
   V It rained every day.
6. E what kind of food / you eat
   What kind of food you eat
   V Nothing special.
7. E you / have / a good time
   Did you have a good time?
   V No!

d ▶ Now go back to p.19

2B Past continuous

a Complete the sentences with the past continuous forms of the verbs.

1. A year ago, I was living (I / live) with my parents.
2. At nine last night, _____ (we / sleep).
3. A What did you (you / do) at midnight on New Year's Eve?
   B We _____ (watch) the celebrations on TV.
4. _____ (she / not study) when I got home, _____ (she / chat) to her friends online.
5. A _____ (Most people / not wear) suits for the job interview.
   B What _____ (they / wear)?

b Choose the best form for each verb. There is one past simple verb and one past continuous verb in each sentence.

1. The Internet *stopped / was stopping* when I *watched / was watching* a film.
2. She *walked / was walking* down the street when she *saw / was seeing* her friend.
3. He *left / was leaving* his job when he *studied / was studying* for his exams.
4. I *did / was doing* some cleaning when I *heard / was hearing* the news on the radio.
5. We *felt / were feeling* tired when we *got / were getting* home.
6. I *didn't visit / wasn't visiting* Cancún when I *worked / was working* in Mexico.
7. I *wasn't looking / didn't look* when I *crashed / was crashing* my bicycle into a tree.

c Use the past continuous and the past simple of the verbs in brackets to complete the sentences about each picture.

1  When I was walking down the street, I found ten pounds. (walk, find)

2  It was raining when she leave the house. (rain, leave)

3  When you call me, I was cooking dinner. (call, cook)

4  They came quietly when the teacher was coming back. (not work, come)

d ▶ Now go back to p.21

3A Present perfect or past simple

We use the present perfect to talk about past experiences.

The present perfect refers to the whole past, not a particular time.

Regular past participles end in -ed, e.g. I have **worked**...
Many past participles are irregular, e.g. I have **bought**...

The past simple and the past participle are often different, e.g. I **drove**; I have **driven**.
See p.176 for a list of irregular verbs.

> **💡 Tip**
>
> **The verb *go* in the present perfect**
> We use *been* instead of *gone* for a past experience:
> I've **been** to China. (= I went there and came back home.)
> We use *gone* to say where other people are now:
> She's **gone** to China. (= She's there now.)

▶ 1.47

	I / You / We / They **have** + past participle	He / She / It **has** + past participle
+	I've **given** a stranger a lift.	He's **given** a stranger a lift.
−	We **haven't done** any charity work.	He **hasn't done** any charity work.
Y/N?	**Have** you ever helped a stranger? Yes, I **have**. / No, I **haven't**.	**Has** she ever helped a stranger? Yes, she **has**. / No, she **hasn't**.

We often use *ever* and *never* with the present perfect to talk about our whole life experience. *ever* and *never* come before the past participle in the sentence.
We can also use *once / twice / three times* etc. at the end of a sentence to say how many times we have had an experience.

A   I've **never** visited the UK. Have you **ever** been there?   ⎫ Present perfect
B   Yes, I have. I've been there **three times**.   ⎭ for experiences in general

When we ask or talk about specific past times we use the past simple.

A   When was **the last time** you went?   ⎫ Past simple for
B   **Two years ago**. I rented a car and drove to Scotland. ⎭ specific events

---

3B Present perfect with *just*, *already* and *yet*

▶ 1.53 We can use the present perfect to talk about the recent past.

Use present perfect with *just* in positive statements to say that something happened a very short time ago.
just comes before the past participle in the sentence.
We also use *just* in present perfect questions.

A   **Has** she **just left**?   B   No, she went a few hours ago.

The present perfect with *already* in positive statements shows that something is complete, often before we expected.

already usually comes before the past participle.
We also use *already* in present perfect questions to show surprise.
Have you **already done** all your work?

Use present perfect with *yet*:
- in a negative statement to show that something is not complete.
- in a question to ask if something is complete.

yet comes at the end of the sentence.

> **💡 Tip**
>
> Don't use a past time expression (e.g. *five minutes ago, last week*) with the present perfect. Change to the past simple to talk about the time when something happened:
> I've **already seen** this film. I **saw** it **last week**.
> NOT ~~I've already seen this film last week.~~

Grammar Focus

3A Present perfect or past simple

a Write the past participles of the verbs.

1. buy _bought_
2. do _____
3. drive _____
4. give _____
5. make _____
6. lend _____
7. ride _____
8. save _____
9. see _____
10. sell _____
11. smile _____
12. spend _____
13. take _____
14. want _____
15. write _____

b Complete the sentences with the present perfect form of the verbs in brackets. Use contractions where they are natural.

1. I _'ve never given_ (never / give) money to charity.
2. **A** _____ (you / ever / sell) anything on eBay?
   B Yes, I have. Several times.
3. She _____ (live) in lots of different countries.
4. I know that restaurant – we _____ (eat) there before. The food's excellent.
5. I _____ (never / sing) in front of a large group of people – and I never want to!
6. **A** _____ (he / ever / cook) for more than ten people?
   B No, he hasn't. What about you?
7. She _____ (help) me several times – she's very kind.
8. My car _____ (never / break) down and it's more than ten years old.
9. How many times _____ (the children / see) this film?
10. We _____ (never / try) this, so it'll be new experience.

c Correct the mistakes in these sentences.

1. Have you ever climb a mountain?
   Have you ever climbed a mountain?
2. I never saw that film.
   _____
3. Have you ever gone to Canada?
   _____
4. Where have you been on holiday last year?
   _____
5. She's broken her leg two times.
   _____
6. I've worked in a hospital a long time ago.
   _____
7. In your life, how many times did you move house?
   _____
8. When we went to London we've visited Kew Gardens.
   _____

d ▶ Now go back to p.29

3B Present perfect with *just*, *already* and *yet*

a Match the questions and answers.

1. [g] Would you like some food?
2. [f] Did you like the movie?
3. [a] Has Junko called yet?
4. [c] Where's Liza?
5. [e] Would you like to go for a walk?
6. [b] Can you email Marc about the meeting?
7. [h] Have you written your essay yet?
8. [d] What did you think of the report?

a Yes, I've just spoken to her.
b I've already emailed him.
c She's just gone out. She'll be back soon.
d I'm afraid I haven't read it yet.
e No, thanks. I've already been out.
f We haven't seen it yet.
g No, thanks. I've already had lunch.
h Not yet. I've just finished the introduction.

b Put the words in the correct order to make sentences or questions.

1. they / have / us / yet? / paid
   Have they paid us yet?
2. already / I've / money / all / spent / my
   I've already spent all my money.
3. arrived / our visitors / have / just
   Our visitors have just arrived
4. shops / I / yet / haven't / to / the / been
   I haven't been to the shops yet.
5. raining / just / started / it / has
   It has just started raining.
6. he / yet? / any / has / money / saved
   Has he saved any money yet.

c Look at Jeff's list of things to do. Write sentences about what he has already done (✓), and what he hasn't done yet. Use *already* / *yet* and the present perfect.

1. _He hasn't done the shopping yet._
2. _____
3. _____
4. _____
5. _____
6. _____
7. _____
8. _____
9. _____
10. _____

Jeff To Do – Wednesday

1. do shopping
2. pay Mark back
3. buy paper for the printer ✓ _He has already_
4. check my emails ✓
5. ask Dad for some money _He hasn't_
6. write to Daniel ✓ _He has already_
7. finish writing my project ✓
8. clean the flat _He hasn't ... yet_
9. take out rubbish _He hasn't taken out yet_
10. have a haircut ✓ _He has already had a haircut_

d ▶ Now go back to p.31

147

4A Present continuous and *going to*

I'm meeting Mary at the library to study tomorrow. After the exams, we're going to celebrate!

We use both the present continuous and *going to* + infinitive to talk about future plans – things we have decided to do in the future. In most situations, both forms are possible.

I'm taking an English exam next year. ✓
I'm going to take an English exam next year. ✓

Present continuous
The present continuous is more natural to talk about **arrangements** – when you have agreed something with other people or you have already spent money.

I'm getting married next week. (We have arranged and paid for everything.)
I'm meeting Mary at the library tomorrow. (We have arranged a time and place for the meeting.)

> **Tip**
> When we use the present continuous with a future meaning, we usually mention the time (e.g. *tomorrow*, *next week*)
> We don't need to mention the time with *be going to*:
> She's leaving **tomorrow**. (future arrangement)
> She's leaving. (right now)
> She's going to leave. (future plan)

(For the form of the present continuous see Grammar reference 1B.)

going to
be going to + infinitive tells people about a **plan** or **intention** – when you have already decided to do something in the future.

We're going to get married next year. (We have decided this, but we haven't booked anything yet.)
After the exams, *we're going to celebrate*. (But we don't know exactly where or what time.)

▶ 1.66 *be going to* + infinitve

	I	He / She / It	You / We / They
+	I'm going to watch TV.	She's going to help.	We're going to work hard.
−	I'm not going to play.	It's not going to arrive today.	They're not going to sleep.
Y/N?	Am I going to pick him up? Yes, I am. / No, I'm not.	Is he going to work late? Yes, he is. / No, he isn't.	Are they going to bring anything? Yes, they are. / No, they aren't.

4B *will / won't / shall*

We use *will* to show we are deciding something while we are speaking:
A *Would you like tea or coffee?*
B *Er … I'll have tea, please.*

This is often to make **offers** and **promises**:
A *Oh no – I've left my money at home!*
B *Don't worry – I'll pay.*
A *Can I tell you a secret?*
B *Of course. I promise I won't tell anyone else.*

We can make a **request** with *will*:
Will you take a photograph?
Will you give me a lift to the cinema tomorrow?

We use *shall* in questions to make **offers** and **suggestions**:
Shall I pay for your food? (= I'm offering to pay.)
Shall we go to the cinema this weekend? (= I'm suggesting this.)

We can also use *shall* to **ask for a suggestion**:
A *What shall we do this evening?*
We often reply to these questions with *Let's* + infinitive:
B *Let's go to a nice restaurant.*

> **Tip**
> Reply to offers with *shall* with *Yes, please. / No, thanks.*
> NOT ~~Yes, you shall. / No, you shan't.~~

will and *shall* are modal auxiliary verbs. They are the same for all persons.

▶ 1.70

	I / You / We / They / He / She / It
+	I'll pay for dinner.
−	We won't be late.
Y/N?	Will you help me? Yes, I will. / No I won't.

Short forms: *will* = 'll, *will not* = *won't*

▶ 1.71

I / You / We / They / He / She / It
Shall I pay for dinner?
Shall we leave soon?
What shall I wear?

148

4A Present continuous and *going to*

a Complete the sentences with the correct form of the present continuous, using the verbs in brackets.

1 My parents _are buying_ (buy) me a computer for my birthday.
2 He _____ (study) French next year.
3 _____ (I / not walk) home tonight.
4 '_____ (you / wear) a suit to the interview?' 'No, _____.'
5 'When _____ (your sister / move) to Italy?' 'In about 2 weeks.'
6 _____ (we / go) to the cinema after work.
7 _____ (I / not come) into the office on Friday morning because _____ (I / go) to the doctor's.

b Look at the sentences in **a** again. What arrangements have the people made for each plan?

1 The parents have already ordered the computer.

c Martina and Anna are planning a party. Complete the conversation with the correct form of *going to*.

A So, how's the party planning going?
M Well … We've made a list of what we need to do. And I ¹ _'m going to invite_ (invite) everybody on Facebook today.
A What ² _____ (you / do) about music?
M I ³ _____ (not play) my music. We ⁴ _____ (ask) Graeme to deal with that. He's a DJ, you know! But ⁵ _____ (we / write) a list of our favourites for him.
A Brilliant! ⁶ _____ (there / be) a lot of food?
M Yes, quite a lot. Rachael loves cooking so ⁷ _____ (she / make) the food the day before the party.
A Cool …
M But ⁸ _____ (she / not pay) for it all! We ⁹ _____ (pay) her back for the ingredients.
A So what ¹⁰ _____ (I / do)?
M ¹¹ _____ (you / clean) the house!
A Oh fantastic … I get all the best jobs …

d Choose the most natural sentence to follow sentences a and b in each pair.

1 a ☐ I'm going to have a party.
  b ☐ I'm having a party.
  1 It's this Saturday. Do you want to come?
  2 I don't know how many people to invite. What do you think?

2 a ☐ They're going to arrive in the afternoon.
  b ☐ They're arriving in the afternoon.
  1 They're not sure what time yet.
  2 They've arranged for a taxi to meet them at the station.

3 a ☐ Are we going to play tennis on Saturday?
  b ☐ Are we playing tennis on Saturday?
  1 Yes, I've booked the court for 2 o'clock.
  2 Yes, what time do you want to play?

4 a ☐ She's going to study all day tomorrow.
  b ☐ She's studying all day tomorrow.
  1 She's got an exam next week, and she wants to pass.
  2 She's got classes at university from 9 am to 6 pm.

5 a ☐ I'm going to fly from Denver to Boston.
  b ☐ I'm flying from Denver to Boston.
  1 Which airline do you recommend?
  2 My plane leaves at 8 am.

e ▶ Now go back to p.38

4B *will / won't / shall*

a Look at the sentences. Is each sentence a promise (*P*), an offer (*O*), a decision (*D*), or a suggestion (*S*)?

1 Shall I help you carry that box? ___
2 Shall we go for a walk? ___
3 I'll drive you to the station if you like. ___
4 I think I'll have spaghetti. ___
5 Don't worry. I'll call you later. ___
6 Let's go to the beach. ___
7 I won't be late for the meeting. ___
8 Shall we have chicken for dinner? ___

b Choose the correct word in *italics* to complete the sentence.

1 **A** I need to go to the station.
  B *I'll / I shall* call a taxi for you.
2 **A** This document is secret.
  B Don't worry – I *won't / shall not* show it to anyone.
3 **A** This box is really heavy!
  B *Shall / Will* I help you carry it?
4 **A** Those shoes are in the sale, madam. They're only £20.
  B Great! *I'll / I shall* take them.
5 **A** *Shall / Will* we go out this evening?
  B Good idea. Let's go to the cinema.
6 **A** I'm working late tonight. *Will / Shall* you cook dinner?
  B Of course.

c Complete the conversation with *will* or *shall* and the correct form of the verbs in brackets.

A ¹ _Shall we go_ (we / go) out for dinner tonight?
B Er … well, I haven't got much money. ² _____ (I / cook) something for you at my flat?
A Don't worry. ³ _____ (I / pay) for the meal.
B Really? Thank you! That sounds great. Where ⁴ _____ (we / eat)?
A Let's go for a curry. ⁵ _____ (I / book) a table?
B No, it's OK. ⁶ _____ (I / do) it. I know a good place near here. ⁷ _____ (I / call) them now.
A OK. ⁸ _____ (you / call) me after you make the booking? I'd like to know what time we're going to meet.
B Yes, ⁹ _____ (I / call) you later. I promise ¹⁰ _____ (I / forget).
A Great. Talk to you later then. Bye.

d ▶ Now go back to p.40

5A must / have to / can

Necessary, a rule	Not allowed, a rule
Visitors **must** wash their hands. We **have to** wash our hands.	You **mustn't** smoke in the building. We **can't** smoke here.
Allowed	Not necessary
You **can** smoke outside.	You **don't have to** wear a uniform.

must and *have to* have very similar meanings.

must is often used in written rules:
All patients **must wash** their hands.

People in authority use *must* when they are speaking, for example, teachers, parents etc.:
You **must switch** off your mobile phone.

We use *have to* when we say what is necessary. It is very common in spoken English:
Doctors **have to work** very long hours.
I **have to leave** for work at 7.00 am.

must not and *don't have to* have very different meanings.

must not means something is not allowed – it is important **not** to do something:
Students **must not talk** in the exam room.
You **mustn't smoke** in here.

don't have to means something is unnecessary:
Teachers **don't have to wear** a uniform.
He **doesn't have to work** because he's rich.

can means something is allowed:
You **can take** a one-hour lunch break.
You **can borrow** up to five books from the library.

can't is similar to *mustn't*.
It means not allowed / not possible:
You **can't smoke** here.
Bankers **can't relax** for a minute.

▶ 2.6 *have to* + infinitive

	I / You / We / They	He / She / It
+	We **have to work** hard.	She **has to leave** early today.
−	They **don't have to** play.	He **doesn't have to work**.
Y/N?	**Do** nurses **have to have** a degree? Yes, they **do**. / No, they **don't**.	**Does** he **have to wear** a uniform? Yes, he **does**. / No, he **doesn't**.

can and *must* are modal auxiliary verbs. They are the same for all persons.

▶ 2.7 *must* + infinitive

	I / You / We / They / He / She / It
+	You **must arrive** on time.
−	Teachers **mustn't be** late.

Questions with *must* are rarely used in modern English.

▶ 2.8 *can* + infinitive

	I / You / We / They / He / She / It
+	You **can leave** work early today.
−	The children **can't go** outside alone.
Y/N?	**Can** I **smoke** here? Yes, you **can**. / No, you **can't**.

5B will and might for predictions

We use *will* and *might* to make predictions about what we expect to happen in the future.
will shows that we are very sure:
I**'ll say** something silly. They **won't give** me the job.

might shows we are less sure:
They **might ask** difficult questions. I **might not get** the job.

will and *might* are modal auxiliary verbs. They are the same for all persons.

▶ 2.10

	I / You / We / They / He / She / It
+	You**'ll get** the job. You **might get** the job.
−	He **won't get** the job. He **might not get** the job.

Short forms: will = 'll, will not = won't

We usually use phrases like *I think ... , I don't think ...* and *Do you think ... ?* to introduce predictions when we speak.

▶ 2.11

	I / You / We / They / He / She / It
+	I think you**'ll get** the job. I think he **might get** the job
−	I don't think I**'ll get** the job.
Y/N?	**Do you think** we**'ll get** the job? I think so. / I don't think so. **Do you think** we **might get** the job? We **might**. / We **might not**.

We can also use *I'm sure ...* before predictions with *will*:
I'm sure I'll say something silly.

150

Grammar Focus

5A must / have to / can

a Flavia works in a call centre. Read her office rules. Complete Flavia's description of her work with *have to*, *can* or *can't* and the words in brackets.

Office Rules
- Employees must wear a uniform at all times.
- Employees must not check emails during working hours.
- You must not talk to other employees during working hours.
- You must answer the phone within 5 seconds.
- Employees must always be polite to customers.

I'm telling you, Jo, it's a terrible place to work! The customers can't see you, but we still ¹ _have to_ wear a uniform all the time. You ² _____ (wear) your normal clothes.
I ³ _____ (check) my emails – it's not allowed – and I ⁴ _____ (speak) to my colleagues during the day! Fortunately, we ⁵ _____ (talk) to each other during our breaks!
When the phone rings, we ⁶ _____ (answer) it very quickly – within 5 seconds. And we always ⁷ _____ (be) polite to customers, but they're often incredibly rude to us! I really ⁸ _____ (find) a new job!

b Choose the correct option.
1. Visitors *must not / don't have to* smoke in the building.
2. It's a relaxed office – you *must not / don't have to* wear a tie.
3. I start at 10 am, so I *mustn't / don't have to* get up early.
4. Employees *must not / don't have to* park in the customer car park. It is for customers only.
5. If there is a fire, you *must not / don't have to* use the lift. You must use the stairs.

c Complete the sentences with one of the expressions from the box. Use each expression once.

can   can't   doesn't have to   has to   must   must not

1. In my office, we _____ eat or drink at our desks. We have to go to the canteen.
2. My job's really nice. I _____ start work when I want and finish when I want.
3. She works from home so she _____ drive to work.
4. Warning! Dangerous work area. Visitors _____ enter without permission.
5. Important! You _____ keep your visitor card with you at all times.
6. He _____ travel a lot in his job. Sometimes he goes to three or four countries in a month.

d ▶ Now go back to p.49

5B will and might for predictions

a Duncan is planning to move to China for a year. Look at his predictions and complete his sentences with *will / won't*, *might / might not*.

	100% sure	50% sure ???
Good	learn about China	learn to speak Chinese?
	meet new people	travel around China?
	try new things	stay more than a year?
Bad	difficult language	tiring job?
	not much money	miss family?
	no friends	not like food?

1. I'm sure I __'ll__ learn a lot about China.
2. They have different food in China, and I _____ like it.
3. I'm sure Chinese _____ be really difficult, but I _____ learn to speak a bit.
4. I _____ have any friends at first, but I _____ meet new people.
5. My job _____ be tiring and I _____ have much money!
6. I _____ try new things and I _____ travel around the country.
7. I _____ want to stay more than a year – I _____ want to come back!

b Correct the mistakes in the sentences below. Sometimes there is more than one possible answer.
1. She thinks she might to go to Spain for her holiday.
2. Which sights do you think you visit?
3. I sure the restaurant will be busy.
4. I'm sure it won't raining today – the sky's blue.
5. Do you think you might buying a new computer?
6. I'm sure I might change jobs next year.
7. He might not to arrive on time. The traffic's bad.
8. I won't think I pass my exam.

c Write questions using *will* and the words in brackets.
1. **A** Are you sure (you / enjoy) it?
   B Yes, I'm sure I will.
2. **A** Do you think (she / leave)?
   B She might.
3. **A** How much do you think (it / cost)?
   B About fifty pounds.
4. **A** When do you think (they / tell) us?
   B I don't know.
5. **A** Are you sure (we / finish) on time?
   B No. We might not.
6. **A** Do you think (I / get) an interview?
   B I think so!

d In which questions in **c** can you replace *will* with *might*?

e ▶ Now go back to p.50

151

6A Imperative; should

We use the imperative and *should* to give advice – to tell other people what we think is the best or the right thing to do.

▶ 2.21 Imperative

The imperative is stronger than *should*. It tells somebody exactly what to do.

We can use it to give…

- advice:
  Try to get a good night's sleep.
  Don't stay up late.
- instructions:
  Don't turn right! **Turn** left!
  Come here!
- warnings:
  Be careful!

The imperative is the infinitive of the verb with no subject. For negative imperatives, use *don't* + infinitive:

▶ 2.22 should

should is a bit less strong than the imperative. It shows that what we are saying is advice, not an instruction.

should is a modal auxiliary verb. It is the same for all persons.

	I / You / We / They / He / She / It
+	You **should get up** early.
–	Children **shouldn't eat** a lot of sweets.
Y/N?	**Should** I **stop** eating sweets? Yes, you **should**. / No, you **shouldn't**.

We often use phrases like *I think …*, *I don't think …* and *Do you think … ?* to introduce advice with *should*:
I think / **I don't think** you should go to bed.
A **Do you think** I should say sorry?
B Yes, **I think so**. / No, **I don't think so**.

> 💡 **Tip**
> Adding *I think … I don't think …* before *should* is more polite because it shows you are talking about opinion, not fact.

6B Uses of to + infinitive

The infinitive is the dictionary form of the verb (*go, swim, be, have* etc.).

We use *to* + infinitive (*to go, to swim, to be*, etc.) in many different patterns.

The negative is *not* + *to* + infinitive (*not to go, not to swim, not to be* etc.).

▶ 2.30

1 Infinitive of purpose
Use *to* + infinitive to give a reason:
A Why did you go to Egypt?
B **To see** the sharks.
I looked in the mirror **to check** my hair.
Read a book **to relax**.

2 verb + to + infinitive
When two verbs go together in a sentence, certain verbs are followed by *to* + infinitive:
I **wanted to visit** Australia.
I **decided not to go** home.
Some of the verbs that follow this pattern are: *choose, decide, want, would like, try, promise, expect, remember, forget, need, plan, learn, offer.*

3 adjective + to + infinitive
Many adjectives can be followed by *to* + infinitive:
I was **surprised to get** the job.
It's **important not to forget** people's names at work.

4 verb + question word + to + infinitive
Some verbs can be followed by a question word + *to* + infinitive:
I **forgot what to do**.
I don't **know who to ask**.
Can you **tell** me **where to go**?
I can't **decide what to wear**.

Some of the verbs that follow this pattern are: *ask, decide, explain, forget, know, show, tell, understand*

Grammar Focus

6A Imperative; should

Tony gets up late every morning and has to get ready for work very quickly. He doesn't have breakfast – he just drinks a cup of strong coffee. He drives to work – it's only about 2 kilometres, but the traffic is terrible. He checks his messages while he's waiting. At work, he drinks coffee all day and he doesn't stop for lunch – he eats a takeaway pizza at his desk. When he gets home after work, he watches TV until about 1 am. Then the next day he does the same all over again.

a Read about Tony's normal daily routine. Write advice for him using *should / shouldn't* and the words in brackets.

1 (get up earlier)
   He should get up earlier.
2 (have breakfast)
   _____
3 (drink less coffee)
   _____
4 (drive to work)
   _____
5 (use his phone in the car)
   _____
6 (stop for lunch)
   _____
7 (eat at his desk)
   _____
8 (go to bed earlier)
   _____

b Tony's friend Andy is giving him advice. Complete Andy's advice with the imperative form of the verbs from the box. Be careful – two verbs need to be negative.

drink   eat   get   go
set   spend   ~~start~~   wake

T I'm always tired these days. What should I do?
A That's easy. [1] ___Start___ the day with a good breakfast. [2] _____ about half an hour on breakfast – it's really important.
T Half an hour? I don't have time in the morning.
A So [3] _____ up earlier. [4] _____ your alarm for six thirty. And then [5] _____ back to sleep – [6] _____ out of bed straight away.
T Six thirty? Are you joking?
A No, I'm serious. Get up early, [7] _____ breakfast and [8] _____ coffee. It's really bad for you.

c Correct one mistake in each sentence.

1 Everybody should to bring warm clothes.
2 How much money do I should take?
3 Don't to be late for the party!
4 He shoulds be more careful.
5 Not spend so much money on the Internet.
6 You don't should check your email every five minutes.
7 What you think I should do to get fit?

d ▶ Now go back to p.58

6B Uses of *to* + infinitive

a Match the sentence halves 1–7 with the best ending.

1 [e] It's dangerous
2 [ ] They went to the gym
3 [ ] He drove to the shops
4 [ ] It will be great
5 [ ] I'm going to bed
6 [ ] She was disappointed
7 [ ] She emailed the company

a to get some sleep.
b to buy some food.
c to visit Paris!
d to apply for the job.
e to text and drive.
f to do some exercise.
g not to pass her exam.

b Complete the sentences with the correct question word + *to* + infinitive.

which to buy   what to watch   where to go
how to use   ~~what to do~~   how to get   who to speak to

1 I don't know ___what to do___ about my problem.
2 Can you show me _____ this computer?
3 I can't decide _____ for my holiday.
4 Do you know _____ to the station?
5 I'm not sure _____ on TV tonight.
6 I like both these dresses. I can't decide _____ .
7 Can you tell me _____ about getting a refund?

c Use the verbs in the box to complete the sentences with a positive or negative *to* + infinitive.

~~read~~   eat   break   listen   wear   receive   go   arrive

1 I bought this book ___to read___ about sharks.
2 It's expensive _____ in restaurants every day.
3 I was annoyed _____ a reply to my email.
4 It's rude _____ when she's talking.
5 We promise _____ anything.
6 I don't know what _____ to the wedding.
7 You should leave now _____ on time.
8 I decided _____ to the party. I was too tired.

d ▶ Now go back to p.61

153

Audioscripts

Unit 1

▶ 1.2

1 A It's a nice day today.
  B Yes, it's a perfect day for a birthday party. It's great that so many people are here.
  A So, how do you know Ana?
  B We were at university together. We did the same course.
  A Oh right. What did you study?
  B English Literature. And you? How do *you* know Ana?
  A I'm her neighbour. I live in the house next door.
  B Really? It's a lovely street.
  A I think so. So did you come …

2 C How's the food?
  D It's great. The pizza is delicious. It's always nice to get good food at a party … Err … So, do you live near here?
  C Yeah, I live down by the river. You know those flats …
  D Oh yeah! The new ones. They're expensive! How much rent do you pay?
  C Err … not much. It's not so … expensive … err …
  D So what do you do?
  C I work for a bank.
  D So, how much do you earn?
  C Erm, is that … er … over there … Sorry, I just have to speak to my friend, because …

3 E What do you think of the party?
  F Yeah, it's great. It's really nice to meet all of Ana's friends. You?
  E It's alright, but the music is a bit boring.
  F Mmm.
  E I like your T-shirt. Is it for a football team?
  F No! At least I don't think so!
  E So, do you play any sports?
  F No, not really. I don't really like sport.
  E Well, what do you like then?
  F I prefer reading, or watching films.
  E Oh.
  F Yeah, so I might go to the cinema after the party. There's a new film about a man who goes to Peru to visit his brother and …
  E Yeah, I saw that last week.
  F Oh. What was it like?
  E Oh, it's an awful film. Really boring.
  F OK, well, I'd like to see it anyway. Perhaps I'll like it.
  E No, I don't think so. It's a really strange story. And in the end, the man can't find his brother and he just goes home again.
  F Oh, thanks a lot!

▶ 1.10

TARA Last year, my ex-boyfriend told me he didn't want to see me any more … by text message! What kind of person does that? It was horrible. I called him for days, but he didn't answer. It made me feel like I wasn't important to him at all. I think he just wanted me to go away. What an idiot.
MAGDA When I want to plan something, I generally just send a text. It's the same when I cancel plans – a text message is easier. You don't need to give a long explanation, you know, a lot of reasons. Or have a difficult conversation. It's better for everyone.
CHRIS Birthdays are different now. I hardly ever get cards or presents from friends, or even my brother, and no one calls. Everyone just writes 'happy birthday' on my wall on Facebook. It's not very friendly, in my opinion.
MIKE My daughter is travelling around South America at the moment. She's writing a blog so we know what she's doing. But she rarely calls. And I'd love to get a postcard or a letter sometimes. Just to know she's thinking about the family.

▶ 1.15 PART 1

RACHEL Annie?
ANNIE Rachel!
R Long time no see! How are you?
A I'm great. What a lovely surprise! Great to see you!
R Yeah! You too.
A When did we last see each other?
R Oh, I think it was about … six years ago! So … where are you living these days?
A Oh, not far from here. I live on Hampton Street. Do you know it?
R Yes, I do. That's really close to the centre.
A Mmm. How about you?
R We live on Compton Road.
A Oh – how nice!
MARK My name's Mark, by the way.
A Hi. Nice to meet you.
M Nice to meet you, too.
R Sorry, yes – Mark's my husband!
A Husband – wow! That's fantastic news. When did you get married?
R Six months ago.
M Eight months ago.
R It was six, Mark.
A Well, congratulations! I want to know all the details! Look – I'm going to the café down the street now to meet Leo, my boyfriend. Would you both like to come?
R Yeah, that sounds good.
A Brilliant! Let's go.

▶ 1.20 PART 2

MARK Do you play much sport?
LEO Not really. I occasionally watch the rugby on TV, but I'm not a big sports fan.
M Did you see the match at the weekend?
RACHEL Oh, not sport again!
ANNIE So, have you got any exciting plans for next week?
M Well, er …
R No, not really. Just work. I've got a lot to do in the shop this week, because we're going to a wedding next weekend.
A Oh, the shop? What do you do?
R I'm a florist.
A What a great job! Where's the shop?
R Not far from here. I'll show you some time.
A That would be great! And are you the manager, or …
R Well, not really – it's my shop.
A Wow. That's amazing! So you're a businesswoman! Do you work on your own?
R No, I have someone to help. Tina. She comes in for a few hours every day.
A Oh, that's good.
R How about you? What do you do?
A Oh, marketing. Boring!
R Same as Mark. He works in marketing.
A Oh, I'm sorry. I find it boring.
R Do you have any plans for the weekend?
A Actually, yes. I'm going to visit my brother, Dan.
R Oh, I remember Dan. How is he?
A He's fine. He's married now. To Martina.
R Anyway, we really must go. I need to get back to the shop.
A Yeah, of course.
M It was really nice to meet you.
A Yeah, you too.
L Nice to meet you, Mark.
R It was great to see you again, Annie.
A Yeah! We must meet up soon!
R Definitely!
A Actually, it's Leo's birthday in a couple of weeks. Perhaps we could meet then.
R OK, great. I'll give you a call. And say hello to Dan for me!

▶ 1.22

CHRIS So, are you good about keeping in touch with people?
NINA Er, not really. I always plan to write to people, but then I forget. I send emails to my parents sometimes, about once a month, but more often I get emails from them saying 'Are you OK? We haven't heard from you for a long time.' Then I always send them a quick email and tell them what I'm doing. How about you?
C Oh, I like keeping in touch. I think it's important to keep in touch with your family. I write emails to my parents sometimes, but I also phone or Skype. I phone my mother every weekend.
N Every weekend!
C Yes, she gets worried about me and she wants to know what I'm doing.
N I hardly ever phone my parents. I wait until I go and see them, and talk to them then.
C Don't you ever phone them to have a chat?
N No, I only phone if it's something important. You don't have to be in touch with people all the time.
C What about friends? Surely you keep in touch with friends?
N Not very much, maybe I should do. I send texts or messages sometimes, but that's about all. I always think if you have good friends you can talk about everything when you meet. It's more fun to tell people your news when you can have a real conversation.
C Oh well, I often send messages to people so they know I'm thinking about them. And sometimes, when I have a particularly good photo, I send it to everyone by email. I think it's a nice thing to do …

Unit 2

▶ 1.23
DAY THREE
So, the next morning, we started with some water skiing practice on the beach. First, they showed us how to stand up on the skis … and then how to fall off safely. The lesson took about an hour, and then we were ready to go out to sea. There were five other people in my group, who were all very excited. But not me – I was really worried. The instructor looked at me and said, "Do you want to go first?" and then everyone looked at me. I felt sick but I said, "Yes" …

Ten seconds after I started, I fell over. I tried again. And I fell over again. Then the third time, something amazing suddenly happened. I didn't fall over. And I found out that I love water skiing. The ten minutes in the water passed very quickly and I didn't want to stop!

When we got back to the hotel, the receptionist asked me, "So, did you enjoy the water skiing course?" I said, "Yes" which, for the first time, was the truth.

And then later on that evening I had a drink in the bar with the other water skiers. I felt really happy. And that was when I realised I was enjoying being a 'Yes Man' after all.

▶ 1.24
DAY SEVEN
On the last day of the holiday, I couldn't wait for midnight. At 12 o'clock I could stop answering 'yes' to every question. The week had been fun but I wanted some control of my life again! That evening I went for one last dinner with some of my new friends. "So, did you have a good week?" one of them asked me. "Yes," I said. "What was your favourite thing?" she asked.

And do you know what? I couldn't really answer her. There were so many things I'd enjoyed. I worked as a waiter for a day – I didn't get any money for it, but I made friends with some interesting people who came to eat at the restaurant. I also spent a day fishing with five Greek fishermen and caught several fish. I stayed at a beach party until six in the morning. Oh, and I won a dancing competition!

Of course, some of my experiences weren't very good. I took the same boat trip three times … I went swimming at midnight – actually, I liked the swimming, but I didn't like the mosquitoes that bit me when I got out of the sea. And I spent over 200 euros on souvenirs that I hate!

166

Audioscripts

It was great to try new things. But I was glad the week was nearly finished. I wanted to get back home and relax for a day before I started work again on Monday. But Day 7 wasn't finished yet! Without thinking, I asked my new friends what they planned to do next. They were all smiling at me. One of them said, "We're flying to Thailand tomorrow. Do you want to come with us? You'd love it!"

I looked at my watch. It was 11.55.

▶ 1.33

Well, I was in a rush that morning and I suppose I set off a bit late. It was raining when I left the house and there was a lot of traffic on the roads. I got to the airport just before the desk closed.

When I boarded the plane, all the other passengers were waiting for me. It was a bit embarrassing, but we took off OK. I had a seat in the middle of the plane and for the first couple of hours it was fine.

So I was reading my book when one of the flight attendants came over and spoke to me. She said that there was something wrong with *her* seat and that she needed to take mine. I was the last passenger to check in, so they chose me.

I asked the flight attendant where I should sit and she told me that the only place was the toilet. At first, I thought it was a joke, but then I realised that she was serious.

So I was sitting on the toilet when the turbulence started. It was quite frightening because of course there was no seatbelt in the toilet. I almost fell off a few times. After the turbulence stopped, I opened the door. About five passengers were waiting outside to use the toilet. I just closed the door again.

And then to top it all, when we landed at Istanbul there was a delay of an hour before we could get off the plane because of a problem in the airport.

I still can't believe they told me to stay in the toilet for two hours. It was terrible. You just can't treat customers like that.

▶ 1.38 PART 1

ANNIE Excuse me … Excuse me!
EMPLOYEE Yes, how can I help you?
A I'm going to Birmingham to visit my brother.
E OK. Erm, which train are you taking?
A Oh, I don't know. What time's the next train?
E The next one leaves in … four minutes.
A How often do the trains leave?
E Every … 30 minutes. So the next one after that is at 15.32.
A OK, great. And er, which platform does it leave from?
E That train leaves from … platform 12. So, it's just over there.
A Sorry, just one more thing.
E Yes, of course.
A Could you tell me where the ticket office is?
E It's over there. But it looks quite busy – there's a long queue. I can sell you a ticket.
A Oh, brilliant! How much is a ticket?
E Well, when do you want to come back?
A Oh, I don't know. Probably tomorrow evening. But on Sunday it's going to be sunny I think and my brother's going to have a party and so maybe I'll stay until Monday.
E The ticket prices change. Sunday is cheaper than Monday.
A Oh, Sunday then. His parties are never very good.
E OK, you want a return to Birmingham. Coming back on … Sunday?
A Yes, that's right.
E So, that's £26.30.
A Can I pay by card?
E Yes, sure … OK, so here's your card, and your ticket. Is there anything else I can help you with?
A Actually, there is one more thing. Where can I buy a magazine? Is there a newsagent's here?
E Yes, look – there's one just over there.
A Great. Thanks so much.
E No problem. Have a good journey.

▶ 1.45 PART 2

ANNIE He doesn't live in Birmingham any more! He doesn't live in Birmingham any more! He doesn't live in Birmingham any more!
EMPLOYEE Sorry?
A My brother. He moved. He doesn't live in Birmingham any more. He lives in Stratford now! Can I change my ticket …?

▶ 1.46

TIM So, when I get to Jakarta, what should I do?
KAREN I'm not really sure. I mean, I left Indonesia about ten years ago and … well … it's probably all changed now.
T So, yeah, I think we'll just get a taxi from the airport to the hostel.
K You could, but if you want to save money, I think there's probably a bus service.
T I suppose so. Is that what you did?
K Well, I was going to Jakarta to work, so someone met us with a car and drove us into the centre of town.
T So what was it like when you arrived?
K It's something I'll never forget. You know, this was the first time I went somewhere that was completely different, the other side of the world. I remember we had a pretty bad flight, there was a long delay at the airport because there was something wrong with the plane. And we had quite a lot of turbulence – and as we were landing I remember thinking 'Is this all a big mistake?'. But no … as soon as we got off the plane and I felt how lovely and warm it was, I began to feel much happier. I loved it there, I'm sure you will too.
T And, so, once you were away from the airport, what did you see?
K Well, the first thing I saw was a traffic jam!
T Oh no.
K Yes, and a traffic jam that was much noisier and longer than in this country. And a storm!
T Oh no! Really?
K Yes, quite often in the spring, the rainy season, there's suddenly a storm with heavy rain and lightning. And you just have to run for the nearest building! For me, it was exciting though. I expect you'll love it, too.
T You must have so many memories of your time there.
K Yeah … yeah I do.
T Did you write them down? You know, do a blog or something.
K No … I didn't have an internet connection in my apartment.
T Or a diary or something like that?
K No, I never did.
T That's a pity. But you seem to remember it pretty well!

Unit 3

▶ 1.49

After leaving his job, Philip Wollen opened up the Kindness Trust, an organisation that finds small charities in countries where a little bit of money can make a big difference. Wollen then surprises these charities with a gift to continue their good work. So far, he has given money to between 400–500 different charities in 40 countries. His money has built schools, children's homes, and homes for animals.

A special charity for Wollen is the Morning Star orphanage in Bangalore. The orphanage started when, 20 years ago, a man called John Samson found a hungry baby boy in the street. He gave him a home and then he looked for more homeless children to help. Today the orphanage looks after 60 children. With money from the Kindness Trust, John has made the Morning Star bigger and opened a new learning centre. Wollen went to India to open the centre, meet the children and hear about their lives. One little girl has won a place at a famous women's college, another child is an excellent chess player and another wants to be a doctor. The little boy that John Samson found in the street has now become a chemist.

And it is not just people that Philip Wollen has helped. He has also given money to a large number of animal charities, such as Edgar's Mission in Australia, a charity that cares for old farm animals and finds new homes for them. The charity also tries to teach people how to look after animals, so they are healthy and happy.

Wollen thinks everyone can help to make the world a better place for other people and animals. He says, 'One man can make a difference and every man should try.'

▶ 1.51

PRESENTER So, in these difficult times, how are people spending their money? Are people still borrowing from the banks? I came to Norwich to talk to shoppers.
Excuse me, sir, do you mind if I ask you a few questions about your spending habits?
SPEAKER 1 Err, OK.
P Can I ask what you've got in your bags?
1 I've just bought my food for the week. They had some special offers on cheese! I think I've got enough for a month.
P Are you saving up for anything at the moment?
1 Yes actually, I'm saving for a car. My girlfriend is moving away to Leeds to study and I want to visit her at weekends. The train is really expensive so in the end, it's cheaper to drive.
P Why didn't you borrow the money for the car?
1 Well, I don't want to owe money to a bank. I generally don't like borrowing. I've got three credit cards and I've never used any of them. I've only got them, because of the free stuff you get – travel insurance, cinema tickets, that kind of thing.

PRESENTER And what have you just bought?
SPEAKER 2 Not much! It was all too expensive. But I found a good price on some suntan lotion. So I bought a lot.
P Are you saving up for anything at the moment?
2 Well, I'm always saving, but there isn't really anything I actually want to buy. I've already got everything I need. Why should I spend my money on new things when the things I have are perfectly OK? Everyone should save for when they're older. I don't want to be working when I'm an old man.
P So, I suppose you don't need to borrow?
2 No, not yet! And I hope I never do. When I can't afford something, I don't buy it. Simple. And I never lend money to other people. Never. You give them money, and you never get it back. Then you lose a friend.

PRESENTER Have you bought anything nice today?
SPEAKER 3 Some perfume … and a small necklace. The necklace was quite expensive … well, very expensive … but I need a new one to go with a dress I've just bought.
P Lovely! And are you saving up for anything at the moment?
3 No, not really. I don't really save up for things, to be honest. If I need something, I just buy it. I've got credit cards. I've already spent my salary this month, but that's OK. Life's too short to worry about money.
P So you don't mind borrowing money?
3 I don't borrow money. Well, I use my credit cards, but that's not really borrowing, is it? Oh! And I got a small loan last year. I haven't paid it back yet.

▶ 1.56 PART 1

RACHEL OK, what's next? Oh, we need to buy a present for Leo.
MARK Really? Why?
R It's his birthday, remember. Annie told us last week.
M Well, we don't know him very well.
R Oh, come on. We need to buy him something. Oh, look – how about this shop? I'm sure we can find something in here.
M Hmm.

167

1.57 PART 2

MARK This place is great! I could stay here all day!
RACHEL Well, we're only here for Leo, remember.
SHOP ASSISTANT Hi, can I help you?
R Er, yes. We're looking for a present for a friend. It's his birthday.
SA OK. Are you looking for anything in particular?
R Umm, I don't know …
M Something fun!
SA OK. What sort of thing does he like? Is he a sports fan?
M Yeah.
R Is he? Does he like sport?
M Yeah, I'm sure.
SA OK … How about this? 'Football in a tin'. Perfect for a birthday present.
R What is it exactly?
SA It's a football game. Look, you put the boots on your fingers, there's a ball …
M This looks perfect! He loves football.
R Does he? I'm not sure. What else do you have?
SA What about this? A weather station.
M Oh – what does it do?
SA Well, it tells you the weather now, and the next day. It's also an alarm clock.
M Do you have anything cheaper?
SA Well … well, this is a great product. A book money bank.
R A book money bank?
SA Well, you open it here and there's a place to put your money. To keep it safe.
R Oh, that's quite nice.
M Yeah, I suppose he might like that.
R OK, we've decided.
SA Great …
M On second thoughts, I really think we should get something sporty. Could you show us something else?
SA Oh, I know. What about this? A football clock.
M Brilliant! Let's get that!
R Well, if you really think he likes football.
M Yeah, of course. He was talking about football last time we saw him. We'll take it.
R Was he? I don't remember that.

1.61 PART 3

SHOP ASSISTANT 2 Who's next, please?
MARK Oh, yes. Just this, please.
SA2 How would you like to pay?
M Cash.
SA2 OK.
M Actually, I think I'll put it on my credit card.
SA2 OK. Can you put your card in, please? … And can you enter your PIN, please? … Thank you. OK, here's your receipt, and here's the clock.
M Thanks a lot.

1.62

SHONA I support Oxfam. You see, I had a really happy childhood myself and I think it's important to help other people in poorer countries have happy childhoods. I haven't got a lot of spare money, but I try and help them in other ways. For example, last year I ran a marathon and people sponsored me, you know, gave me money for doing the run. I made just over a hundred pounds. And then, once a month, I make cakes and take them to my office. I sell pieces of cake to my colleagues for morning tea and give the money to Oxfam.
JACK Well, giving to charity is quite easy really. You can go online and pay with your credit card. I've given money to Greenpeace that way a few times recently. And once a year, I sell their calendars – mostly to friends and the people I work with. I think that helping to save our natural world is the most important thing you can do. I think I should do something now – so that my children and my children's children can enjoy the kind of world that I live in.
JESSICA Of course, I think it's important to … well, that people give money to charities. But actually, I haven't got a lot of money myself. I owe money to my parents and I have to pay back the government for my university study and … In fact, I've never given any money to a charity. I can't really afford it.
WILLIAM Our history is really important and we need to protect it. When I think of all the old buildings that we've already lost, it's terrible. So, once every six months I go around my neighbourhood and collect money door to door for the National Trust. I tell people about local places the National Trust want to protect and they are usually very generous.

Unit 4

1.65

INTERVIEWER So Marta, what exactly is a May Ball?
MARTA Well, it's a huge party at our college. They have it every summer after we finish our exams because we need to celebrate after all that stress. Everyone gets dressed up, and there's food and drink and entertainment. There are eight different stages and over 70 bands. This year one of my favourite DJs is playing. I really can't wait.
I What are you going to wear?
M I've just bought the dress I'm going to wear – it's dark blue and I feel really good in it. I'm going to wear it with high heels and some nice jewellery!
I Is there anything else you need to do?
M Get ready and sleep! I need to look my best … I'm going to the hairdresser's tomorrow. And a beautician is doing our make-up. Apart from that, I'm not going to leave the house on Saturday. I'm going to get as much sleep as possible!
I What time are you leaving?
M The ball doesn't start until 9 pm but I'm meeting the others at 7 pm so we can start queuing. Everyone says it takes a really long time to get in … but then we're going to stay the whole night – until 6 am, when they serve breakfast!

CRAIG So, hi, everyone – welcome to today's audio blog. Well, today is the fourth day of my wedding. Everyone's going to be back here again in a few hours. There's going to be more dancing and food, of course. And today they're going to make a special cream from a spice called turmeric and rub it on my face and arms. The idea is that it cleans your skin and makes you ready for marriage. I hope it doesn't hurt …
Then tomorrow is the wedding day. It starts at 9 am, so quite early. But it finishes in the afternoon, after lunch. My friends are arriving early tomorrow to help me get ready and take me there. I'm going to wear a traditional Indian suit called a 'kurta pajama'. It's actually really comfortable.
I'm really excited now. I'm looking forward to seeing all my friends and relatives, and, of course, my new wife! But I need to be patient … the first part of an Indian wedding is breakfast with all the guests. The bride eats in a separate room with some of her friends. So, I'm not going to see Monisha until the ceremony actually begins, later in the morning.

1.68 PART 1

HARRY Hello?
MIKE Hi, Harry! It's me! I'm here! I've just arrived at my hotel.
H Welcome to Tokyo! Did you have a good journey?
M Yeah, it was fine. I was so lucky to get a stopover in Japan!
H And lucky that I'm here to show you around! I've already got a few ideas about what we can do.
M OK, but I really don't want to go where all the tourists go. I want to see the real Tokyo.
H OK, so we won't go to Disneyland then! And I won't take you to the Imperial Palace, either.
M OK.
H I mean, the palace is nice but it's so crowded. It's really just a place for tourists.
M Fine.
H So … shall we start with something to eat?
M OK.
H There's a great noodle restaurant I know. The noodles are delicious, some of the best in Tokyo. And it's also really simple. You just eat quickly and then you leave. So we won't waste any time!
M Brilliant.
H After that, I'll take you to Yoyogi Park. It's a huge park and it'll be really busy at the moment because everyone's going to see the cherry blossom.
M The cherry blossom?
H Yeah, it's beautiful. You see young people, businessmen in suits, families – everyone goes to look at the pretty flowers. There are also lots of musicians there, and the teenagers doing 'cosplay' …
M Who?
H Well, basically they're people who dress up as characters from computer games and cartoons. That kind of thing. They just do it for fun but they spend a lot of time and money on it so they look incredible.
M Wow – I think I've seen pictures of them before. I'd love to see them in real life. And after that?
H Well, do you want to do any shopping?
M Actually, yeah – I want to look for a new camera.
H Excellent. I'll take you to Akihabara, then. There are lots of electronics shops there. And they often have special offers.
M Perfect. And what are we doing in the evening?
H I've already booked a room for karaoke.
M Really? I don't really like karaoke that much. I'm a terrible singer.
H Yeah, but you haven't tried karaoke Japanese-style! I've booked a private room for six people. So, you, me and four of my friends. You'll love them – they're really good fun. Anyway, I've booked it till 2 am.
M 2 am?! Remember my flight leaves at 7 am tomorrow!
H Don't worry – you won't miss your flight! I promise. Anyway, we won't be finished at two. After that we're going to the Tsukiji fish market!
M A fish market? In the middle of the night?
H Yeah, it's the best time to go. They bring in all the fish they've just caught. Trust me, it's an amazing sight.
M OK. This is going to be an interesting day …
H So, shall I come to your hotel in about an hour?
M OK, see you in a bit.
H Bye!

1.75 PART 2

HARRY Airport, please.
TAXI DRIVER OK.
M Ooof!
H Tired?
M Yes, and I'm a bit worried about my flight. It leaves in two hours …
H Don't worry – you'll be fine. It only takes half an hour to get there. We've got plenty of time.
M Hmm.
H So, what was your favourite part of the day?
M Difficult question. I liked all of it. The food was great. The fish market … well, I've never seen anything like that.
H Yep!
M But I think I liked the karaoke best. It's such good fun in a private room. I hate it in England, when you do it in front of 50 strangers.
H Yeah, absolutely.

1.76 PART 3

MIKE Can you ask the taxi driver to go a bit faster? I really am worried about this flight.
HARRY Yeah, he is a bit slow. Can you go a bit faster?
M This is a nightmare now! The flight leaves in an hour!
H Yeah, I'm really sorry about this. We stayed too long at the fish market. And I didn't know there'd be so much traffic.
M Mmm.
H Look – I've got an idea. You enjoyed your day, right?
M Definitely. Well, until now anyway.
H Well, change your flight and stay another day. I'll take the day off work. There are lots more places in Tokyo I want to show you.

Audioscripts

M I don't know … what about the flight?
H You can change the flight! Come on, it'll be great!
M Yeah, but …
H Come on … shall I tell the taxi driver to turn round?
M Well …

▶ 1.77 PART 1

RACHEL Hello, Fantastic Flowers.
ANNIE Oh, hi. Rachel?
R Yes?
A It's Annie.
R Oh, hi Annie! How are you?
A I'm OK, thanks. You?
R I'm great.
A Listen – you know it's Leo's birthday this week?
R Of course!
A Well, are you doing anything on Wednesday? Would you like to come round for a meal?
R Oh, that sounds nice. I'll just check. No, we can't do Wednesday. Sorry. We're meeting some friends.
A Oh, OK. How about Thursday? Is that OK for you?
R Thursday … hang on a minute … oh, no, sorry. I'm working on Thursday evening.
A Oh.
R This week's really busy for us. Next week?
A OK. What are you doing on … Monday?
R Just a moment … Nothing! We can do Monday – perfect.
A Great!
R What time shall we come round?
A Let's say … seven o'clock.
R OK – and would you like us to bring anything?
A No, nothing! See you on Monday then!
R Great! See you then.
A Bye!

▶ 1.81 PART 2

MARK That was great!
RACHEL Yeah, thanks, Annie. You're a great cook.
ANNIE Thanks! I'm glad you enjoyed it.
M Enjoyed it? I don't think I can move!
A Excuse me for a moment.
M I think I need to go for a run tomorrow.
R I always tell you not to eat so much.
A Rachel, can you come here for a second? I need you to help me carry something.
R I'll send Mark. He needs the exercise! Go on.
LEO I think I need to get some exercise as well!
R Mark said you're a big sports fan.
L No, not really. I mean – I like to keep fit, so I go to the gym. But I don't really like sport. It's a bit boring. And I can't stand football.
R Oh.
A Happy birthday, Leo!
M & R Happy birthday!
L Thanks, everyone. What an amazing cake!
M Oh … we've got this for you, Leo.
R Yes, happy birthday!
L Oh, you really didn't need to! . . . Ha, thanks . . . Wow, that's great. I love it! That's very kind of you.
M I knew you'd like it! Actually, Leo, I was thinking … since you're a sports fan, maybe we could do something together some time. Maybe go to a football match?
L Well … sure, or how about a workout? I like going to the gym. How about that? Do you want to come with me some time?
M Oh, OK. Why not? The gym sounds great.
L When are you free? I normally go in the evening.
M Well, are you going next Tuesday? I'm free then.
L I can't Tuesday. How about Thursday?
M OK. Sounds great!

▶ 1.85

SUSANNA I don't really like having a party at home to celebrate. It's too much work. I think it's better to go out together and find a nice place where you can celebrate. Then you can all have a good time together.
This weekend, it's my 21st birthday and we're going to book a function room at a hotel and have a big party there. All my friends are coming and we're going to have a band and a DJ. Everyone's going to look their best – all the men are going to wear suits and I'm going to buy a new dress. I'm really excited about it!
BARBARA I like inviting friends to my home, but I'm not a very good cook. I always get very stressed if I have to cook meals for people. Everyone else is having a nice time, but I'm just worrying if the food's OK. So, I don't really enjoy it. What I do like is if we all cook something together, or if everyone makes something and brings it. I think that makes it more relaxed.
We're doing that on Saturday. We're having a barbecue, but I'm just making some salads and I'm going to ask everyone to bring something for the barbecue. I'm looking forward to it.
SVEN I sometimes enjoy parties, but they're all the same really: you just sit around and talk to people about all the usual stuff until it's time to go home. With friends, I think it's better to do something together, then you don't get bored – like going to the cinema or bowling maybe, or going out somewhere nice together.
This weekend, I'm going to the countryside with some old friends I haven't seen for a long time. We're going to a lake to swim and have a picnic together, and maybe we'll play volleyball. That'll be fun.

Unit 5

▶ 2.5

ALISHA I love my job … working with people and helping them … but it's often stressful. I have to work long hours including weekends, and sometimes deal with very serious problems. These days, to become a nurse you have to do well at school – especially in maths, science and English. Then you have to do a nursing degree before you can get a job. You also need to be good at making decisions and working in a team. There are lots of rules to remember. You can't enter a room without washing your hands. You can't lift a patient on your own. When you work with people who are very sick, every decision you make is so important.
JOHN For my job, you need to do two or three years training – usually while you are working with a company. You can't go to people's houses on your own and start fixing things without a qualification. Now I have my own company, I usually work about 45 to 50 hours a week. It can be tiring. And, of course, you have to be careful, especially when you're tired. There are a lot of health and safety rules … for example, you always have to switch off the mains power. I heard of one guy who forgot and nearly died. Anyway … there are good things, too – you don't have to wear a suit or go to many meetings and I enjoy being my own boss.
MIRIAM I'm in investment banking … and to get in I needed a good university degree, and, also, to be a good communicator. You have to enjoy working really hard … I work very long hours, a hundred hours or more a week … And, well … I have to deal with a lot of stress … especially when millions of pounds of other people's money. You also can't relax because if something goes wrong, you lose money – other people's money. I suppose I also like that – it's exciting. But it's not an easy job and sometimes I feel that what I do isn't really that useful.

▶ 2.9

INTERVIEWER Are you enjoying the careers fair?
SARA It's not bad. It's good to meet people from different companies.
I Are you looking for work at the moment?
S Yes. But it won't be easy to find a job I'll enjoy. There just aren't enough jobs – you have to take what you can find. I applied for a job this week but I don't think I'll get an interview. They won't be interested in me, because I don't have any experience.

I Are you enjoying the fair today?
MARCO Yeah, it's great. I'm sure I'll make some really useful contacts. There are people from some really interesting companies here.
I And are you applying for jobs at the moment?
M Yes. I don't think it'll take long to find work. You never know … I might get a job today! I know someone who found a job at an event just like this last year.

I Are you enjoying it today?
KATE Yes, it's good. It's useful because I'm not sure what kinds of jobs I'm interested in.
I So are you looking for work at the moment?

K Not yet. I'm still studying and then I'll try to get some work experience when I finish my course. After that, I can start looking for a job. I might not get my perfect job, because not many people do, straight out of university.
I And how do you feel about that?
K Well … I just need to pay the bills, you know. I'm sure I'll find some kind of work because I'm happy to do anything they'll pay me for. I can work my way up. I've got time!

▶ 2.15 PART 1

RACHEL Oh dear.
TINA Is everything OK?
R I'm not sure really. I've just got a text message from my friend Annie. Do you remember her?
T Yeah, of course.
R Yeah, well she says she's had some bad news and she needs to talk to me.
T Oh dear. I hope she's OK.
R Hmm, I'd better give her a ring. Or maybe I should go and see her.
T Yeah, maybe you should. I'll finish things here, if you want.
R But I can't leave you here on your own.
T I'll be fine! Don't worry about it.
R But we've still got so much to do.
T Oh, it doesn't matter. Honestly, I'll be OK.
R I don't want to leave you with too much work. It doesn't seem very fair. It means you won't be able to leave early today.
T Oh, never mind. Look, why don't you tell me what we still need to do? And I'll write a list. Then you can go and see Annie.
R OK, well if you're sure.
T Of course. It's no problem.
R Well, …

▶ 2.17 PART 2

RACHEL Right, and after that …
TINA Shall I finish off those flowers? The ones you were doing?
R OK. That would be great.
T And would you like me to prepare some of the orders for tomorrow?
R Yeah. You could start with that order for Mrs Thompson, because she's picking it up early.
T OK.
R And then maybe you should start on the order for that big birthday party.
T OK.
R Actually, no – we can do that tomorrow morning – we'll have time.
T Yeah, fine.
R OK, I think that's everything. Oh, when you leave, you'll need to put the alarm on. I'll write down the code for you.
T OK. Oh – do you want me to take out the rubbish when I leave?
R Er, no, don't worry. The bag's not full yet. I'll do it tomorrow.
T OK, fine.
R OK, great. I'll text Annie to say I'm coming.
T Oh, how about taking her some flowers? That'll cheer her up.
R Good idea … Oh, hello. How can I help?
CUSTOMER Hi, yeah. Er, I just wanted to make an order for some flowers.
R Of course. What would you like?
C Well, actually, it's for my daughter's wedding. So … er … some red roses …
R Yep.
C Some white roses …
R Hmmhmm.
C Some lilies …
T Rachel – why don't I deal with this?
R Are you sure?
T Yes! Just go!
R OK – bye!
C Oh, bye.
T So, that was some red roses …
C Three dozen, please.
T Three dozen …
C Er, white roses, three dozen.
T OK.

169

2.20

PENNY Are you working this summer?
JOHN Yeah, I've got a job in a café, same as last year. How about you?
P I don't know. I usually work in a supermarket, but I don't like it much. It's so tiring and you have to start really early in the morning. I might look for a different job this summer. What's working in a café like?
J Oh, it's good. It gets quite busy, so you need to be good at working really fast. But I like that.
P Well, that's the same as a supermarket.
J Yeah. But it's good fun, too. You're working in a team and you meet lots of people. It's great!
P Is the pay good?
J Not bad and you can sometimes make quite a lot from tips.
P Really? How much do you make in tips?
J It depends. I can sometimes make £20 in one day!
P Wow! That sounds good.
J It's not always that much though. Listen, why don't you apply for a job? I'm sure they'll give you one. They're always looking for new people.
P Yeah, I don't know. I've never worked in a café. I don't know anything about it.
J Oh, that doesn't matter; they'll give you training. You don't need to know anything.
P Really?
J No, you just have to smile a lot and be nice to people. It's easy.
P Hmm, OK. What are they called?
J Cuba Coffee Company, they've got a website.
P OK thanks, I'll have a look tomorrow, update my CV and apply!
J Great – good luck!

Unit 6

2.28

INTERVIEWER So what did you do?
CAROLINE Well, I was really confused. I thought I was going to die. I didn't really know what to do – I just wanted to get out of the water. But then I saw a shark; then another, and another. And suddenly I stopped feeling frightened. I forgot about dying, and watched those amazing fish moving through the water. Seeing those sharks probably saved my life, because they made me feel relaxed. I started breathing better and – very slowly – I made my way to the top.
I And how did you feel when you got back to the surface?
C Well, once we were back on the fishing boat, I felt a lot of different things. I was happy to be alive, but I was also embarrassed because I used most of my air. And I was shocked and angry with my instructor for taking me down to 40 metres and then disappearing.
I And how has the whole experience changed you?
C After that experience, every time I tried to dive, I got really worried. In the end, I stopped scuba diving. I still love sharks, but I'll never go that deep again to see them.

2.31

INTERVIEWER So, Aaron, your story is pretty amazing. What happened to you?
AARON Well, I think I'm very lucky to be alive today. I was pulled along under a plane when we were flying at a height of 6,000 metres.
I Wow! That's unbelievable! How did it happen?
A So, there were three people in the plane that day. Me, and two other jumpers, Monica and Ben. I wasn't an experienced parachute jumper at the time. I had only done about 15 jumps.
I So, what went wrong?
A Well … Monica told me I should go first … I stood up and put my foot outside the plane door, but then the wind pushed me to the side. I was stuck, flat against the side of the plane. I tried to push myself away, but it didn't work. Then, part of my parachute got stuck on the plane, I couldn't move my leg so I couldn't fall. I was hanging under the plane, hanging from my parachute, and there was nothing I could do. The others couldn't see me. The plane was just pulling me along in the sky and nobody knew I was there.
I That sounds terrifying! How did you feel?
A Obviously, I was very frightened. I knew how dangerous it was. I knew I could die if I hit the back of the plane.
I So, did the others help you?
A At first, they didn't know I was there. But when Monica was getting ready to jump, she saw me and shouted 'Aaron's under the plane!' The pilot slowed the plane down and they freed my parachute. When I started to fall, I felt better, but when I landed I was shocked to think about what had happened.
I Did that experience stop you from jumping?
A No, but I realised how serious it was. Because I jumped first, Monica saw me and saved me, but if I had been the last one to jump, I would have died. Because the pilot couldn't have saved me while he was flying the plane.

2.32 PART 1

RACHEL Hi, Annie.
ANNIE Oh, hi Rachel. Thanks for coming.
R That's OK. Here, I brought you some flowers.
A Oh, thank you. They're lovely.
R Oh, that's OK. What's happened?
A It's work. My boss asked to see me this afternoon. And she told me I'm going to lose my job.
R Oh, how awful! I'm really sorry to hear that. Did she say why?
A She just said the company's having problems.
R That's terrible.
A Yeah … anyway, I'll make some tea.

2.34 PART 2

RACHEL So, what happened when you talked to your boss? Did you ask when you're going to lose your job? Or if it's completely certain?
ANNIE No, I didn't say much. I was too upset.
R Of course you were.
A I didn't really ask anything. What do you think I should do?
R OK, well, I'd get all the details first.
A Right.
R So I think you should speak to your boss again. Maybe there'll be other jobs there.
A I don't think that's a good idea. I don't know if I want to stay. Lots of people are unhappy there. And I don't think there are any other jobs anyway.
R OK, but I think it's a good idea to ask. You don't know what she'll say.
A I suppose so.
R And why don't you speak to some of the people you work with? Ask them what they're doing?
A Mmm, I don't think I should do that. My boss told me not to talk to anyone else. Because other people are going to lose their jobs too.
R Mmm. You work in marketing, right?
A Yeah.
R Well, Mark works in marketing, too. His company's often looking for new people.
A Really? Do you think I should speak to him about it?
R Definitely. I'll speak to him, too.
A OK. Great.
R And I wouldn't worry too much – changing jobs could be a good thing. You'll have the chance to do something new.
A Yeah – you're right.

2.38 PART 3

RACHEL Is that everything, Annie? Has something else happened?
ANNIE No, it's stupid …
R Come on – you can tell me.
A Well, it's just – I called Leo to talk about my job but he didn't answer the phone. I sent him a text but he still hasn't replied.
R Don't worry. I'm sure he'll call you soon.
A Yeah. Maybe he's not interested in me any more. Oh, I don't know.
R Oh, you shouldn't worry. He's probably just busy at work!
A You're right, you're right.
R Everything will be fine. Call Mark tomorrow. I'll tell him what's happened when he comes home tonight.
A OK.
R And I'm sure Leo will ring you soon!
A Thanks, Rachel … for your help.
R That's OK! That's what friends are for!

2.39

CHLOE The problem is that I think about my job even in my free time. I'm so busy during the day I don't have time to think and then when I get home I spend all my time thinking and worrying. You see, my old boss had to leave in a hurry – a family problem – and they gave me his job. But I haven't had any training and I don't feel ready to be a manager and make decisions. Friends tell me I should do something relaxing after work, like go for a walk on the beach. But I still can't stop thinking about meetings I've been to or meetings I'll have to go to the next day. And all the reports I have to write! There's so much to do and I just feel so stressed.
BOB At first, I was excited about doing something new. I've never done anything like this before. Well, I'm sorry to say I've stopped feeling excited, I'm just generally confused. I don't feel like I'm improving at all. The thing is my wife is Polish and I want to be able to speak to people in her family when we go to Poland. I wasn't very good at languages at school. I mean, I learnt a little bit of French and that was quite hard. But I find Polish really difficult. My wife says 'don't worry – when we go to Poland you'll really start to learn'. But, to be honest, I'm not so sure. I don't think I'm the kind of person who can just listen to a language and learn it.
MARISA I feel really tired, because I haven't been sleeping well for the past week. I stay up late most nights and drink coffee to stay awake. I read the books on my booklist and the notes I've made during the year again and again. And I test myself all the time to help me remember information. My parents tell me I should take more breaks. They forget that I didn't do very well in my exams last year and I was very disappointed with my results. I really want to do well this year, so I need to do all this work. So, I think I'm just going to have to continue like this until I'm sure that I can remember everything.

Phonemic Symbols

Vowel sounds

Short

/ə/	/æ/	/ʊ/	/ɒ/
teach**er**	m**a**n	p**u**t	g**o**t
/ɪ/	/i/	/e/	/ʌ/
ch**i**p	happ**y**	m**e**n	b**u**t

Long

/ɜː/	/ɑː/	/uː/	/ɔː/	/iː/
sh**ir**t	p**ar**t	wh**o**	w**al**k	ch**ea**p

Diphthongs (two vowel sounds)

/eə/	/ɪə/	/ʊə/	/ɔɪ/	/aɪ/	/eɪ/	/əʊ/	/aʊ/
h**air**	n**ear**	t**our**	b**oy**	f**i**ne	l**a**te	c**oa**t	n**ow**

Consonants

/p/	/b/	/f/	/v/	/t/	/d/	/k/	/g/	/θ/	/ð/	/tʃ/	/dʒ/
picnic	**b**ook	**f**ace	**v**ery	**t**ime	**d**og	**c**old	**g**o	**th**ink	**th**e	**ch**air	**j**ob
/s/	/z/	/ʃ/	/ʒ/	/m/	/n/	/ŋ/	/h/	/l/	/r/	/w/	/j/
sea	**z**oo	**sh**oe	televi**si**on	**m**e	**n**ow	si**ng**	**h**ot	**l**ate	**r**ed	**w**ent	**y**es

Irregular verbs

Infinitive	Past simple	Past participle
be	was /wɒz/ / were /wɜː/	been
become	became	become
begin	began	begun
blow	blew /bluː/	blown /bləʊn/
break /breɪk/	broke /brəʊk/	broken /ˈbrəʊkən/
bring /brɪŋ/	brought /brɔːt/	brought /brɔːt/
build /bɪld/	built /bɪlt/	built /bɪlt/
buy /baɪ/	bought /bɔːt/	bought /bɔːt/
catch /kætʃ/	caught /kɔːt/	caught /kɔːt/
choose /tʃuːz/	chose /tʃəʊz/	chosen /ˈtʃəʊzən/
come	came	come
cost	cost	cost
cut	cut	cut
deal /dɪəl/	dealt /delt/	dealt /delt/
do	did	done /dʌn/
draw /drɔː/	drew /druː/	drawn /drɔːn/
drink	drank	drunk
drive /draɪv/	drove /drəʊv/	driven /ˈdrɪvən/
eat /iːt/	ate /et/	eaten /ˈiːtən/
fall	fell	fallen
feel	felt	felt
find /faɪnd/	found /faʊnd/	found /faʊnd/
fly /flaɪ/	flew /fluː/	flown /fləʊn/
forget	forgot	forgotten
get	got	got
give /gɪv/	gave /geɪv/	given /ˈgɪvən/
go	went	gone /gɒn/
grow /grəʊ/	grew /gruː/	grown /grəʊn/
have /hæv/	had /hæd/	had /hæd/
hear /hɪə/	heard /hɜːd/	heard /hɜːd/
hit	hit	hit
hold /həʊld/	held	held
keep	kept	kept
know /nəʊ/	knew /njuː/	known /nəʊn/

Infinitive	Past simple	Past participle
leave /liːv/	left	left
lend	lent	lent
let	let	let
lose /luːz/	lost	lost
make	made	made
meet	met	met
pay /peɪ/	paid /peɪd/	paid /peɪd/
put	put	put
read /riːd/	read /red/	read /red/
ride /raɪd/	rode /rəʊd/	ridden /ˈrɪdən/
ring	rang	rung
run	ran	run
sit	sat	sat
say /seɪ/	said /sed/	said /sed/
see	saw /sɔː/	seen
sell	sold /səʊld/	sold /səʊld/
send	sent	sent
set	set	set
sing	sang	sung
sleep	slept	slept
speak /spiːk/	spoke /spəʊk/	spoken /ˈspəʊkən/
spend	spent	spent
stand	stood /stʊd/	stood /stʊd/
steal /stiːl/	stole /stəʊl/	stolen /ˈstəʊlən/
swim /swɪm/	swam /swæm/	swum /swʌm/
take /teɪk/	took /tʊk/	taken /ˈteɪkən/
teach /tiːtʃ/	taught /tɔːt/	taught /tɔːt/
tell	told /təʊld/	told /təʊld/
think	thought /θɔːt/	thought /θɔːt/
throw /θrəʊ/	threw /θruː/	thrown /θrəʊn/
understand	understood /ˌʌndəˈstʊd/	understood /ˌʌndəˈstʊd/
wake /weɪk/	woke /wəʊk/	woken /ˈwəʊkən/
wear /weə/	wore /wɔː/	worn /wɔːn/
win	won	won
write /raɪt/	wrote /rəʊt/	written /ˈrɪtən/

Acknowledgements

The publishers would like to thank the following teachers and ELT professionals for the invaluable feedback they provided during the development of the B1 Student's book:

Andre Alipio, Brazil; Peggy Altpekin, Turkey/Gulf; Kate Chomacki, UK; Leonor Corradi, Argentina; Sandra Aliotti, Argentina; Ludmila Gorodetskaya, Russia; Ralph Grayson, Peru; Ludmila Kozhevnikova, Russia; Catherine Morley, Spain; Antonio Mota Cosano, Spain; Julian Oakley, UK; Litany Pires Ribeiro, Brazil; Elena Pro, Spain; Michael Ward, UK

The publishers are grateful to the following contributors: Gareth Boden: commissioned photography; Leon Chambers: audio recordings; Hilary Luckcock: picture research, commissioned photography; Rob Maidment and Sharp Focus Productions: video recordings

The authors and publishers acknowledge the following sources of copyright material and are grateful for the permissions granted. While every effort has been made, it has not always been possible to identify the sources of all the material used, or to trace all copyright holders. If any omissions are brought to our notice, we will be happy to include the appropriate acknowledgements on reprinting. The publisher has used its best endeavours to ensure that the URLs for external websites referred to in this book are correct and active at the time of going to press. However, the publisher has no responsibility for the websites and can make no guarantee that a site will remain live or that the content is or will remain appropriate.

The publishers are grateful to the following for permission to reproduce copyright photographs and material: p. 18 Book cover of 'Yes Man'(Eallace,D), Artwork © *Two Associates* Published by arrangement with The Random House Group Limited; p. 21 adapted from 'Passengers on broken-down National Express coach get out and push it to bus depot' *Daily Mail*; pp. 28-29 adapted from 'Have you ever stopped to help a stranger or been helped by a stranger?'(Webb,G) 24/10/2012 with kind permission from Gretchen Webb; p .34(Oxfam Logo) reproduced with the permission of Oxfam GB, Oxfam House, John Smith Drive, Cowley, Oxford OX4 2JY, UK www.oxfam.org.uk. Oxfam GB does not necessarily endorse any text or activities that accompany the materials; p .34 (Greenpeace Logo) with permission from Greenpeace; pp .48-49 (2b-d) adapted from 'City & Guilds' with permission, The City and Guilds of London Institute accepts no liability for the contents of this book; pp. 60-61 adapted from 'Experience: Sharks saved my life'(Spence,C) 26/09/2009, *The Guardian*, © Guardian News & Media Ltd 2009.

Key: L = left, C = centre, R = right, T = top, B = bottom

p7: Panos/Piotr Malecki; p8: Shutterstock/Yayayoyo; p9(T): Shutterstock/Yayayoyo; p9(B): Shutterstock/Yayayoyo; p10(TL): Shutterstock/Charlotte Purdy; p10(TR): Shutterstock/Travis Manley; p10(BL): Shutterstock/Ilaszio; p10(BR): Shutterstock/beboy; pp14/15(background): Alamy/Randolph Images; p14(T): Thinkstock/Stockbyte; p14(B): Alamy/Tetra Images; p15: Alamy/Blend Images; p17: Magnum Photos/Ian Berry; p18(T)(inset): pp18(T)/19(L): Shutterstock/Kodentseva; pp18/19(B): Alamy/Shirley Kilpatrick; p19(R): Corbis/Christine Pemberton/LatitudeSt; p20(T): Getty/AFP; p20(C): Alamy/Sergio Azenha; p20(B): Thinkstock/Fuse; p21: Albanpix.com; p24(T): Corbis/SUPRI/Reuters; p24(CL): Shutterstock/Dimos; p24(CR): Getty/AFP; p24(BL): Shutterstock/Ziye; p24(BR): Shutterstock/Matek Hudovernik; p25: Alamy/Jack Malipan Travel Photography; p27: Getty/ArabianEye; p28: Alamy/Jim West; p29: KindnessTrust; p30(T): Shutterstock/Sergey Mironov; p30(BL): Alamy/incamerastock; 30(BR): Alamy/Paul Rapson; p31(BR): Shutterstock/Sergey Mironov; p34(T)(inset): Oxfam; p34(T): Oxfam/Abbie Trayler-Smith; p34(C)(inset): National Trust; p34(C): Rex/Sefton Samuels; p34(B)(inset): Greenpeace; p34(B): Greenpeace/Markus Mauthe; p37: Panos/Andrea Gjestvang; p38(L): Rex /Geoffrey Robinson; p38(R): Simon Lamb; p39(TL): Shutterstock/Bui Viet Hung; p39(TR): Corbis/Issei Kato/Reuters; p39(BL): South American Pictures/Tony Morrison; p39(BR): Alamy/Ian Shaw; p40: Shutterstock/Neale Cousland; p41(TL): Getty/Bloomberg; p41(TC): Superstock/JTB Photo; p41(TR): Shutterstock/Perati Komson; p41(BL): Thinkstock/istockphoto; p41(BR): Alamy/Paul Brown; pp44/45(B): Alamy/Jiri Hubatka; p44(TL): Getty/nullplus; p44(TR): Getty/Jake Curtis; p44(BL): Superstock/Fancy Collection; p44(BR): Corbis/Image Source; p47: Corbis/Louie Psihoyos; p49(TL): Thinkstock/istockphoto; p49(TR): Science Photo Library/Dan Dunkley; p49(CL): Corbis/Image Source; p49(CR): Corbis/Erik Isakson/Tetra Images; p49(B): Shutterstock/Lurin; p50(L): Shutterstock/arek_malang; p50(C): Shutterstock/Monkey Business Images; p50(R): Shutterstock/arek_malang; p51(a): Shutterstock/Dmitry Kalinovsky; p51(b): Shutterstock/Andreas G Karelias; p51(c): Alamy/Peter Titmuss; p51(d): Alamy/aber CPC; p51(e): Alamy/David J Green - Lifestyle themes; p55: Alamy/Images-USA; p57: Alamy/IML Image Group Ltd; p58(TL): Shutterstock/gpointstudio; p58(TR): Corbis/Dinuka Liyanawatte/Reuters; p58(UCL): Shutterstock/stockkete; p58(UCR): Alamy/Janine Wiedel Photo Library; p58(LCL): Thinkstock/shironosov; p58(LCR): Getty/Chris Fertnig; p58(BL): Alamy/Lev Dolgachov; p58(BR): Shutterstock/Marcin Balcerzak; p60(L): Guardian News & Media Ltd/Joel Redman; p60(e): Shutterstock/Rich Carey; p60(f): Shutterstock/Rich Carey; p60/61: Shutterstock/Rich Carey; p61(T): Rex/Cultura; p61(BL): Shutterstock/f9 Photos; p61(BR): Shutterstock/Rich Carey; p64(TL): Shutterstock/Nadino; p64(CR): Thinkstock/Hemera Technologies; p64(TR): Thinkstock/istockphoto; p127(lips telephone): Alamy/Paul Springett 03; p127(spice rack): Alamy/PhotoSlinger; p127(football mug): Alamy/Lenscap; p127(candles): Alamy/Mouse in the House; p127(clock): Alamy/James Jackson; p127(slippers): Alamy/Andrew Twort; p128: Albanpix.com; p129: Alamy/Lev Dolgachov; p130(L)(lips telephone): Alamy/Paul Springett 03; p130(L)(spice rack): Alamy/PhotoSlinger; p130(L)(football mug): Alamy/Lenscap; p130(L)(candles): Alamy/Mouse in the House; p130(L)(clock): Alamy/James Jackson; p130(L)(slippers): Alamy/Andrew Twort; p130(R): Alamy/Lev Dolgachov; p135(1): Shutterstock/PhotoBlink; p135(2): Shutterstock/Coprid; p135(3): Shutterstock/Jacek Bieniek; p135(4): Shutterstock/Peter Djordjevic; p135(5): Thinkstock/istockphoto; p135(6): Thinkstock/Photodisc; p135(7): istockphoto/gsermek; p135(8): Shutterstock/Sagir; p135(9): istockphoto/PeJo29; p135(10): Shutterstock/Elnur; p135(11): Shutterstock/Ivaschenko Roman; p135(12): Shutterstock/bemashato; p136(T)(a): Corbis/Blend; p136(T)(b): Shutterstock/Lurin; p136(T)(c): Corbis/Rubberball; p136(T)(d): Masterfile/Chad Johnston; p136(T)(e): Science Photo Library/Dan Dunkley; p136(T)(f): Thinkstock/Elena Elisseeva; p136(T)(g): Corbis/Image Source; p136(T)(h): Corbis/Cardinal; p136(T)(i): Thinkstock/istockphoto; p136(B)(a): Shutterstock/Faraways; p136(B)(b): Alamy/Peter Titmuss; p136(B)(c): Corbis/ocean; p136(B)(d): Alamy/aber CPC; p136(B)(e): Shutterstock/Andreas G Karelias; p136(B)(f): Shutterstock/Dmitry Kalinovsky; p136(B)(g): Shutterstock/Chad McDermott; p136(B)(h): Shutterstock/Monkey Business Images; p136(B)(i): Alamy/Geraint Lewis; p136(B)(j): Thinkstock/istockphoto; p136(B)(k): Alamy/David J Green - Lifestyle themes.

Commissioned photography by Gareth Boden: pp31(TL,TC,TR), 32(CL,CR,BL,BR), 35, 64.

We are grateful to Grand Arcade, Cambridge and Stephen Perse Senior School, Cambridge for their help with the commissioned photography.

The following stills were taken on commission by Rob Maidment and Sharp Focus Productions for Cambridge University Press: pp12, 13, 22, 23, 32(T), 33, 42, 43, 52(T,B), 62, 63.

Front cover photograph by Superstock/Scott Dickerson/Alaska Stock - Design Pics.

The publishers would like to thank the following illustrators: Mark Bird; Mark Duffin; Sean KJA; Jo Goodberry; Dusan Lakicevic; Carrie May; Jerome Mireault; Roger Penwill; Gavin Reece; Gregory Roberts; Martin Sanders; Sean Sims; Marie-Eve Tremblay

Corpus Development of this publication has made use of the Cambridge English Corpus (CEC). The CEC is a computer database of contemporary spoken and written English, which currently stands at over one billion words. It includes British English, American English and other varieties of English. It also includes the Cambridge Learner Corpus, developed in collaboration with the University of Cambridge ESOL Examinations. Cambridge University Press has built up the CEC to provide evidence about language use that helps to produce better language teaching materials.

English Profile This product is informed by the English Vocabulary Profile, built as part of English Profile, a collaborative programme designed to enhance the learning, teaching and assessment of English worldwide. Its main funding partners are Cambridge University Press and Cambridge ESOL and its aim is to create a 'profile' for English linked to the Common European Framework of Reference for Languages (CEFR). English Profile outcomes, such as the English Vocabulary Profile, will provide detailed information about the language that learners can be expected to demonstrate at each CEFR level, offering a clear benchmark for learners' proficiency. For more information, please visit www.englishprofile.org

CALD The Cambridge Advanced Learner's Dictionary is the world's most widely used dictionary for learners of English. Including all the words and phrases that learners are likely to come across, it also has easy-to-understand definitions and example sentences to show how the word is used in context. The Cambridge Advanced Learner's Dictionary is available online at dictionary.cambridge.org. © Cambridge University Press, Third Edition, 2008 reproduced with permission.

This page is intentionally left blank

This page is intentionally left blank

Cambridge English

EMPOWER

Combo A
Workbook
with Answers

B1

Peter Anderson

Contents

	Unit 1 Communicating			Page
1A	Do you play any sports?	**Grammar** Question forms **Vocabulary** Common adjectives		4
1B	I'm really into Facebook	**Grammar** Present simple and present continuous **Vocabulary** Adverbs	**Pronunciation** Long and short vowels	5
1C	It was really nice to meet you	**Everyday English** Greeting people; Ending a conversation	**Pronunciation** Sentence stress	6
1D	I'm sending you some photos	**Reading** An email about a holiday	**Writing skills** Correcting mistakes **Writing** A reply to an email asking about a holiday	7
	Reading and listening extension	**Reading** An article about internet dating	**Listening** A conversation about making friends	8
	Review and extension	**WORDPOWER** *like*		9
	Unit 2 Travel and Tourism			
2A	We had an adventure	**Grammar** Past simple **Vocabulary** Tourism	**Pronunciation** *-ed* endings	10
2B	Everyone was waiting for me	**Grammar** Past continuous **Vocabulary** Travel collocations	**Pronunciation** Sentence stress: vowel sounds	11
2C	What time's the next train?	**Everyday English** Asking for information in a public place	**Pronunciation** Joining words	12
2D	This city is different, but very friendly	**Reading** A travel blog	**Writing skills** Linking words **Writing** A blog post	13
	Reading and listening extension	**Reading** An article about a race	**Listening** A conversation about travel problems	14
	Review and extension	**WORDPOWER** *off*		15
	Unit 3 Money			
3A	Have you ever helped a stranger?	**Grammar** Present perfect or past simple **Vocabulary** *make / do / give* collocations		16
3B	I've already spent my salary this month	**Grammar** Present perfect with *just*, *already* and *yet* **Vocabulary** Money		17
3C	Do you have anything cheaper?	**Everyday English** Talking to people in shops	**Pronunciation** Sentence stress	18
3D	We've successfully raised £500	**Reading** An email about raising money for charity	**Writing skills** Paragraphing **Writing** An email to colleagues about a charity	19
	Reading and listening extension	**Reading** An article about saving money	**Listening** A conversation about helping people	20
	Review and extension	**WORDPOWER** *just*		21
	Unit 4 Social Life			
4A	I'm going to the hairdresser's tomorrow	**Grammar** Present continuous and *going to* **Vocabulary** Clothes and appearance	**Pronunciation** Sound and spelling: *going to*	22
4B	Shall we go to the market?	**Grammar** *will / won't / shall* **Vocabulary** Adjectives: places	**Pronunciation** Sound and spelling: *want* and *won't*	23
4C	Are you doing anything on Wednesday?	**Everyday English** Making arrangements	**Pronunciation** Sentence stress	24
4D	Are you free on Saturday?	**Reading** An email invitation	**Writing skills** Inviting and replying **Writing** A reply to an invitation	25
	Reading and listening extension	**Reading** An article about a film director's day	**Listening** A conversation about summer plans	26
	Review and extension	**WORDPOWER** *look*		27

Unit 5 Work				
5A	I have to work long hours	**Grammar** *must / have to / can* **Vocabulary** Work		28
5B	I might get a job today!	**Grammar** *will* and *might* for predictions **Vocabulary** Jobs		29
5C	I'll finish things here, if you want	**Everyday English** Offers and suggestions	**Pronunciation** Sentence stress: vowel sounds	30
5D	I am writing to apply for a job	**Reading** A job advert and a letter	**Writing skills** Organising an email **Writing** A letter applying for a job	31
Reading and listening extension		**Reading** An article about studying and careers	**Listening** A conversation about jobs	32
Review and extension		**WORDPOWER** *job* and *work*		33
Unit 6 Problems and Advice				
6A	You should have a break	**Grammar** Imperative; *should* **Vocabulary** Verbs with dependent prepositions	**Pronunciation** Sound and spelling: /uː/ and /ʊ/	34
6B	I was very frightened	**Grammar** Uses of *to* + infinitive **Vocabulary** *-ed / -ing* adjectives		35
6C	What do you think I should do?	**Everyday English** Asking for and giving advice	**Pronunciation** Main stress	36
6D	I often worry about tests and exams	**Reading** An email asking for advice	**Writing skills** Linking: ordering ideas and giving examples **Writing** An email giving advice	37
Reading and listening extension		**Reading** A magazine advice column	**Listening** A conversation about problems with studying	38
Review and extension		**WORDPOWER** verb + *to*		39
Vox pop video				76
Audioscripts				82
Answer key				87

1A Do you play any sports?

1 VOCABULARY Common adjectives

a Underline the correct words to complete the sentences.

1 The new building opposite the university is *rude / ugly / alright*. I hate it!
2 Our new teacher is always very *serious / silly / rude*. We work very hard in her lessons and she never smiles or laughs.
3 The cakes in the new baker's are *silly / serious / delicious*!
4 My brother's new girlfriend is *ugly / gorgeous / delicious*. I think she's a fashion model.
5 We played lots of *silly / horrible / perfect* games at Sarah's birthday party. I've got some really funny photos on Facebook.
6 Lily's a *perfect / strange / lovely* person. Her grandchildren love visiting her.

b Complete the sentences with the adjectives in the box.

| boring | alright | awful | amazing |
| delicious | rude | strange | perfect |

1 I'm not interested in football. It's so _boring_.
2 Thanks for the chocolates. They were _____!
3 Look at this beautiful weather – it's a _____ day to go to the beach.
4 The film we saw last night was really _____. I didn't understand it at all.
5 **A** How was the restaurant?
  B Oh, it was _____. There are better Italian restaurants in my town.
6 The weather in Scotland was _____. It rained every day.
7 The band were _____! It was the best concert I've ever been to.
8 The waiter in the hotel was _____. He said we were stupid because we couldn't speak English very well!

2 GRAMMAR Question forms

a Underline the correct words to complete the questions.

1 How many children *he does have / does he have / does have he*?
2 Where *did you meet / did meet you / you met* your husband?
3 *Did he grow up / He grew up / He did grow up* in this area?
4 What *was like the film / was the film like / the film was like*?
5 How much *paid you / you did pay / did you pay* for your smartphone?
6 *Why she go / Why she went / Why did she go* to the USA?
7 How many films *he made / did he make / did make he* last year?
8 How *was your holiday / your holiday was / did your holiday be*?

b Put the words in the correct order to make questions.

1 you / Sarah's friend / are ?
   Are you Sarah's friend?
2 work / a bank / he / does / in ?
   _____
3 you / last month / to New York / go / did / why ?
   _____
4 like / that new Brazilian / what / restaurant / is ?
   _____
5 with your sister / who / that man / was ?
   _____
6 TV programmes / you / do / watch / what type of ?
   _____
7 go to / did / which university / you ?
   _____
8 did / how much / cost / the tickets ?
   _____

1B I'm really into Facebook

1 VOCABULARY Adverbs

a Put the words in brackets in the correct place in each sentence.

1 They see their grandchildren now that they live in Australia. (hardly ever)
   They hardly ever see their grandchildren now that they live in Australia.
2 I enjoy watching old Hollywood movies. (particularly)
   _____
3 She hates it when people are late for meetings. (absolutely)
   _____
4 We go to Italian restaurants, but sometimes we also go to Turkish ones. (generally)
   _____
5 We're sure his flight arrives at Terminal 2, but I need to check it. (pretty)
   _____
6 I hope she brings her gorgeous brother to the party! (really)
   _____

b Underline the correct adverbs to complete the sentences.

1 I love rock music, but I *absolutely / especially / fairly* like The Rolling Stones. They're my favourite band.
2 He *hardly ever / never / especially* phones his mother – maybe once or twice a month.
3 I *rarely / pretty / normally* enjoy horror films, but this one was awful!
4 She's *fairly / absolutely / rarely* good-looking, but I don't think she's beautiful.
5 I *never / really / hardly ever* hate maths. I just don't understand it!
6 She *generally / particularly / rarely* takes her family out for dinner – only when it's her birthday.
7 They love all sports, but they're *fairly / mainly / pretty* interested in football. They watch all the matches on TV.
8 It's *pretty / normally / rarely* cold today, so why don't you take your gloves?

2 PRONUNCIATION Long and short vowels

a ▶ 1.1 Listen to the words. Do the letters in **bold** make long or short vowel sounds? Tick (✓) the words with long vowel sounds.

1 ✓ b**i**rthday
2 ☐ b**a**nk
3 ☐ c**i**nema /sinəmə/
4 ✓ f**oo**d /fu:d/
5 ✓ p**a**rty /pa:ti/
6 ☐ s**i**lly /sɪli/
7 ☐ m**u**sic /mu:zɪk/
8 ☐ sp**o**rt /spɔt/
9 ☐ fr**ie**ndly /frend/
10 ☐ bl**o**g /blog/

3 GRAMMAR Present simple and present continuous

a Underline the correct verb forms to complete the sentences.

1 She *is loving / loves / love* reading fashion magazines at the hairdresser's.
2 We usually *are going / goes / go* to the café opposite the hotel.
3 I *'m reading / read / reading* a great book in English at the moment.
4 He *'s wanting / does want / wants* to phone his family in Tokyo. Can he use this phone?
5 Why *are you waiting / do you wait / you waiting* for the bus? Let's walk home.
6 I hardly ever *am visiting / visit / visits* my cousins in Ireland.
7 She *studies / studying / 's studying* French politics at university this term.
8 Yes, they're here. They *play / 're playing / playing* a computer game in the living room.

b Complete the conversation with the present simple or present continuous forms of the verbs in brackets. Use contractions where possible.

ALICE   What ¹*'s Sarah doing* (Sarah, do) in that shop?
NAOMI   She ² _____ (buy) some postcards to send to her family.
ALICE   Really? I ³ _____ generally ⁴ _____ (not send) postcards. I usually ⁵ _____ (write) a message on my Facebook wall. And sometimes I ⁶ _____ (put) a few photos of my holiday on my wall.
NAOMI   Yes, me too, but Sarah's grandparents ⁷ _____ (not have) a computer, so she ⁸ _____ (send) them postcards instead.
ALICE   Oh, and what ⁹ _____ (Tom and Jack, do) this morning?
NAOMI   They ¹⁰ _____ (spend) the day at the beach.
ALICE   But Tom ¹¹ _____ (not like) swimming in the sea. He says the water's too cold.
NAOMI   Yes, but it ¹² _____ (be) really hot today!

c ▶ 1.2 Listen and check.

5

Everyday English
It was really nice to meet you

1 USEFUL LANGUAGE
Greeting people; Ending a conversation

a Underline the correct words to complete the conversation.

SAM   Hi, James! ¹*Much / Long / Very* time no see! How are you?
JAMES Hi, Sam. I'm fine, thanks. ²*What a / What / How* lovely surprise! Great to see you!
SAM   Yes, it's really nice ³*see you / to see you / you see*, too.
JAMES Where are you living ⁴*today / this day / these days*?
SAM   Oh, not ⁵*far from / far of / far away* here. In Park Road, near the sports centre.
JAMES Oh, ⁶*what / how / who* nice!
SAM   And ⁷*she is / it is / this is* my wife, Jackie.
JAMES Your wife – wow! That's fantastic ⁸*new / news / notices*! Nice to ⁹*meet / meat / meeting* you, Jackie.
JACKIE Nice to meet you, ¹⁰*two / too / to*.

b ▶1.3 Listen and check.

c Complete the sentences with the words in the box.

surprise   hello   meet   news   again
time   last   ~~nice~~   must   up

1 Sea View Road? Oh, how _nice_!
2 Your husband – wow! That's fantastic _news_!
3 We really _must_ go. We're late.
4 What a lovely _surprise_!
5 Say _hello_ to Roger for me.
6 Long _time_ no see!
7 It was really nice to _meet_ you.
8 We must meet _up_ soon.
9 It was great to see you _again_.
10 When did we _last_ see each other?

d ▶1.4 Listen and check.

2 PRONUNCIATION
Sentence stress

a ▶1.5 Listen to the sentences and underline the stressed words.

1 I'm pretty sure it was two months ago.
2 What a lovely surprise!
3 It was really nice to meet you.
4 I'm sorry, but I really must go.
5 Where are you living these days?
6 I'm late for a meeting.

1D Skills for Writing
I'm sending you some photos

1 READING

a Read Nandeep's email to Hannah and tick (✓) the correct answer.

   a ☐ Nandeep is staying at the Taj Mahal hotel in Delhi.
   b ☐ Nandeep is visiting his cousins in Boston.
   c ☐ Nandeep is on holiday at his aunt and uncle's house in Delhi.

b Read the email again. Are the sentences true or false?

   1 Nandeep mainly speaks in Hindi to his cousins.
   2 He's visiting lots of places while he's in India.
   3 The Taj Mahal is in Delhi.
   4 Nandeep didn't enjoy visiting the Taj Mahal.
   5 Nandeep often uses his aunt and uncle's pool.
   6 Nandeep isn't enjoying his holiday.

2 WRITING SKILLS
Correcting mistakes

a Correct the sentences.

   1 I'm having a lovely time here in france.
      I'm having a lovely time here in France.
   2 Yesterday we visitted the Palace of Versailles near Paris.

   3 In the mornings, I usually going to the beach with my Portuguese friends.

   4 I hope your having a lovely time in Canada with your family.

   5 Their English are very good, but we always speak in German.

Hi Hannah,

I hope you're enjoying your stay in Boston.

I'm spending a month on holiday in India. I'm staying with my aunt and uncle and my two cousins in Delhi. I don't speak much Hindi, but they all speak English very well, so communication isn't a problem. They're taking me to see lots of really interesting places. Yesterday we drove to Agra and visited the Taj Mahal. It took two hours to get there. This is a photo I took – what an amazing building!

It's really hot here all the time, but my aunt and uncle have a swimming pool, so we spend a lot of our time in the water – it's so relaxing! In the evenings I usually go to cafés with my cousins and their friends.

I'm having a great time here in India!

See you soon.

Nandeep

---

3 WRITING

a Read the email from Paul. Use the notes in brackets to write Becky's reply.

Hi Becky

Hope you're having a nice holiday. Tell me all about it! (*Describe my holiday*)

What's the hotel like? (*Not in a hotel – staying with my family!*)

What do you do every day? (*Explain and send a photo*)

See you soon (*he OK? Ask.*)

Love
Paul

UNIT 1
Reading and listening extension

1 READING

a Read the article. Match the statements 1–3 with the people a–c.
1 I don't think internet dating is a good way to meet people. — a Joanna
2 Most people I've met online are friendly. — b Stephen
3 I'm very happy with the person I met online. — c Colm

INTERNET DATING:
How is it for you?

Are you looking for that special person? Do you want to meet new people? Lots of people meet their new partner over the Internet. It is particularly popular in the U.S.A., where about 30% of people meet their partner online. We talked to some young people in Ireland about their experiences of internet dating.

JOANNA, 23, CORK
I am dating a man I met on the Internet. His name is Gavin and he is lovely. We have the same hobbies and we laugh about the same things. We rarely argue and our relationship is perfect. I'm so happy.

STEPHEN, 28, DUBLIN
I normally wouldn't meet someone through the Internet. I prefer to meet people face-to-face. I think it's difficult to know what a person is like from a photo or some information online. I want to get to know someone properly, and I don't think you can do that on the Internet.

COLM, 22, GALWAY
I have several friends who I have met online. It's a great way to meet new people who have similar interests to you. Sometimes people can be rude but most people are very friendly – it's great fun! I recommend it as a good way of meeting new people.

There might be some problems with meeting people online, but lots of people are doing it these days, and it helps people meet new people and make new friends. Good luck!

b Read the article again and tick (✓) the best endings for the sentences.

1 In the U.S.A. ...
   a ☐ people rarely use the Internet to find love.
   b ✓ internet dating is a normal way to meet people.
   c ☐ 30% of young people have a boyfriend or girlfriend.

2 Joanna ...
   a ☐ has met several people online.
   b ☐ is very happy in her relationship.
   c ☐ doesn't think internet dating is right for her.

3 Stephen ...
   a ☐ would like to meet a girl online.
   b ☐ doesn't want to put a photo of himself online.
   c ☐ doesn't think that you can get to know people online.

4 Colm thinks that ...
   a ☐ it's difficult to meet people online.
   b ☐ people are often unfriendly.
   c ☐ the Internet is a good way to meet people and have fun.

5 The writer of the article thinks that ...
   a ☐ people hardly ever meet someone they like online.
   b ☐ internet dating can be a good way to meet people.
   c ☐ internet dating is the best way to meet people.

c Write a paragraph about different ways of meeting new people. Think about:
- different places to meet new people
- some problems with meeting people for the first time
- the stories in the article
- your own experience.

8

2 LISTENING

a ▶1.6 Listen to the conversation. Match 1–3 with a–c to make true sentences.

1 Sophia — a goes to a club every week.
2 Richard — b is friends with the people he lives with.
3 Peter — c meets people in a café every week.

b ▶1.6 Listen to the conversation again and tick (✓) the best endings for the sentences.

1 The radio programme is about …
  a ☐ starting university.
  b ☐ moving to a new city.
  c ✓ how people make friends.
2 Richard doesn't …
  a ☐ usually go to bars.
  b ☐ like making friends with new people.
  c ☐ find it difficult to meet people at university.
3 Richard likes …
  a ☐ going to parties with his friends.
  b ☐ people who like similar things to him.
  c ☐ the countryside near where he lives.
4 Sophia is interested in …
  a ☐ making friends with people studying Drama.
  b ☐ joining a club.
  c ☐ meeting lots of different people.
5 Peter doesn't …
  a ☐ use the Internet to meet people.
  b ☐ like the people he lives with.
  c ☐ usually go out in the evenings.
6 Which of the sentences is true about the students?
  a ☐ The university is helping all the students to make friends.
  b ☐ The students are making friends in different ways.

c Write questions and answers about what you do in your free time and who you spend it with. Think about these questions:
  • Where do you spend your free time?
  • What do you do and how often?
  • Who do you spend your free time with?

Review and extension

1 GRAMMAR

Correct the sentences.

1 Where you went on holiday last year?
  Where did you go on holiday last year?
2 At the moment, she works in the café by the station.
3 Why you missed the bus?
4 I can't talk to you now because I do my homework.
5 What kind of music you usually listen to?
6 They waiting for the bus to London.

2 VOCABULARY

Correct the sentences.

1 The new Iron Man film is amaizing!
  The new Iron Man film is amazing!
2 We very enjoyed the film last night.
3 We had a lovly time at the party last night.
4 I think our History lessons are so borring.
5 I think that man's a bit extrange. Look, he's talking to himself.
6 New York's allright, but I prefer living in London, actually.

3 WORDPOWER like

Match 1–8 with a–h to make sentences.

1 [e] We can go for a walk in the park
2 ☐ What was the party
3 ☐ What gorgeous weather! It looks
4 ☐ The boy in the white T-shirt looks
5 ☐ He loves films with superheroes, you know,
6 ☐ I absolutely love this singer. She sounds
7 ☐ I want to buy a computer
8 ☐ Thanks for your email. It sounds

a like the perfect day for the beach.
b like this one. How much is it?
c like Philip. They've got the same smile.
d like you're having a great holiday.
e if you like.
f like Katy Perry.
g like Batman or Spider-Man.
h like last night?

REVIEW YOUR PROGRESS

Look again at Review your progress on p.16 of the Student's Book. How well can you do these things now?
3 = very well   2 = well   1 = not so well

I CAN …

ask and answer personal questions	☐
talk about how I communicate	☐
greet people and end conversations	☐
write a personal email.	☐

2A We had an adventure

1 GRAMMAR Past simple

a Tick (✓) the correct sentences. Correct the wrong sentences.

1. ☐ The train not arrived until 22:30, so we got home around midnight.
   The train didn't arrive until 22:30, so we got home around midnight.
2. ☐ I slept very badly on the plane, so I feeled very tired the next day.
3. ☐ Did you took the train from New York to Washington?
4. ☐ We flew from London to Manchester because it was really cheap.
5. ☐ They spended two nights in a hotel and then they stayed at a friend's house for three days.
6. ☐ I didn't enjoyed my trip to Scotland because the weather wasn't very good.
7. ☐ When I got back to my hotel, I found a message from my sister.
8. ☐ We unpacked our suitcases and ate dinner in the hotel restaurant. It cost 100 euros!

b Complete the exchanges with the past simple form of the verbs in brackets. Use contractions where possible.

1. **A** How __was__ (be) your flight?
   B Fine, thanks, but I __didn't sleep__ (not sleep) because the seats __wasn't__ (not be) comfortable.
2. **A** What __you did__ (you, do) last summer?
   B We __hadn't__ (not have) much money, so we __decided__ (decide) to stay in the UK.
3. **A** Where __Ben went__ (Ben, go) on holiday last year?
   B He __went__ (go) to Canada.
4. **A** __Did you bringed__ (you, bring) back any souvenirs from Jamaica?
   B Yes, I __did__. (do) I __bought__ (buy) some Blue Mountain coffee.
5. **A** __did you meet__ (you, meet) your French friends when you were in Paris?
   B Yes, we __did__. (do) We __met__ (meet) them for dinner one evening.
6. **A** _____ (you, visit) your cousins in Los Angeles?
   B No, we _____ (not have) time.

she had a friend over/round for coffee
a friend came over/round for tea.

2 VOCABULARY Tourism

a Match 1–8 with a–h to make sentences.

1. [d] We decided to go to China on holiday, so we had to get
2. [e] I'm really bored. Why don't we do
3. [a] James decided to go away
4. [f] Going to the Olympics is great, but you need to book
5. [h] It's a good idea to buy
6. [b] Come on! Let's unpack
7. [c] My daughter didn't have much money so she stayed
8. [g] On the day you leave, you need to check out of

a to Scotland for the weekend.
b our bags and go out for lunch.
c in hostels when she went travelling for a year.
d a visa from the embassy.
e some sightseeing this afternoon?
f your accommodation before you go.
g your hotel by 11 o'clock.
h souvenirs here – they're very expensive at the airport.

b Write the names of the holiday items under the pictures.

1 suntan lotion   2 passport   3 backpack

4 dictionary   5 money   6 suitcase

3 PRONUNCIATION -ed endings

a Tick (✓) the verbs that have an extra syllable when we add -ed.

Infinitive	+ -ed	Extra syllable?
depart	departed	✓
love	loved	
listen	listened	
hate	hated	
sound	sounded	
look	looked	
post	posted	
invite	invited	
enjoy	enjoyed	
like	liked	

b ▶ 2.1 Listen and check.

10

2B Everyone was waiting for me

1 VOCABULARY Travel collocations

a Complete the sentences with the correct forms of the verbs in the box.

> miss   take off   get to   change   give   land
> set off   board   hitchhike   travel around

When I was a student, my best friend and I ¹travelled around Europe for a month. We didn't want to travel by train, so we ²_____. Once, a lorry driver ³_____ us a lift from Paris to Cannes – over 900 kilometres!
She ⁴_____ from her house at six o'clock in the morning. However, she ⁵_____ the 06:30 train because there was a traffic jam in the town centre.
Our plane ⁶_____ from Beijing 45 minutes late, but we ⁷_____ in Sydney ten minutes early!
Our journey from London to Glasgow was terrible! We ⁸_____ our train in London at two o'clock, but then we ⁹_____ trains in Birmingham and also in Manchester. In the end, we ¹⁰_____ Glasgow just after midnight!

b Underline the correct words to complete the sentences.

1. **A** Why was there a big *strike / traffic jam / lift* on the motorway this morning?
   B Because there was a *crash / strike / queue* between two cars at 7:30.
2. **A** Why did you *lose / miss / delay* your train?
   B Well, my friend was driving us to the station, but her GPS wasn't working, so we *set off / broke down / got lost*. In the end, we bought a map!
3. **A** Why were there *traffic jams / long delays / long queues* to all the flights from Heathrow Airport today?
   B Because there was a pilots' *strike / turbulence / delay* yesterday, so lots of planes are at the wrong airport today.
4. There was *a turbulence / something wrong / a strike* with our coach, so we waited for two hours at the service station.
5. It took me over an hour to get my ticket because there was a long *delay / queue / crash* at the ticket office. Then the train *got lost / took off / broke down* just outside Paris, so that's why I'm so late.
6. **A** It sounds like you had a bad flight between Washington and London.
   B Yes, there was a lot of *turbulence / queues / strikes* over the Atlantic because of the bad weather.

2 GRAMMAR Past continuous

a Complete the sentences with the past continuous forms of the verbs in brackets.

1. When we arrived at the station, my uncle __was waiting__ (wait) for us in the car park.
2. It _____ (snow) hard when we got to our hotel.
3. _____ (you, fly) over the Alps when the turbulence started?
4. How fast _____ (you, drive) when the accident happened?
5. Where _____ (you, stand) when the thief stole your handbag?
6. Did you get lost because your GPS _____ (not work)?

b Complete the text with the past simple or past continuous forms of the verbs in brackets.

My mother and I ¹ __had__ (have) a terrible journey from London to Edinburgh last weekend. First, when my brother ² _____ (drive) us to the airport on Saturday evening, his car ³ _____ (break down) on the motorway. In the end, we ⁴ _____ (miss) our plane and ⁵ _____ (buy) some new tickets for the flight on Sunday morning instead. However, on Sunday morning we ⁶ _____ (wait) for our flight when it ⁷ _____ (start) snowing heavily, and they ⁸ _____ (decide) to close the airport. So we ⁹ _____ (take) a taxi to Euston Station and ¹⁰ _____ (buy) tickets for the 2 pm train to Edinburgh.

3 PRONUNCIATION
Sentence stress: vowel sounds

a ▶ 2.2 Listen to the sentences. Do the letters in **bold** sound like /ə/ as in *computer*, /ɒ/ as in *dog* or /ɜː/ as in *her*? Tick (✓) the correct box for each sentence.

	Sound 1 /ə/ (e.g. *computer*)	Sound 2 /ɒ/ (e.g. *dog*)	Sound 3 /ɜː/ (e.g. *her*)
1 W**e**re you waiting for the bus?	✓		
2 I w**a**sn't driving the car.			
3 They w**e**re watching TV.			
4 We w**e**ren't having dinner.			
5 She w**a**s talking on her phone.			
6 W**a**s she listening?			
7 He w**a**sn't smoking.			
8 They w**e**ren't playing chess.			

11

2C Everyday English
What time's the next train?

[Handwritten notes on yellow sticky note:]
3) How much is a return ticket to Edinburgh?
4) How often do the buses leave for the airport?
5) What time is the next coach to Barcelona?
6) Can I pay for my ticket in euros?
7) Where can I buy a sandwich for the journey?
8) How much does it cost to get a taxi to the airport?

HW

...e questions.
...can?
...the / could?
...formation desk?
...ow?
...w / the?
...is?

7 can / a sandwich / the journey / for / where / buy / I ?
_____

8 a taxi / to the airport / much / it / does / cost / to get / how ?
_____

b ▶ 2.3 Listen and check.

c Complete the conversation with the words in the box.

| can   near   here   have   over there   could you   ~~excuse~~ |
| anything else   actually   from   what time |

A ¹ _Excuse_ me.
B Yes, how ² _can_ I help you?
A ³ _Could you_ tell me which platform the next train to London leaves ⁴ _from_ ?
B Certainly, madam. It leaves from Platform 2.
A OK, thanks. And ⁵ _what time_ does it leave?
B It leaves at 10:32, in twelve minutes.
A Brilliant. Thanks.
B Is there ⁶ _anything else_ I can help you with?
A ⁷ _actually_ , there is one more thing. Where can I buy a cup of coffee? Is there a café ⁸ _near here_ ?
B Yes, there is. There's a café on the platform, ⁹ _over there_
A Great. Thanks so much.
B No problem. ¹⁰ _have_ a good journey.

d ▶ 2.4 Listen and check.

e Match the traveller's sentences 1–8 with the ticket seller's responses a–h.

1 [c] Hello.
2 [b] Could you tell me what time the next bus to Folkestone leaves, please?
3 [f] Great, thanks! And where does it leave from?
4 [d] I will be. Can I have a ticket, please?
5 [h] Here you are. Also, is there somewhere I can buy a newspaper?
6 [e] That's OK. I can run fast.
7 [g] Yes, I think that's it. Thank you for your help!
8 [a] Thanks! Bye!

a Goodbye!
b Yes, of course. It leaves in five minutes.
c Good afternoon. How can I help you?
d Certainly. That'll be £9.50.
e No problem, sir. Now hurry, or you'll miss your bus!
f From stop number 4, but you'll need to be quick!
g You'll need to! Is that all, sir?
h Yes, at the newsagent over there, but I'm not sure you'll have time.

2 PRONUNCIATION Joining words

a ▶ 2.5 Listen to the questions. Tick (✓) the two words that are joined together.

1 When did you check into your hotel?
   a [✓] che**ck i**nto   b [ ] you**r h**otel
2 How can I help you?
   a [ ] ca**n I**   b [ ] hel**p y**ou
3 Did you get a visa when you went to China?
   a [ ] ge**t a**   b [ ] whe**n y**ou
4 What time did you set off from home?
   a [ ] di**d y**ou   b [ ] se**t o**ff
5 What time is your plane?
   a [ ] tim**e i**s   b [ ] i**s y**our
6 How much is a return ticket to Bath?
   a [ ] mu**ch i**s   b [ ] t**o B**ath

2D Skills for Writing
This city is different, but very friendly

1 READING

a Read Roberto's blog and tick (✓) the correct answers.

1 Roberto and Ana are staying in …
   a ☐ a hotel in the centre of London.
   b ☐ a hostel near Heathrow Airport.
   c ☐ a hotel in Earl's Court.
   d ✓ a hostel near the centre of London.

2 On Sunday, Roberto and Ana …
   a ☐ had fish and chips for lunch.
   b ☐ spent all day at the British Museum.
   c ✓ went to the British Museum and Covent Garden.
   d ☐ thought the British Museum was boring.

SATURDAY
Ana and I got to London at 11:30 this morning. It was a very long flight from São Paulo. When we got off the plane, the first thing we noticed was the cold – six degrees! I'm glad I brought a warm coat! In São Paulo, it was 35 degrees when we left. Everything they say about Londoners is true! The people at the airport weren't very friendly and they couldn't understand our English. And we couldn't understand what they were saying. In the end, we took the underground from Heathrow Airport to our hostel in Earl's Court, near the centre of London. The hostel is full of young tourists from all over the world and everyone was very friendly and helpful. We were very tired, so we decided to sleep for a few hours. Ana's telling me to get ready to go and eat, so I have to finish now – more tomorrow.

SUNDAY
Ana and I had our first experience of British food last night. We went to a little café near the hostel. We decided to try fish and chips. It's a typical British dish and it was delicious with a hot cup of tea (with milk!). Today we visited the British Museum and Covent Garden. The British Museum is amazing – there are lots of interesting things to see. We spent two hours there and only saw a few of the rooms. We bought some sandwiches for lunch and then we went to Covent Garden market. There were lots of musicians and magicians in the street. We had a lovely afternoon and Ana took lots of photos. You can see them on Facebook.

b Read the blog again. Are the sentences true or false?
1 On Saturday, it was warmer in London than in São Paulo. F
2 It was difficult for Roberto and Ana to understand the people at the airport. T
3 When they got to the hostel, they went to bed. T
4 They didn't enjoy their fish and chips. F
5 They didn't see all the rooms in the British Museum. F
6 They had lunch in a restaurant in Covent Garden. F

2 WRITING SKILLS Linking words

a Underline the correct words to complete the sentences.
1 There was a long queue for the museum, and / *so* / but we decided to go to the market instead.
2 We didn't visit the Tower of London *because* / so / but the tickets were very expensive.
3 The hotel looked really nice, because / *and* / but they didn't have any free rooms that night.
4 Yesterday I visited Ellis Island so / *and* / because the Statue of Liberty.
5 There weren't any flights today but / so / *because* there was a snow storm.
6 Because / *When* / So we got to our hotel, I phoned my wife to wish her 'Happy Birthday'.
7 It started raining hard, but / because / *so* we didn't go to the mountains.
8 We wanted to go to the concert, *but* / so / because we couldn't get any tickets.

3 WRITING

a Read the notes. Write Maite's blog post about her holiday in New York.

Maite's blog: New York post (notes)

Monday, 25th January

Madrid: left 12:20
New York: arrived 14:30
Very tired – (why?)
Weather: very cold – minus 6 degrees!
People = (?)
Hotel = (?)
Dinner = (?)

13

UNIT 2
Reading and listening extension

1 READING

a Read the article. How did the couples travel? Tick (✓) the correct ways. Sometimes there is more than one possible answer.

1 Carl and Sam
   a ☐ on foot
   b ✓ on two wheels
   c ✓ on four wheels
   d ☐ by sea
2 Ashish and Bryony
   a ☐ on foot
   b ☐ on two wheels
   c ☐ on four wheels
   d ☐ by sea
3 Yvette and Rob
   a ☐ on foot
   b ☐ on two wheels
   c ☐ on four wheels
   d ☐ by sea

b Read the article again and underline the correct words to complete the sentences.

1 Carl and Sam / Ashish and Bryony / <u>Yvette and Rob</u> stayed in Bristol for most of the week.
2 Carl and Sam / Ashish and Bryony / Yvette and Rob enjoyed the first day of the race.
3 Carl and Sam / Ashish and Bryony / Yvette and Rob stopped when they didn't know where they were.
4 Carl and Sam / Ashish and Bryony / Yvette and Rob finished their journey on foot when something happened to the vehicle they were in.
5 Carl and Sam / Ashish and Bryony / Yvette and Rob stopped after the first day.

c Complete the words to make sentences about the article. Write one word in each space.

1 During the race, the students c_ouldn't_ spend any money.
2 When they started the race, the weather was s_____.
3 Carl and Sam got a l_____ home with Carl's dad.
4 It c_____ money for Ashish and Bryony to stay in a hotel.
5 Yvette and Rob got to Spain early in the m_____.

d Write about a long journey you went on. Remember to include:
- where you went
- a description of how you travelled there
- what you thought of the place.

In July, a group of students from Bristol University, in England, had a race. It started at the university at 9 am on 20 June. The winners were the pair who travelled the longest distance in seven days without spending any money.

CARL AND SAM

We decided to cycle. The sun was shining when we set off and it was fun. But on the third day, it started raining and we got lost. It was awful. We slept under a tree in a field. The next morning Carl phoned his dad and he came to get us and drove us home.

DISTANCE TRAVELLED: 110 MILES

ASHISH AND BRYONY

We hitchhiked. A lorry stopped and we got in. There were long delays and we didn't go far for hours. That evening as we were driving north the lorry broke down and we had to get out. We didn't know what to do. We were tired and hungry so we decided to walk to a village and stay in a hotel. But we had to pay. The next day we went home.

DISTANCE TRAVELLED: 130 MILES

YVETTE AND ROB

We decided to walk to the port in Bristol and try to board a ship. We went to the office and asked if any ships would take us for free. For five days no one would. On the sixth day we found a ship to take us to Spain. We boarded the ship and the next day we arrived in Bilbao as the sun was rising. It was amazing.

DISTANCE TRAVELLED: 640 MILES

Review and extension

1 GRAMMAR

Correct the sentences.

1 When I did some housework, I heard the news on the radio.
   When I was doing some housework, I heard the news on the radio.
2 When we were getting to the station, the train was just arriving.
3 My wife phoned me while I waited for my plane.
4 A man was taking my wallet while I was waiting in the queue for my ticket.
5 Last year, we were going on holiday to Greece for two weeks.
6 I was driving to the airport when I was seeing the accident.

2 VOCABULARY

Correct the sentences.

1 They missed their flight because Rob's car broke on the way to the airport.
   They missed their flight because Rob's car broke down on the way to the airport.
2 My travel from Berlin to London took fifteen hours.
3 Last week, I went to Rome on a business travel.
4 The trafic was terrible because it was the rush hour.
5 By the time they checked away the hotel, it was 2 pm.
6 In the afternoon, they went sighseeing in the old town.

3 WORDPOWER *off*

Complete the sentences with the words in the box.

| 75% | I'm | set | ~~switched~~ | drove | took | are | fell |

1 He was tired when he went to bed, so he _switched_ off the light and went to sleep.
2 They _____ off from Paul's house at 3:00 and arrived in Paris at 11:30.
3 When I got to the hotel, I _____ off my shoes.
4 She _____ off her motorbike and broke her arm.
5 Those jeans are cheap! They're _____ off the original price.
6 He got in his car and _____ off without speaking.
7 Goodnight. _____ off now. I'm meeting a friend.
8 Ladies and gentlemen: the film is about to start, so please make sure your phones _____ off.

REVIEW YOUR PROGRESS

Look again at Review your progress on p.26 of the Student's Book. How well can you do these things now?
3 = very well   2 = well   1 = not so well

I CAN ...

talk about past holidays	☐
describe difficult journeys	☐
ask for information in a public place	☐
write a travel blog.	☐

2 LISTENING

a ▶2.6 Listen to the conversation. Match problems a–e with where they are happening 1–5.

1 M3 ——— a crash and delays
2 M4   b long delays
3 M1   c no delays
4 Trains   d problems this weekend
5 Gatwick   e traffic jam

b ▶2.6 Listen to the conversation again and tick (✓) the correct answers.

1 Why were there delays on the M3 this morning?
   a ✓ There was a crash.
   b ☐ The police closed the road.
   c ☐ It was raining.
2 What happened three hours ago near Swindon?
   a ☐ There was an accident.
   b ☐ There was a very long queue.
   c ☐ A lorry stopped working.
3 Who should use the A429 this evening?
   a ☐ People who are going to Swindon.
   b ☐ Lorries.
   c ☐ Everyone on the M4.
4 Who did the police say can't go on the motorway?
   a ☐ People going to a music festival.
   b ☐ Hitchhikers.
   c ☐ People who want to camp.
5 What is unusual about the trains today?
   a ☐ There aren't any trains working.
   b ☐ The trains are mainly working well.
   c ☐ There are lots of delays.
6 Where did Jackie and Bob stay last night?
   a ☐ In a hotel at the airport.
   b ☐ On the floor at the airport.
   c ☐ In India.

c Write about a long journey you took. Remember to include:
- how you travelled
- how long it took
- what problems you had.

3A Have you ever helped a stranger?

1 GRAMMAR
Present perfect or past simple

a Put the words in the correct order to make sentences.

1 has / that old lady's / done / shopping / James / lots of times .
   James has done that old lady's shopping lots of times.

2 you / have / to / been / in / Rio de Janeiro / carnival / the / ever ?
   _____

3 twice this week / I / to charity / money / given / have .
   _____

4 have / you / my / with / helped / homework / me / never .
   _____

5 they / volunteer work / ever / done / have / any ?
   _____

6 big / never / a / for the waiter / left / tip / has / she .
   _____

7 money / have / any / you / homeless person / to / given / ever / a ?
   _____

8 several times / I / visited / this month / my / have / grandmother .
   _____

b Complete the exchanges with the present perfect or past simple forms of the words in brackets.

1 A *Have you ever given* money to charity? (you, ever, give)
   B Yes, I *gave* £10 to a cancer charity last week. (give)

2 A *Has she ever done* volunteer work in Africa before? (she, ever, do)
   B Yes, she *did* some volunteer work in Mali last year. (do)

3 A *Have you ever helped* someone who was hurt? (you, ever, help)
   B Yes, I _____ a woman who fell off her bike last week. (help)

4 A I _____ tips in that restaurant lots of times. (leave)
   B Really? How much _____ the last time you came? (you, leave)

5 A _____ drinks for 20 people? (he, ever, buy)
   B Yes, he _____ a drink for all his friends on his birthday in July. (buy)

2 VOCABULARY
make / do / give collocations

a Match 1–8 with a–h to make sentences.

1 [d] She was a very confident girl, so she made
2 [h] When she read the email from her nephew, it made
3 [e] Are you doing anything
4 [b] He's a really funny guy. He always makes
5 [g] Your daughter's very clever. Is she doing
6 [c] My grandfather always gives us
7 [f] We gave the American tourists
8 [a] He didn't use his camera any more, so he gave it

a away to his grandson.
b silly jokes when he's with friends.
c a big hug when we go to see him.
d lots of friends at her new school.
e nice for your birthday?
f directions to the train station.
g well at school this term?
h her smile because it was so funny.

b Underline the correct words to complete the sentences.

1 I love those old black-and-white films. Charlie Chaplin always *does* / *makes* / *gives* me smile.
2 You're so mean. You never *do* / *make* / *give* the waiters a tip.
3 He *made* / *did* / *gave* volunteer work for a charity in Africa last year.
4 She was so happy to see him again that she *gave* / *made* / *did* him a big hug.
5 Do your parents usually *make* / *give* / *do* something nice when it's their wedding anniversary?
6 I'm having a great time in Paris. I've *made* / *done* / *given* some new friends in the hostel.
7 The doctors say that she's *making* / *giving* / *doing* well and that she can leave the hospital tomorrow.
8 I've never *made* / *given* / *done* anyone directions in French – all the tourists who come here speak English.

16

3B I've already spent my salary this month

1 VOCABULARY Money

a Match 1–8 with a–h to make sentences.

1. [f] My company pays my salary
2. [g] That holiday sounds fantastic, but
3. [b] My brother lent me £50 yesterday
4. [h] If you can't afford to buy a new car,
5. [e] She's just spent £150
6. [c] I only buy clothes from that shop
7. [d] If you buy two jackets,
8. [a] When I borrow money

a so I could buy some new jeans.
b from my parents, I always pay it back quickly.
c when they have special offers.
d we can give you a 20% discount.
e on two pairs of shoes.
f into my bank account.
g it costs £5,000 just for a week!
h why don't you get a loan from the bank?

b Complete the text with the words in the box.

~~into~~ afford lend spend bank account
~~up for~~ borrow back loan

I'm saving [1] _up for_ a car at the moment. I pay £200 [2] _into_ my [3] _bank account_ each month. I can't [4] _afford_ to buy a new car, so it will have to be second-hand – probably three or four years old. My parents have offered to [5] _lend_ me some money but I don't want to [6] _borrow_ any money from them. They've just bought a very old house in the country and they need to [7] _spend_ a lot of money on repairs. So I'm going to ask the bank for a [8] _loan_ of £5,000. I think I can pay it [9] _back_ in two years.

2 GRAMMAR Present perfect with *just*, *already* and *yet*

a Underline the correct adverbs to complete the sentences.

1. I've *just* / **already** / *yet* spent £100 this weekend, so I'm afraid I can't afford to go to a restaurant for dinner.
2. It's Mum's birthday tomorrow – have you bought her a present *already* / *just* / **yet**?
3. Look, I've **just** / *already* / *yet* bought a new mobile phone. It's brilliant, isn't it?
4. He's *yet* / *just* / **already** saved up £3,000 because he wants to travel round the world next summer.
5. A Why does she look so upset?
   B Because she's *already* / **just** / *yet* lost her wallet.
6. No, I can't lend you any more money. You've **already** / *just* / *yet* borrowed £100 from me.
7. Oh, no! We can't play tennis now because it's **already** / *yet* / *just* started raining.
8. She hasn't opened a new bank account *already* / **yet** / *just*.

b Correct the sentences.

1. Mike just has spent £400 on a new camera.
   Mike has just spent £400 on a new camera.
2. He's borrowed already £2,000 from his bank.
   ___
3. Have you yet paid Louise back?
   ___
4. Sue already has spent the money she borrowed from me.
   ___
5. We've bought just a new TV in the sales.
   ___
6. Has she saved yet enough money to buy a tablet?
   ___
7. I've bought already a present for my wife.
   ___
8. They've opened a new bank account in France just.
   ___

17

3C Everyday English
Do you have anything cheaper?

1 USEFUL LANGUAGE
Talking to people in shops

a Put the conversation in the correct order.

☐ **B** Yes, I suppose she might like them. On second thoughts, maybe I should get something else.
[1] **A** Good morning. Can I help you?
☐ **B** Do you have anything cheaper?
☐ **A** OK. Er, let me see … what about this necklace?
☐ **B** Yes, it's lovely. OK, I'll take it.
☐ **A** Are you looking for anything in particular?
☐ **B** Er, yes. I'm looking for a present for my wife.
☐ **A** Really? How about these earrings? They're really beautiful. A perfect present …
☐ **B** Well, she loves earrings.
☐ **A** Well, these earrings here are cheaper. They're only £50 with the discount.

b  Listen and check.

c <u>Underline</u> the correct words to complete the sentences.
1. How would you like to *cost / pay / buy*?
2. We're looking *for / at / after* a present for my grandfather.
3. Did you want something *on / in / at* particular?
4. Who's *then / after / next*, please?
5. *In second thoughts / On second thoughts / My second thought*, I really think we should get her a book.
6. Can you *enter / write / touch* your PIN, please?
7. Do you have this in a different *size / till / receipt*? Thanks.
8. Could you show us *something more / something else / something other*?

d Put the words in the correct order to make sentences.
1. for / jacket / looking / a / I'm .
   I'm looking for a jacket.
2. a / 14 / size / I'm / I / think .

3. same / in / have / one / blue / do / the / you ?
   _____
4. much / tell / can / it / how / is / you / me ?
   _____
5. a bit / too / that's / expensive .
   _____
6. one / you / cheaper / do / have / a ?
   _____

2 PRONUNCIATION Sentence stress

a  Listen to the sentences and <u>underline</u> the stressed syllables or words.
1. Can you <u>show</u> us something <u>else</u>?
2. Can you enter your PIN, please?
3. I'm looking for a present for my husband.
4. Do you have any black jeans?
5. Thanks. I'll take it.
6. Actually, I think we should buy her a book.

18

3D Skills for Writing
We've successfully raised £500

1 READING

a Read David and Philip's email and tick (✓) the correct answer.

David and Philip are writing to …
a ☐ ask their colleagues for more money.
b ☐ invite their colleagues to a party.
c ☐ tell their colleagues about Cancer Research and how they have all helped.
d ☐ ask their colleagues to swim a kilometre.

b Read David and Philip's email again. Are the sentences true or false?

1 In the last year they have given £2,500 to Cancer Research.
2 In April, 30 people swam a kilometre to raise money.
3 The party in June was very popular.
4 4,000 people with cancer get money from Cancer Research.

Mail

Hello everyone,

We'd like to say a big 'Thank you!' to everyone who has helped us to raise money for Cancer Research over the past six months. We've successfully raised £2,500!

We really hope you have enjoyed the various events that we have organised this year. First we had a 'Swimathon' in April. Thirty of us swam a kilometre and raised over £1,000. Then 200 people came to our fantastic summer party in June. And don't forget to come to our special quiz night in September. There are some amazing prizes!

Cancer Research will use the money to do important research. This includes the work of over 4,000 scientists, doctors and nurses who are fighting cancer in this country. Cancer Research helps thousands of people with cancer every year.

Would you like to help us raise more money for Cancer Research? Please look out for the next event. Thanks again for all your help.

David and Philip

---

2 WRITING SKILLS Paragraphing

a Read the sentences. Put them in the correct order to make an email with four paragraphs. The paragraphs should be in the following order:

- Introduction
- How the team has raised / raises money
- Information about ActionAid
- Closing the email

☐ Thanks again for all your help. Please look out for our next event.
☐ ActionAid will use the money to help poor people around the world, to educate them and to protect them. In the past ten years, they have helped thousands of children start school.
☐ We have successfully raised £750.
☐ And, of course, next Friday there is the book and DVD sale at lunchtime.
[1] We'd like to thank everyone for helping to raise money for ActionAid over the past year.
☐ Most of you came to the 1970s party in September. A lot of people also came to our karaoke night in November.
☐ So remember that a small amount of money can make a big difference. For example, only £4 per week gives a child in Africa clean water, education and medicine.

3 WRITING

a Read the notes and write Sam's email to his colleagues about the Save the Children charity.

Email to colleagues about Save the Children

Introduction:
Thank you – everyone who helped raise money – past 12 months. How much?

How the team has raised money and future events:
September: sports day
October: 1990s karaoke evening
Next week: quiz night + prizes!

Information about Save the Children:
Our money = save children's lives + better future
Last year STC helped 10m children around world
Small amount of money = big difference, e.g. £3 saves lives of 8 children with stomach virus

Closing the email
Help raise more money for STC?
Email me for info about future events
Thanks again

UNIT 3
Reading and listening extension

1 READING

a Read the magazine article. Complete the sentences with the numbers in the box.

> 100   10 million   13 million   ~~87 million~~

1 A company bought the website for £ _87 million_.
2 He started the website with £_____.
3 The website has more than _____ regular users.
4 Charities got £_____ from Martin after he sold the website.

Martin Lewis is a British journalist, TV presenter and writer. He knows a lot about money: how to spend it, where to use it, and, most of all, how to save it!

Martin was always interested in saving money and helping other people to save money. He gave tips to friends about it, he talked about it on television and he wrote about it in a national newspaper. In 2003, he decided to start a website, *moneysavingexpert.com*. He paid a man in Uzbekistan £100 to design the site and soon thousands of people were using it. The website gave lots of useful information. It told people which times of the day supermarkets had the most special offers. It helped people get discounts on everything from clothes to holidays. It told people when shops had sales on. The website helped people to buy things that they couldn't afford to buy before. And if you needed to borrow money to buy a new car or a house, it told you which banks were the best to lend it to you. Lots of people started using *moneysavingexpert.com* and started telling their friends about it.

The website has been a huge success and Martin has done very well. Over 13 million people now use *moneysavingexpert.com* every month and in 2012, Martin Lewis sold the site to another company for £87 million. But Martin hasn't stopped helping people. Since selling the website, he has given away over £10 million to charities that help people look after their money. He's certainly made a lot of people smile. And it all started with £100.

b Read the magazine article again. Are the sentences true or false?

1 Martin Lewis is an expert on how to spend less money.
2 It took a long time before anyone used the website.
3 People can save money by going to supermarkets at a particular time of the day.
4 Martin Lewis still owns the website.
5 *Moneysavingexpert.com* has made Martin a very rich man.

c Complete the summary of the magazine article with the correct forms of the verbs in the box.

> borrow   buy   call   cost   get
> save   spend   ~~work~~   write

Before 2003, Martin Lewis [1] _worked_ as a journalist and [2] _____ about how to save money. In 2003, it [3] _____ him £100 to start a website, which he [4] _____ *moneysavingexpert.com*. It was soon very popular. It has lots of information about how to [5] _____ less money in shops, how to open a bank account, how to [6] _____ a discount on products and where to [7] _____ money from. The website has helped millions of people to [8] _____ money or get a loan since 2003. A company [9] _____ the website in 2012 for £87 million.

c Write about something that you have borrowed from or lent to someone. Include answers to these questions:
- What was it?
- Who did you lend it to or borrow it from?
- How long for?

2 LISTENING

a ▶ 3.3 Listen to the conversation. Underline the correct people to complete the sentences.

1 *Anita / Gary / Mike* gave a man something that he didn't have.
2 *Anita / Gary / Mike* is helping a friend who doesn't have much money.
3 *Anita / Gary / Mike* does something nice for other people every week.
4 *Anita / Gary / Mike* asked other people to lend her things.
5 *Anita / Gary / Mike* made friends with the person he helped.

20

b 🔊 3.3 Listen to the conversation again and tick (✓) the correct answers.

1 Why is Anita's neighbour having a party?
   a ✓ It's her daughter's birthday.
   b ☐ It's her son's birthday.
   c ☐ It's her husband's birthday.
2 Where is the birthday party going to be?
   a ☐ At the local beach.
   b ☐ In the back garden.
   c ☐ In the local park.
3 What did the Greek man do?
   a ☐ He borrowed an umbrella from Gary.
   b ☐ He lent an umbrella to Gary.
   c ☐ He borrowed Gary's coat.
4 What happened when Gary saw the man again?
   a ☐ They had lunch.
   b ☐ They had a cup of tea.
   c ☐ They went on holiday together.
5 What has Gary just bought?
   a ☐ A ticket to the theatre.
   b ☐ A ticket to Adelaide.
   c ☐ A ticket to Greece.
6 How does Mike try and make people smile?
   a ☐ He gives them money.
   b ☐ He puts his arms around them.
   c ☐ He makes friends with them.

c Write about the nicest thing that you've ever done. Remember to include:
   • who you helped
   • why you helped them
   • what you did
   • how they felt and how you felt afterwards.

Review and extension

1 GRAMMAR

Correct the sentences.

1 I never left a big tip in a restaurant.
   I've never left a big tip in a restaurant.
2 Did you ever give money to charity?
3 I've been to China on business last year.
4 I just bought a new mobile phone.
5 I haven't bought yet a birthday present for my brother.
6 I already spent £200 this weekend.

2 VOCABULARY

Correct the sentences.

1 I've just opened an account bank in the UK.
   I've just opened a bank account in the UK.
2 Can you borrow me 50 euros, please?
3 Joe did a really funny joke, but nobody laughed.
4 James is saving on for a new computer.
5 Our taxi driver was very friendly, so we made him a big tip.
6 I bought a new laptop in the sells – it was only £150!
7 Have you ever made any volunteer work?
8 Tony owes to me £50, but he hasn't paid it back yet.

3 WORDPOWER *just*

Complete the sentences with the words in the box.

about   spoken   in time   like   ~~coming~~
a beginner   over   under

1 I'm just ___coming___. I'll be there in two minutes!
2 There was a lot of traffic but we got to the airport just _____ for our flight.
3 My watch cost just _____ €100. Not cheap at all!
4 You're just _____ your mother – you have the same blue eyes!
5 Dinner is just _____ ready. It'll be five minutes.
6 The film is 125 minutes long. It's just _____ two hours.
7 I've just _____ to him. He'll meet us at 9.00.
8 No, she can't give a presentation in English yet. She's just _____.

REVIEW YOUR PROGRESS

Look again at Review your progress on p.36 of the Student's Book. How well can you do these things now?
3 = very well   2 = well   1 = not so well

I CAN ...

talk about experiences of generosity	☐
talk about spending and saving money	☐
talk to people in shops	☐
write an update email.	☐

4A I'm going to the hairdresser's tomorrow

1 VOCABULARY
Clothes and appearance

a Match the pictures with the words in the box.

underwear   tights   sweatshirt   tie   high heels
tracksuit   ~~gloves~~   sandals   earrings   jumper
flat shoes   bracelet

1 _gloves_   2 _____   3 _____
4 _____   5 _____   6 _____
7 _____   8 _____   9 _____
10 _____   11 _____   12 _____

2 GRAMMAR
Present continuous and *going to*

a Put the words in the correct order to make sentences.

1 buy / going / a new dress / I'm / the party / for / to .
   I'm going to buy a new dress for the party.

2 going / your wedding / you / are / invite / your / to / cousin / to ?
   _____

3 aren't / going / they / get married / to / this / year .
   _____

4 going / are / do / after university / you / what / to ?
   _____

5 visit / Spain next year / going / we're / in / my relatives / to .
   _____

6 to / you / are / wear / to / the party / what / going ?
   _____

b Complete the conversation with the present continuous forms of the verbs in the box. Use contractions where possible.

stay   come   bring   not fly   ~~arrive~~   take   meet (x2)

A So what have you arranged for this evening?
B Well, my parents ¹ _are arriving_ at the station on the 6:30 train from Paris.
A So, ² _____ you ³ _____ them at the station?
B Yes, we are. We ⁴ _____ a taxi from our house at 6:00. I booked it this morning.
A Good. So where ⁵ _____ they ⁶ _____ ?
B At the Hilton Hotel. They've got a double room with a balcony.
A Great. And what about the restaurant?
B I've reserved a table for eight at eight o'clock. Everyone ⁷ _____ to the restaurant at 7:45 so we can all be there when they arrive.
A Brilliant. Have you told the restaurant that it's your father's birthday?
B Yes, they've made him a special cake with HAPPY 60TH on it. They ⁸ _____ it to our table at ten o'clock, together with the coffee.
A And what about tomorrow?
B They ⁹ _____ to Scotland until the afternoon, so there's plenty of time. Their flight's at 3:30.
A Great, so it's all arranged. I have to go now because I ¹⁰ _____ Sally for a coffee in ten minutes. See you later!

c ▶ 4.1 Listen and check.

3 PRONUNCIATION
Sound and spelling: *going to*

a ▶ 4.2 Listen to *going to* in the sentences. Do you hear /ˈɡəʊɪŋ tə/ (*going to*) or /ˈɡənə/ (*gonna*)? Tick (✓) the correct box for each sentence.

	/ˈɡəʊɪŋ tə/	/ˈɡənə/
1 Are you going to go out tonight?	☐	✓
2 What are you going to do for your birthday?	☐	☐
3 He isn't going to have a holiday this year.	☐	☐
4 We're going to try to find a taxi.	☐	☐
5 I'm going to have a shower after breakfast.	☐	☐
6 They aren't going to do their homework.	☐	☐
7 She's going to phone her brother.	☐	☐
8 I'm not going to go to Ibiza this year.	☐	☐

4B Shall we go to the market?

1 GRAMMAR will / won't / shall

a Match 1–8 with a–h to make sentences.

1. [c] Let's go on holiday to Greece next summer.
2. [ ] You know I don't really like hot food.
3. [ ] Which film shall we see with the kids?
4. [ ] Let's invite your parents for lunch next Sunday.
5. [ ] Hello. I'm at the supermarket, but I can't carry all the shopping on the bus.
6. [ ] Oh, no! We've just missed the last bus.
7. [ ] Hi, Dad. I'm afraid I've lost my mobile phone.
8. [ ] Oh, no. I haven't got enough money to buy this tablet today.

a OK, shall I phone for a taxi, then?
b Good idea. I'll call them this evening to see if they're free.
c Good idea. I'll go to the travel agent's tomorrow.
d Don't worry. I'll buy you a new one for your birthday.
e Oh, that's a pity. Shall I lend you some money?
f Don't worry. I'll bring the car and meet you there in ten minutes.
g Shall we go to the new Harry Potter film?
h OK, so we won't go to an Indian restaurant, then.

b Underline the correct words to complete the sentences.

1. **A** *Will* / <u>Shall</u> / *Won't* we go to the cinema tonight?
   B Yes, OK. I *'ll* / *won't* / *shall* check which films are on and phone you back.
2. **A** Hi, Dad. I've missed the last bus home!
   B Don't worry. I *shall* / *won't* / *'ll* bring the car into town and meet you by the cinema.
3. What *will* / *shall* / *won't* we do this weekend?
4. Don't worry. The station's very near here, so you *'ll* / *shall* / *won't* miss your train.
5. **A** *Shall* / *Will* / *Won't* we try and get tickets for The Rolling Stones concert?
   B Good idea. I *won't* / *shall* / *'ll* phone the ticket office.
6. Look, I know you're a vegetarian, so I *'ll* / *won't* / *shall* cook steak for dinner.
7. *Will* / *Won't* / *Shall* I help you do the washing-up?
8. **A** Let's take Monica and Sara to that new Chinese restaurant this evening.
   B Yes, that's a great idea. I *'ll* / *won't* / *shall* call them and reserve a table for 7:30.

2 VOCABULARY Adjectives: places

a Complete the crossword puzzle.

→ **Across**

4. Stonehenge is an __ancient__ monument in Wiltshire in England. It's about 5,000 years old.
5. When the weather is really bad, we play on the i_____ tennis court at my local sports centre.
7. There are lots of h_____ mountains in Switzerland. For example, the Matterhorn is about 4,500 metres above sea level.
8. I live in a very o_____ town. Tourists never come here!
10. We live in a p_____ village. There's no traffic at all!

↓ **Down**

1. My school's in a really m_____ building. It's only five years old.
2. This road is very n_____. It isn't wide enough for a bus.
3. The view from the top of the Empire State Building is m_____.
6. It's very n_____ in this café, isn't it? It's difficult to hear you.
9. The British Museum is h_____. There are nearly 600 rooms!

b Choose the opposites of the adjectives in **bold**. Use the words in the box.

| modern | high | pretty | outdoor | quiet | ~~wide~~ |

1. The streets in the old part of town are very **narrow**. __wide__
2. I think the new houses they've built are really **ugly**. _____
3. There is a big **indoor** swimming pool in my town. _____
4. That restaurant's always very **crowded**. _____
5. This is one of the most **ancient** cities in Greece. _____
6. The hills in the South of England are quite **low**. _____

3 PRONUNCIATION
Sound and spelling: *want* and *won't*

a ▶4.3 Listen and underline the correct words to complete the sentences.

1. We *won't* / *want to* go swimming today.
2. They *want to* / *won't* take you to the old castle.
3. I *won't* / *want to* go to that restaurant again.
4. You *want to* / *won't* wait for the next train.
5. I *won't* / *want to* study English again next year.
6. Tom and I *want to* / *won't* invite him to our party.

4C Everyday English
Are you doing anything on Wednesday?

1 USEFUL LANGUAGE
Making arrangements

a Put the conversation in the correct order.

- [ ] **A** Oh, OK, never mind. How about Friday? Is that OK for you?
- [ ] **B** Brilliant! 11 o'clock. See you then.
- [ ] **A** OK, so you can't do this week. What are you doing next Monday?
- [ ] **B** Oh, that sounds nice. I'll just check. No, sorry, I can't do Wednesday. I'm going shopping with my mother.
- [1] **A** Are you doing anything on Wednesday? Would you like to go for a coffee?
- [ ] **B** Next Monday? Just a moment, I'll just check. Nothing! I can do next Monday. Perfect!
- [ ] **A** Great! So we can meet for a coffee on Monday?
- [ ] **B** Friday … hang on a minute … no, sorry. I'm going to London for the day. This week's really busy for me.
- [ ] **A** Shall we meet at The Coffee Place at 11.00?
- [ ] **B** Yes, Monday's fine. Where shall we go?

b ▶ 4.4 Listen and check.

c Put the words in the correct order to make sentences.

1 like / would / bring / me / anything / you / to ?
   Would you like me to bring anything?
2 anything / doing / you / Saturday / this / are ?
   _____
3 busy / us / week's / really / this / for .
   _____
4 come / we / what / round / shall / time ?
   _____
5 you / on / doing / next week / Tuesday / are / what ?
   _____
6 round / you / come / would / for / to / lunch / like ?
   _____
7 can't / Thursday / I / this week / do .
   _____
8 for / Sunday / is / OK / you / this ?
   _____

d ▶ 4.5 Listen and check.

Debbie's diary

Monday	am	9–11 meeting at work
	lunch	1–2 lunch with Mum
	pm	
Tuesday	am	7–9 fitness class
	lunch	
	pm	6–8 cinema with Joe
Wednesday	am	8–9 yoga
	lunch	
	pm	6.30 doctor's appointment
Thursday	am	
	lunch	12–1 shopping with Karen
	pm	7–8.30 dance class
Friday	am	all day – work conference
	lunch	
	pm	
Saturday	am	day off!
	lunch	
	pm	
Sunday	am	☆ day trip to Blackpool ☆
	lunch	
	pm	

e Read Debbie's diary and underline the correct words to complete the telephone conversation.

SANDRA Hi, Debbie! Are you free to meet on Monday morning?
DEBBIE I'll just check my diary. I'm sorry, I have a ¹*fitness class / meeting / doctor's appointment* then.
SANDRA Oh, that's a shame. How about Monday lunchtime?
DEBBIE No, I'm having lunch with ²*Joe / Mum / Karen* then.
SANDRA Never mind. Are you doing anything on Tuesday evening?
DEBBIE I'm afraid I'm going ³*shopping / to the cinema / to a dance class*.
SANDRA That sounds like fun! Let's see. I'm busy on Wednesday and Thursday. Could we meet on Friday?
DEBBIE Unfortunately, I'm busy all day on Friday. I've got a ⁴*doctor's appointment / dance class / work conference*.
SANDRA OK. What are you doing on Sunday?
DEBBIE Oh, dear. On Sunday I'm ⁵*at a work conference / in Blackpool / in a meeting* all day.
SANDRA So you don't have any free time this week?
DEBBIE Yes, I do! I have the whole day off on ⁶*Wednesday / Thursday / Saturday*!

2 PRONUNCIATION Sentence stress

a ▶ 4.6 Listen to the sentences and underline the stressed words or syllables.

1 I can't meet you tomorrow.
2 He can meet us at the station.
3 I didn't understand him.
4 She hasn't seen that film.
5 I must start cooking dinner.
6 They don't like basketball.

24

4D Skills for Writing
Are you free on Saturday?

1 READING

a Read Abby's email to Tony and his reply, and tick (✓) the correct answer.
- a ☐ Abby invites Tony and Laura to come to a birthday party at her house.
- b ☐ Abby and Mike would like to go to a Chinese restaurant with Tony and Laura.
- c ☐ Abby wants to see Tony and Laura's new house.
- d ☐ Abby invites Tony and Laura to celebrate Mike's birthday at a Chinese restaurant.

Hi Tony

How are things? We haven't seen you for ages. I hope you and Laura are well and that you're enjoying your new house.

Are you doing anything on Friday, 21st June? It's Mike's 40th birthday and we're going to our favourite Chinese restaurant, Xian, with some friends. We're going to book a table for eight o'clock. Can you come? It would be lovely to see you both and have a chance to chat.

Everyone's bringing an old photo of Mike. Could you bring your favourite photo of Mike from when he was at school or university?

Love

Abby

Hi Abby

Lovely to hear from you. Yes, we're well and we love our new house. We've just finished painting our bedroom and we're going to start on the kitchen next weekend.

Thanks for inviting us to Mike's birthday party. We're free on the 21st and we'd love to come. I'll bring some really funny photos of Mike when he was at school! We're looking forward to seeing you and Mike and having a chat.

All the best

Tony

---

b Read the emails again. Are the sentences true or false?
1 Abby and Mike have seen Tony and Laura recently.
2 Tony and Laura have recently moved to a new house.
3 Abby wants Mike's friends to take photos of him at the restaurant.
4 Tony and Laura are making some changes to their new house.
5 Tony doesn't have any old photos of Mike.

2 WRITING SKILLS Inviting and replying

a Correct the sentences. Use contractions where possible.
1 Hope you're well and your enjoying your new job.
   <u>Hope you're well and you're enjoying your new job.</u>
2 Thanks for invite me to your party.
   _____
3 It would be lovely to seeing you.
   _____
4 We're free on Saturday and we love to come.
   _____
5 This is just to say that we have a party on Saturday.
   _____
6 We didn't see you for ages!
   _____

3 WRITING

a Read Sam's email to Jess inviting her to his birthday party, and the notes below. Decide whether Jess can or can't go to the party and write her reply.

Hi Jess

How are you? I haven't seen you for over six months. I hope you are well and enjoying your new job.

Are you doing anything next Saturday? I'm having a birthday party at my house and I'm inviting a few friends. People are arriving at 7:30. Everyone is bringing some food for the party. Could you bring a salad?

It would be lovely to see you and have the chance to chat.

Love Sam

Notes for reply:
She CAN go to the party
1 Me? Fine. Give information about new job
2 Thanks for invitation
3 Free next Sat, love to come
4 Bring a huge salad!
5 Looking forward, nice chat

Notes for reply:
She CAN'T go to the party
1 Me? Fine. Give information about new job
2 Thanks for invitation
3 Party = fun! Can't come
4 Visit cousin in Paris next weekend
5 Enjoy the party!

25

UNIT 4
Reading and listening extension

1 READING

a Read the magazine article. Put the events in the correct order that Julia does them.

- ☐ Arriving at the theatre
- ☐ Getting a new outfit
- ☐ Going to the hairdresser's
- ☐ Having lunch
- ☐ Meeting my friend
- ☑ 1 Running on Venice Beach

b Read the magazine article again. Are the sentences true or false?

1 There are lots of people on Venice Beach in the morning.
2 Julia thinks she will spend all day shopping.
3 There are lots of people at the shopping mall.
4 Julia doesn't want to have lunch until she's bought a new dress.
5 Julia is looking forward to the evening because she has never been to a premiere before.

c Complete the sentences with the correct forms of the verbs in brackets.

1 Julia ___is meeting___ her friend at the shopping mall today. (meet)
2 At 1:15 Julia is _____ lunch. She _____ anything yet. (have, buy)
3 At 4:22 Julia _____ the hairdresser's in a taxi. (go)
4 At 6:35 Julia _____ to go out. (get ready)
5 At 7:15 she _____ at the theatre. (arrive)

d Write an email to a friend about your plans for the weekend. Remember to include:

- where you are going
- what you are going to do
- who you are going with
- what you think will happen.

12 HOURS IN LOS ANGELES
with film director Julia Fitzgerald

7:15 am The sun is shining, and I'm going to put my tracksuit on and go for a run. I love this time of the day as it's so peaceful and quiet down on Venice Beach.

10:00 am I'm going to a film premiere tonight so I have to look my best. I've arranged to meet my friend at an indoor shopping mall in Santa Monica, but she's not here yet. It's a modern place with lots of great shops and some pretty little cafés. I'd like to buy a new dress. It's crowded today, so I'm sure we'll be here all day!

1:15 pm We've stopped for lunch at an ordinary LA diner. I haven't bought anything yet, but all this walking around is making me hungry. I'm going to get a burger and fries.

2:20 pm My friend's taking me to a huge new department store, which sells everything. She thinks we'll find something in here.

3:05 pm Success! I've found a gorgeous red dress and matching high heels. We've decided to celebrate with coffee and cake at my favourite outdoor café near the beach.

4:22 pm I'm in a taxi now. I've got an appointment at the hairdresser's at 4:30 pm. I hope I won't be late. I think I might be!

6:35 pm I'm nearly ready. Shall I wear the gold bracelet and necklace or the black one? I can't decide. The car is coming at 7:00 pm so I have a bit of time.

7:15 pm We're driving up to the theatre for the premiere. It's crowded and noisy as everyone is hoping to see all the stars. It's my first time at a premiere so I'm so excited. It's going to be a brilliant night!

2 LISTENING

a ▶4.7 Listen to the conversation. Complete the sentences with the names in the box.

| Alex | Giles's mum | Gavino | Giles | Isaac |

1 ___Giles___ is going to finish university this summer.
2 _____ is marrying an Italian woman.
3 _____ is teaching Giles Italian next week.
4 _____ wants to go sightseeing in Rome.
5 _____ is going on a date tonight.

b ▶4.7 Listen to the conversation again and tick (✓) the correct answers.

1 Why is Giles going to Italy this summer?
   a ✓ He is going to a wedding.
   b ☐ His girlfriend is Italian.
   c ☐ He wants to visit Rome.
2 Who is Laura?
   a ☐ Giles's girlfriend.
   b ☐ Alex's fiancée.
   c ☐ A student in their class.
3 What is Giles's dad going to do if Giles passes his exams?
   a ☐ He's going to pay for Italian lessons.
   b ☐ He's going to buy him a new suit.
   c ☐ He's going to take him to Rome.
4 What does Isaac like about Rome?
   a ☐ The new buildings.
   b ☐ The history.
   c ☐ The mix of old and new architecture.
5 Where is Isaac going now?
   a ☐ He is going to meet a girl.
   b ☐ He is going to get a haircut.
   c ☐ He is going home.

c Write about what you're going to do when you finish your English course. Include the answers to these questions:
   • Where are you going to go?
   • What would you like to do?

Review and extension

1 GRAMMAR

Correct the sentences.

1 I going to look for a job in a hotel this summer.
   I'm going to look for a job in a hotel this summer.
2 Don't worry. I pay the money back tomorrow.
3 He'll go to buy a new car next month.
4 Will I come to your house in half an hour?
5 Will we go to that café for a cup of tea?
6 Are you going to doing your homework this evening?

2 VOCABULARY

Correct the sentences.

1 They've got a fantastic outside swimming pool in my town.
   They've got a fantastic outdoor swimming pool in my town.
2 Are you going to buy a new suit case in the sales?
3 I love it here in the country. It's so peacefull!
4 He always uses a tie when he goes for a job interview.
5 I love coming to this park because you can't hear the traffic. It's so quite here.
6 That restaurant's so noise. It's really hard to talk there.

3 WORDPOWER look

Complete the sentences with the words in the box.

| after | forward | up | around | at | for |

1 He looked ___at___ the timetable to see when the next train left for London.
2 Excuse me. I'm looking _____ a bank. Is there one near here?
3 We're really looking _____ to seeing our Spanish friends tomorrow.
4 We have a lovely babysitter that looks _____ our children when we go out for the evening.
5 I'm tired! Do you really want to look _____ the museum again?
6 If you aren't sure what it means, look _____ the word in your dictionary.

REVIEW YOUR PROGRESS

Look again at Review your progress on p.46 of the Student's Book. How well can you do these things now?
3 = very well   2 = well   1 = not so well

I CAN ...

talk about my plans for celebrations	☐
plan a day out in a city	☐
make social arrangements	☐
write and reply to an invitation.	☐

27

5A I have to work long hours

1 VOCABULARY Work

a Complete the sentences.
1. This person looks after the plants and cuts the grass. g*ardener*
2. When your hair gets too long, you make an appointment with this person. h_____
3. If you have a problem with your central heating, you need to call this person. p_____
4. This person works in a laboratory and might have a university degree in chemistry or biology. s_____
5. Somebody whose job is to look after people's money. b_____
6. If you have a problem with the lights in your house, you call this person. e_____
7. If the police arrest you, this person can help you. l_____
8. This person can help you to manage your money. a_____
9. This person checks your teeth to make sure they are in good condition. d_____
10. When you are in hospital, this person looks after you. n_____

b Complete the sentences with the words in the box.

> team   people   environment   self-employed   skills
> salary   university degree   qualifications   training
> ~~long hours~~

1. He's usually in his office from 8 am until 8 pm, but he doesn't mind working *long hours*.
2. She works for an important bank in London, earns a very good _____ and drives a company car.
3. You need to have several years of _____ to become a doctor.
4. They have a really nice working _____ – their offices are modern with good air conditioning and plenty of light.
5. I really enjoy working on big projects with lots of other people. It's good to work in a _____.
6. You need to have a _____ to become a lawyer.
7. Receptionists have to deal with _____, so they need to be friendly and polite.
8. Some people prefer to be _____ and work for lots of different companies.
9. Secretaries need to have a lot of _____ – they need to be organised, and good with computers.
10. You need to have good _____ if you want to get a job at this university.

2 GRAMMAR must / have to / can

a Complete the sentences about the signs with *have to* or *can't*.

ALL VISITORS MUST WASH THEIR HANDS BEFORE ENTERING THIS ROOM.

PASSENGERS MUST NOT STAND UP UNTIL THE PLANE HAS COMPLETELY STOPPED.

1. You __*have to*__ wash your hands before you go into this room.
2. Excuse me, madam. You _____ stand up until the plane has stopped.

VISITORS MUST NOT TAKE PHOTOS USING FLASH PHOTOGRAPHY.

PASSENGERS MUST WEAR THEIR SEAT BELTS AT ALL TIMES.

3. I'm sorry, sir. You _____ take photos in here with a flash.
4. Excuse me. I'm afraid you _____ wear your seat belt all the time.

YOU MUST WEAR A HARD HAT AT ALL TIMES ON THIS CONSTRUCTION SITE.

YOU MUST NOT SMOKE IN THIS TOILET.

5. Visitors _____ wear hard hats when they come to this building site.
6. I'm sorry. You _____ smoke in the toilet.

b Underline the correct words to complete the text.

I work as a receptionist in a big hotel, so I [1]*must* / mustn't / can always be polite to the guests. During the week, I [2]don't have to / can't / must go to bed late because I have to start work early. Fortunately, I [3]don't have to / mustn't / can't wear a uniform, but I [4]can / mustn't / have to dress smartly.

My sister's a student, so she [5]mustn't / doesn't have to / can't get up early most days. However, she [6]doesn't have to / mustn't / has to study very hard at the moment because she's got important exams next month.

My dad's a taxi driver, so he often [7]has to / mustn't / can't work in the evenings and at weekends. He [8]doesn't have to / mustn't / must drive fast because there are speed cameras everywhere in my town.

My mum's a nurse, so she [9]has to / mustn't / can't wear a uniform when she's at work. Sometimes she starts work very early but my dad usually takes her to work in his taxi, so she [10]must / doesn't have to / mustn't get the bus.

28

5B I might get a job today!

1 GRAMMAR
will and *might* for predictions

a Match 1–8 with a–h to make sentences.

1. [c] She might
2. [ ] I think I'll
3. [ ] Spain might not
4. [ ] I don't think she'll
5. [ ] I'm sure he'll
6. [ ] France won't
7. [ ] He might not
8. [ ] I might not

a win the match on Saturday. The Brazilian team are just as good as them.
b pass his exams. He's very clever and he's worked really hard all year.
c feel better tomorrow. She says she's taken some medicine.
d get to school on time. I've only just woken up!
e pass his exams. He hasn't worked very hard this year.
f win the match on Saturday. They haven't got any good players in their team and Brazil are a fantastic team.
g come this evening. She's not feeling well.
h see them tonight. We all usually go to the gym on Thursdays.

b Complete the sentences with *will* (or *'ll*), *won't*, *might* or *might not*.

1 I'm sure you ___will___ pass your exams. You've worked very hard this year.
2 Don't go on holiday next week. They _____ invite you for a second interview.
3 I know they _____ offer me a good salary. A friend of mine works there and he doesn't earn a lot of money.
4 You _____ get a job immediately when you finish university – 50% of university graduates don't have a job three years after finishing their studies.
5 She doesn't think she _____ go travelling after university. She wants to find a job as soon as possible.
6 **A** Do you think he _____ pass all his exams?
   B Yes, I'm sure he _____. Don't worry.
7 Who knows? You _____ make some useful contacts at the conference.
8 I'm sure he _____ get the job. He doesn't have any experience.

2 VOCABULARY Jobs

a Write the names of the jobs under the pictures.

1 __builder__ 2 _____ 3 _____ 4 _____

5 _____ 6 _____ 7 _____ 8 _____

9 _____ 10 _____ 11 _____ 12 _____

b Complete the sentences with the correct jobs.

1 When I was little, I wanted to be a v__et__ because I loved looking after animals.
2 I'm looking for a good b_____ to fix the roof on my house.
3 Nick is a fantastic m_____. He can play the piano, the guitar, the cello and the saxophone.
4 Christopher Wren was the a_____ who designed St Paul's Cathedral in London.
5 Louise works in a department store as a s_____ a_____.
6 Johnny Depp is an American film a_____, famous for his role as Jack Sparrow in the *Pirates of the Caribbean* films.
7 Val works as a c_____, looking after old people in their homes.
8 Sarah works in our IT Department as a c_____ p_____.
9 James was a well-known j_____ who worked for *The New York Times* newspaper.
10 Yves St Laurent was a famous French fashion d_____.
11 Our p_____ always delivers the mail to our house at ten o'clock.
12 I hope that the p_____s in the UN can solve the world's problems one day.

29

5C Everyday English
I'll finish things here, if you want

1 USEFUL LANGUAGE
Offers and suggestions

a Put the words in the correct order to make sentences.
1 money / I / you / some / lend / the bus / for / shall ?
   Shall I lend you some money for the bus?
2 off / maybe you / ask / manager / for / your / should / the day .
   _____
3 Internet / look up / I'll / the / the / train times / on .
   _____
4 do / a taxi / guest / you / our / me / to / want / for / book ?
   _____
5 drive / airport / don't / the / why / I / to / you ?
   _____
6 arranging / about / a / in / meeting / Milan / how ?
   _____
7 money / don't / why / borrow / from / some / you / your father ?
   _____
8 Rome / could / direct flight / you / a / to / catch .
   _____

b ▶5.1 Listen and check.

c Complete the sentences with the words in the box.

   fine   about   could   mind   ~~shall~~   sorry   matter
   don't   maybe   would   idea   worry

1 A _Shall_ I book a room for your meeting?
   B Yes, good _____.
2 A _____ you like me to drive you to the station?
   B No, I'll be _____. Don't _____ about it. I can take the bus.
3 A But you won't be able to have any lunch.
   B Oh, never _____. I'm not really hungry.
4 A I'm really _____. I can't come to the cinema tonight.
   B Oh, it doesn't _____. We can go another time.
5 How _____ asking your boss if you can have more time for the report?
6 Why _____ I book the train tickets on the Internet?
7 _____ you should invite your boss to the meeting, too?
8 You _____ send her some flowers for her birthday.

d ▶5.2 Listen and check.

2 PRONUNCIATION
Sentence stress: vowel sounds

a ▶5.3 Listen to the sentences. Tick (✓) which vowel sounds you hear for the modal verbs in **bold**.

	Strong vowel /ʊ/	Weak vowel /ə/
1 **Would** you like a coffee?		✓
2 Yes, I **would**. Thanks.		
3 **Could** you help me with my report?		
4 Yes, of course I **could**.		
5 You **should** get a taxi.		
6 Yes, you're right. I **should**.		
	/æ/	/ə/
7 **Shall** I book a meeting room?		
8 Well, what do you think? **Shall** I?		

5D Skills for Writing
I am writing to apply for a job

1 READING

a Read the job advert and Martin's job application, and tick (✓) the correct answer.
a ☐ The job is for 12 months.
b ☐ The job is in a hotel in Bristol.
c ☐ The hotel needs a receptionist.
d ☐ The hotel needs a waiter.

b Read the job advert and job application again. Are the sentences true or false?
1 The hotel will give the receptionist a bedroom and food.
2 People who apply for this job don't need experience of working in hotels.
3 Martin is free to work this summer.
4 Martin would like to learn some new skills.
5 Martin doesn't have any previous experience of working in hotels.
6 Martin would like more details about the job.

2 WRITING SKILLS Organising an email

a Match 1–8 with a–h to make sentences.
1 [g] I'm writing to
2 ☐ I have five years'
3 ☐ I would like to work for your company
4 ☐ I have a lot of experience of
5 ☐ My experience of working in a busy hospital
6 ☐ I attach a copy of my CV with
7 ☐ Could you please send me information
8 ☐ I look forward to

a working in a team and dealing with customers.
b about the working hours and the training programme?
c more information about my past employment.
d because it would be a good opportunity to learn some new skills.
e hearing from you.
f experience of working as a secretary in a busy hospital.
g apply for the job of secretary.
h will be very useful for this job.

BRISTOL EVENING POST — jobs section

HOTEL RECEPTIONIST WANTED
We're looking for a hard-working and friendly receptionist to work in a hotel in Devon this summer. You will need to speak a foreign language.
We prefer someone with experience of working in hotels.
Accommodation and meals provided.
Apply online at www.bayviewdevonhotel.com by 31 May.

Subject: Hotel Receptionist

Dear Sir/Madam,
I am writing to apply for the job of receptionist at the Bay View Hotel, which you advertised in the Bristol Evening Post.
I am studying French and Spanish at Bath University and am available to work in July and August.
I would like to work for you because it would be a good opportunity for me to learn new skills and to work in a team. I have worked in a hotel before, as a waiter, so I have experience of dealing with customers and working in a busy hotel environment.
I attach a copy of my CV with details of my previous experience.
Could you please send me information about the salary, the working hours and the accommodation?
I look forward to hearing from you.
Yours faithfully,
Martin Evans

3 WRITING

a Read the job advert and write a letter applying for the job.

The Argus – jobs section

SALES ASSISTANT WANTED
T-World are looking for a hard-working sales assistant to sell all types of computers, tablets, game consoles, smart TVs and smartphones in our brand-new superstore in Brighton.
We are offering a good salary plus sales bonus to the right person.
You will need previous sales experience and a good understanding of the latest technology.
We prefer someone with experience of working in a busy environment.
Full training programme given.
Apply by 30 September to salesassistant@tworld.co.uk

31

UNIT 5
Reading and listening extension

1 READING

a Read the article. Match the people 1–4 with pictures a–d.
1. ☐ Malcolm
2. ☐ Freya
3. ☐ Cara
4. ☐ James

a  b  c 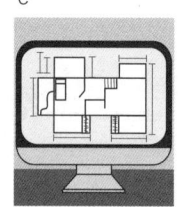 d

b Read the article again and tick (✓) the correct boxes. Sometimes there is more than one possible answer.

	gets paid well	works and studies	is doing something he/she loves	has to work many hours every day
1 Malcolm		✓		
2 Freya				
3 Cara				
4 James				

c Read the article again and underline the correct answer. Sometimes there is more than one possible answer.
1. Who works for themselves?
   a Malcolm   b Freya   c <u>Cara</u>   d James
2. Who doesn't earn any money?
   a Malcolm   b Freya   c Cara   d James
3. Who has free weekends?
   a Malcolm   b Freya   c Cara   d James
4. Who likes the place where he/she works?
   a Malcolm   b Freya   c Cara   d James
5. Who studies and works in a different place?
   a Malcolm   b Freya   c Cara   d James

d Write a paragraph about a job you'd like to do. Remember to include:
- the things you'd like to do in the job
- the hours
- the salary
- the environment.

Which way now?

When you leave school or university you must think carefully about what you would like to do next. Here, some young people tell us their experiences.

I thought about my skills and qualifications, and then about me. I've always liked working in a team, I like being outside and I decided I can't work in an office every day. Someone suggested I train to be a builder. I go to college Monday and Friday, and work Tuesday to Thursday. I have to get up early so I can't go out in the evenings, but I'm learning a useful skill.

Malcolm, 19

I work for a number of companies as a book designer. I'm self-employed, which means I work on my own and not in a team. When I'm very busy I have to work long hours, in the evenings and sometimes at weekends. But I really like my job, and I can work at home, so I can say that I have a really nice working environment! I don't have to deal with customers or a manager! When I'm busy I can earn a very good salary, but I'm not always busy.

Cara, 28

I love art and design and I've always wanted to do something I enjoy. I decided to study to become an architect. I'm learning so much and I'm doing what I want, which is really important. I have to study every day of the week and I just hope I can find a job when I leave university.

Freya, 21

I've always liked animals. Earning a really good salary is important to me too, so I studied to be a vet. I have to work long hours and I must study at home most weekends, but I know it is worth it when I'm helping sick animals.

James, 24

32

2 LISTENING

a ⏵5.4 Listen to the conversation. What did Josh say about these jobs? Tick (✓) the correct boxes. Sometimes there is more than one possible answer.

	Postman	Hairdresser	IT worker	Bank clerk
1 Work long hours	✓			
2 Nice working environment				
3 Deal with people				
4 Earn a good salary				
5 Work in a team				

b ⏵5.4 Listen to the conversation again and complete the table to show what Josh liked and disliked about the jobs. Write one word in each space.

	He liked …	He disliked …
1 Postman	working _outside_.	starting work _____.
2 Hairdresser	learning new _____.	dealing with _____.
3 IT worker	_____ work when he wanted.	working at _____.

c Choose one of the following:
1 Write a conversation between two people. Person A is interviewing Person B for the job of a journalist. Person B explains why he/she is the right person for the job, and asks five questions about the job. Person A asks questions and answers the questions Person B asks.
2 Write about the parts of a job you would be happy to do and what you definitely wouldn't like to do.

⊙ Review and extension

1 GRAMMAR

Correct the sentences.
1 Tomorrow's Sunday, so I mustn't get up early.
   Tomorrow's Sunday, so I don't have to get up early.
2 Excuse me, sir. You don't have to smoke on the plane. It's against the law.
3 Do you must wear a suit to work?
4 When I finish school, I can go to university. It depends on my grades.
5 I've to start work at 7 o'clock in the morning in my new job!
6 I'll take my umbrella. It can rain this afternoon.

2 VOCABULARY

Correct the sentences.
1 In your new job, I'm sure they'll give you lots of trainings.
   In your new job, I'm sure they'll give you lots of training.
2 My sister works as a shop assistent in a big department store.
3 You need good qualification if you want to become a doctor.
4 He works as a disigner for a top fashion magazine.
5 If you want to become a plummer, you'll need to go to college.
6 My brother wants to become a professional music.

3 WORDPOWER job and work

Underline the correct words to complete the sentences.
1 My GPS doesn't _work_ / job very well when I drive through the mountains.
2 I've found a really good job / work in the local newspaper.
3 No, I can't go to the cinema. I've got to stay late at job / work.
4 My headache's a bit better, so I think that aspirin's beginning to work / job.
5 What time do you start job / work in the mornings?
6 He's got to work / job all weekend on that report.
7 I'm studying for my final exams – it's really hard job / work.
8 My dad's got a lot of small jobs / works to do in the garden.
9 My dad can't work / job out how to use the camera on his new phone.

◷ REVIEW YOUR PROGRESS

Look again at Review your progress on p.56 of the Student's Book. How well can you do these things now?
3 = very well   2 = well   1 = not so well

I CAN …

talk about what people do at work	☐
talk about my future career	☐
make offers and suggestions	☐
write a job application.	☐

33

6A You should have a break

1 GRAMMAR Imperative; should

a Complete the text with the words in the box.

| should go | don't use | eat | should read | shouldn't drink |
| go | don't sit | should have | shouldn't have | ~~get~~ |

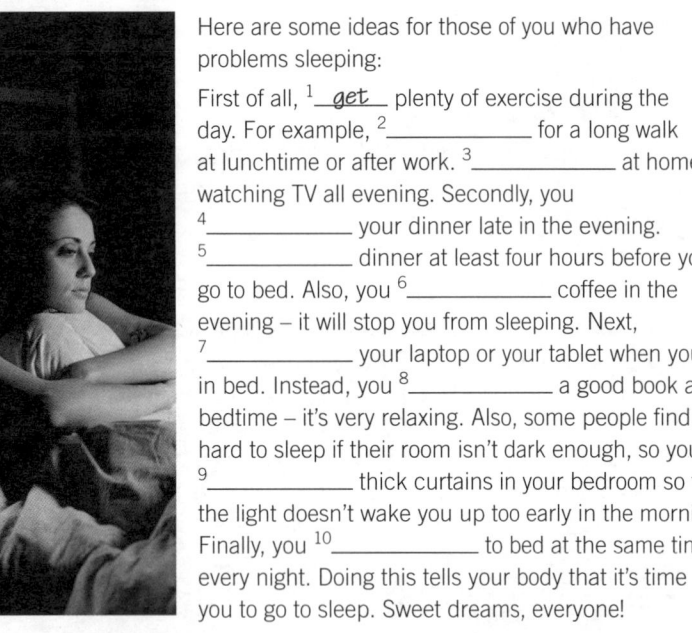

Here are some ideas for those of you who have problems sleeping:

First of all, ¹_get_ plenty of exercise during the day. For example, ² _____ for a long walk at lunchtime or after work. ³ _____ at home watching TV all evening. Secondly, you ⁴ _____ your dinner late in the evening. ⁵ _____ dinner at least four hours before you go to bed. Also, you ⁶ _____ coffee in the evening – it will stop you from sleeping. Next, ⁷ _____ your laptop or your tablet when you're in bed. Instead, you ⁸ _____ a good book at bedtime – it's very relaxing. Also, some people find it hard to sleep if their room isn't dark enough, so you ⁹ _____ thick curtains in your bedroom so that the light doesn't wake you up too early in the morning. Finally, you ¹⁰ _____ to bed at the same time every night. Doing this tells your body that it's time for you to go to sleep. Sweet dreams, everyone!

b Rewrite the sentences. Use *should*, *shouldn't* or the imperative.

1 He shouldn't listening to music while he's studying.
   He shouldn't listen to music while he's studying.
2 To eat lots of fruit and vegetables every day.
   _____
3 Not use your computer for very long in the evenings.
   _____
4 You should to try to relax for an hour before you go to bed.
   _____
5 I think she should getting more exercise during the day.
   _____
6 You don't should go swimming immediately after lunch.
   _____
7 When you've got a headache, to take an aspirin.
   _____
8 Don't stay you at work after 6 o'clock.
   _____

2 VOCABULARY Verbs with dependent prepositions

a Match 1–8 with a–h to make sentences.

1 [e] When you called me, I was looking
2 [ ] The train from Manchester arrived
3 [ ] Can you think
4 [ ] He was listening
5 [ ] Could you deal
6 [ ] He asked his father
7 [ ] Matthew decided to talk
8 [ ] My father wants to pay

a for £50 because he needed a new shirt for the wedding.
b to his son's teacher about his exam results.
c for the meal with his credit card.
d of a nice present for your grandfather's birthday?
e at an old photo of when we were at school.
f with this order for six takeaway pizzas, please?
g to the football match on the radio.
h at Euston Station 25 minutes late.

b <u>Underline</u> the correct words to complete the sentences.

1 In my job I have to deal *about / for / <u>with</u>* customers all day long.
2 It's hard to concentrate *with / on / for* my homework when you're listening to the radio.
3 This bus is crowded! I'll wait *for / to / from* the next one.
4 His girlfriend's gone to Paris for a month, so he thinks *from / about / for* her all the time.
5 They don't pay you much, do they? You should ask your boss *from / on / for* more money.
6 Jackie says she spends about £200 a month *at / on / to* clothes!
7 If you want to buy a new car now, you should borrow some money *with / for / from* your bank.
8 He's really generous. He paid *with / for / of* my plane ticket to New York!

3 PRONUNCIATION Sound and spelling: /uː/ and /ʊ/

a ▶6.1 Listen to the sentences. Are the vowel sounds in **bold** long /uː/ or short /ʊ/? Tick (✓) the correct box for each sentence.

	long /uː/	short /ʊ/
1 We t**oo**k my grandmother to the theatre.	☐	✓
2 The children wanted to go to the z**oo**.	☐	☐
3 Where did you l**o**se your mobile phone?	☐	☐
4 W**ou**ld you like a cup of coffee?	☐	☐
5 Wh**o** did you invite to the party?	☐	☐
6 I don't think you sh**ou**ld go to work today.	☐	☐
7 C**ou**ld I borrow £5, please?	☐	☐
8 What did you think of the f**oo**d?	☐	☐

34

6B I was very frightened

1 VOCABULARY -ed / -ing adjectives

a Underline the correct words to complete the sentences.
1. I thought the Tokyo metro was really *confused* / <u>*confusing*</u>. All the signs were in Japanese!
2. The football match was very *exciting* / *excited*. It finished 4 – 4.
3. Tracy isn't very *interesting* / *interested* in computer games.
4. I was *shocked* / *shocking* when I saw him. He looked very ill.
5. She was very *annoyed* / *annoying* when he asked her for some more money.
6. The flight from London to Mexico City was very *tired* / *tiring*.
7. I thought the view from the top of the Eiffel Tower was *amazing* / *amazed*.
8. He felt *embarrassing* / *embarrassed* when his mother kissed him in front of his friends.

b Complete the sentences with adjectives ending in *-ed* or *-ing*.
1. The people in the flat above me are so a*nnoying*. They play loud music when I'm trying to get to sleep.
2. He looked really c_____ when he woke up. He said, 'Where am I?'
3. I thought that TV documentary about Martin Luther King was so i_____.
4. The exam results were very s_____. Nobody got more than 50%!
5. She was very f_____ when she saw the spider, but she calmed down when we told her it was made of plastic.
6. He was very d_____ that his father didn't bring him a present from Spain.
7. They couldn't speak a word when they heard the s_____ news that the king was dead.
8. She felt very e_____ when he told her that they were going on holiday to Florida.

2 GRAMMAR Uses of to + infinitive

a Put the words in the correct order to make sentences.
1. job / I / to / disappointed / get / not / was / the .
   <u>I was disappointed not to get the job.</u>
2. sharks / was / learn / interesting / it / to / about .
   _____
3. our cars / you / tell us / park / where / can / to ?
   _____
4. wear / is / not / dangerous / to / a seat belt / it .
   _____
5. her / relax / to / she / a bath / help / had .
   _____
6. the station / went / to / meet / aunt / to / they / their .
   _____
7. her father / she / him / to / some money / ask / for / phoned .
   _____
8. didn't / he / what / to the party / know / wear / to .
   _____

b Correct the sentences.

1. They wanted buy him a nice birthday present.
   <u>They wanted to buy him a nice birthday present.</u>
2. He asked me how getting to the airport.
   _____
3. She was annoyed to not receive an invitation to his wedding.
   _____
4. They went to the supermarket for buy some food for dinner.
   _____
5. We couldn't remember which bus catching for the airport.
   _____
6. John and Angela decided to have not their wedding in Scotland.
   _____
7. It was embarrassing fail my driving test again.
   _____
8. She went to the library for borrow a book on dinosaurs for her son.
   _____

6C Everyday English
What do you think I should do?

1 USEFUL LANGUAGE
Asking for and giving advice

a Match sentences 1–8 with responses a–h.
1. [d] I think it's a good idea to book a table. The restaurant might be full.
2. [ ] Someone stole my handbag when I was at the beach this afternoon.
3. [ ] I'd speak to your boss about it.
4. [ ] I wouldn't worry too much. You can get a new passport at the embassy.
5. [ ] Do you think I should invite Steve to the surprise party?
6. [ ] What do you think I should do?
7. [ ] I didn't get the job in marketing.
8. [ ] I broke my finger on Saturday.

a Oh, what a pity. I'm sure you'll get another job soon.
b Oh, that's a shame. So that means you can't play tennis today?
c No, I don't think that's a very good idea. Anna doesn't like him very much.
d Yes, I suppose so. Saturday night can be very busy.
e How awful! I'm really sorry to hear that.
f I don't think I should do that. She'll be angry with me.
g Yes, you're right. I can go there one day next week.
h I think you should go to the police station.

b ▶6.2 Listen and check.

c Put the words in the correct order to make sentences.
1. apply for / which / should / do / job / you / I / think ?
   Which job do you think I should apply for?
2. colleagues / should / I / your / you / think / ask .
   _____
3. sorry / really / that / hear / to / I'm .
   _____
4. new job / a / should / do / think / I / you / look / for ?
   _____
5. I / a / think it's / to / your boss / speak / to / good idea .
   _____
6. about / talk / I'd / your parents / it / to .
   _____
7. apply / I / for / marketing job / new / the / wouldn't .
   _____
8. think / I / you / your / don't / job / leave / should .
   _____

d ▶6.3 Listen and check.

2 PRONUNCIATION Main stress

a ▶6.4 Listen to the sentences and tick (✓) the stressed words.
1. You're from Canada, right?
   a [ ] You're   b [✓] Canada
2. Elena works in the Spanish Embassy.
   a [ ] Spanish   b [ ] Embassy
3. Would you like to work in London?
   a [ ] work   b [ ] London
4. We're having a surprise party for Anna.
   a [ ] party   b [ ] Anna
5. My boss wants to speak to me.
   a [ ] boss   b [ ] me

36

6D Skills for Writing
I often worry about tests and exams

1 READING

a Read Anthony's email to Sue and Sue's reply. Tick (✓) the correct answer.

a ☐ Anthony is looking for a new job.
b ☐ Anthony doesn't want Jim to leave his job.
c ☐ Sue gives Anthony some ideas to help him.
d ☐ Sue works as a manager in a bank in London.

Dear Sue

The problem is that I'm feeling very stressed about my job at the moment. You see, Jim, one of the people in my team, has just left. They haven't replaced Jim yet and so my boss has given all of his work to the other people in the team, including me. Do you have any advice for me?

Regards

Anthony

Dear Anthony

Thank you for your email. I'm very pleased that you have written to me for advice.

This kind of situation is very common in companies when somebody leaves. I remember this happened when I was working in a bank in London. One summer, two of the people in my team left the bank at the same time. We had to do all of their work and it took three months to replace them! Anyway, here are some ideas that might help you.

First of all, try not to get too stressed about the situation. I think you should discuss the problem with your colleagues. Maybe they will have some ideas about how to make the situation a bit easier? Secondly, when you've got too much work to do, I think it's a good idea to try to prioritise your work carefully. For example, are there some less urgent jobs that you could do later?

Next, I think you should speak to your boss about this problem. He might not realise how much work he has given you and maybe he can find some other people to help you with it. Finally, I'd try to do something relaxing after work, such as going to the gym or swimming. It's important to relax when you aren't at work and to get plenty of sleep.

I hope this helps you and please feel free to come and talk to me in my office.

Best wishes

Sue Smith

HR Manager

---

b Read the emails again. Are the sentences true or false?

1 Anthony is doing all of Jim's work.
2 Sue was the manager of a team of two people at the bank.
3 Sue thinks that Anthony should talk to his colleagues about the problem.
4 Sue doesn't think Anthony should discuss the problem with his manager.
5 Sue thinks it's a good idea for Anthony to relax after work.

2 WRITING SKILLS Linking: ordering ideas and giving examples

a Put *for example* or *such as* in the correct place in each sentence. Add capital letters and punctuation (. , ') and make any other necessary changes.

1 There are lots of ways to make new friends joining a sports club.
   There are lots of ways to make new friends, such as joining a sports club.

2 It's a good idea to read something in English every day. You can read the BBC news pages on the Internet.

3 Why don't you do something relaxing this evening going for a swim after work?

4 There are more enjoyable ways of preparing for an exam. You could revise with a friend on the same course.

5 You could start a new hobby to help you relax dancing or swimming.

3 WRITING

a Read Kento's message to his English teacher, Tina. Use the notes below to write Tina's reply.

Dear Tina

I think I'm quite good at reading and writing in English, but listening is very hard for me. I really want to improve my listening. Do you have any ideas?

Thank you

Kento

Notes for message to Kento:
Paragraph 1: say thanks
Paragraph 2: me: learning Japanese – listening v. difficult – explain why – ideas to help …
Paragraph 3:
1) impossible to understand every word – concentrate on most important words
2) extra practice – study centre – CDs, e.g. CDs from Student's Book
3) radio / TV in English, films (+ subtitles)
4) podcasts – short stories?
5) pop songs + read words – find internet sites
Paragraph 4: hope this helps – talk to me after class?

37

UNIT 6
Reading and listening extension

1 READING

a Read the magazine article and underline the correct people to match the adjectives.

1 annoyed — Petra / <u>manager</u> / Sue
2 embarrassed — Petra / customers / Sue
3 confused — manager / Sue / Petra
4 frightened — Petra / manager / customers
5 not disappointed — customers / Petra / Sue
6 surprised — Petra / customers / Sue

b Read the magazine article again. Tick (✓) the correct answers.

1 What is Petra's problem?
   a ☐ She doesn't like spending time with customers.
   b ✓ Her manager thinks she works too slowly.
   c ☐ She gets confused by what the customers say to her.

2 Who is Toni?
   a ☐ One of Petra's customers.
   b ☐ Petra's manager.
   c ☐ Another hairdresser.

3 When does Petra get embarrassed?
   a ☐ When her manager gets angry with her in front of customers.
   b ☐ When the customers talk to her.
   c ☐ When her manager looks at her.

4 What surprises Sue?
   a ☐ That Toni talks to Petra in front of customers.
   b ☐ That Toni doesn't understand the customers.
   c ☐ That Toni doesn't understand what good customer service is.

5 What does Sue suggest?
   a ☐ She suggests that Petra tells her manager how she feels.
   b ☐ She suggests that Petra doesn't think about it.
   c ☐ She suggests that Petra's customers speak to Toni.

c Read the magazine article again. Match 1–5 with a–e to make sentences.

1 [c] Petra thinks that a customer who
2 ☐ Toni thinks that Petra
3 ☐ Petra can't concentrate when Toni
4 ☐ Petra is confused because she
5 ☐ Sue thinks that Toni

a keeps looking at her.
b shouldn't spend so much time talking to customers.
c spends a lot of money should get good service.
d thinks she is very good at her job.
e will change his mind after the customers speak to him.

d Write an email to Petra giving her some advice about her problem. Remember to include:
- some advice
- some instructions
- a similar situation from your own life.

Ask Sue

Every week, our experts answer your problems. This week, Sue Taylor, our writer and management expert, answers a question about a problem at work.

Dear Sue

I need to ask you for some help.

I'm a hairdresser and I work in a very fashionable salon. I'm very good at dealing with the customers and I like to talk to them when I cut their hair. They pay a lot of money for their haircuts, and I think it's important to spend time with them and make sure they're happy. But my manager, a man called Toni, gets really annoyed with me and keeps telling me to work faster. He sometimes talks to me in front of the customers, which makes me really embarrassed. He looks at me all the time when I talk to them and now I find it really difficult to concentrate on what I'm doing.

I'm really confused. I'm a really good hairdresser, none of the customers are ever disappointed with my work and I get on well with all my colleagues. I'm frightened of losing my job if I say anything.

Can you help me?

Petra

Dear Petra

You're right. When customers spend a lot of money on a haircut, they should enjoy the experience, feel relaxed and get excellent service. I'm surprised Toni doesn't understand this. How many of your customers would come back if you spent less than 15 minutes with them?

I think you should ask your customers for help. Ask them to speak to or write an email to your manager telling him what they like about the service you give them. I think your manager will soon change his mind.

Good luck!

Sue

2 LISTENING

a ▶6.5 Listen to three friends talking about studying. Tick (✓) the people that match the statements.

	Georgia	Marsha	Max
1 I can't study at home.	✓		
2 I study in the library.			
3 I haven't got a good memory.			
4 I listen to a recording of myself to help me remember.			
5 I can help someone with their revision.			

b ▶6.5 Listen to the three friends talking about studying again. Tick (✓) the correct answers.

1 What is Georgia's problem?
  a ✓ Her brother is disturbing her.
  b ☐ She hasn't got a laptop to use for studying.
  c ☐ She doesn't want to go to the library to study.
2 What does Max suggest Georgia do?
  a ☐ She should go to the library to study.
  b ☐ She must tell someone to stop.
  c ☐ She should ask her parents to help her with the problem.
3 What is Georgia going to do?
  a ☐ Talk to someone about the problem.
  b ☐ Go somewhere else to avoid the problem.
  c ☐ Talk to someone and go somewhere else.
4 Who has a problem with History?
  a ☐ Georgia.
  b ☐ Max.
  c ☐ Marsha.
5 What is Georgia embarrassed about?
  a ☐ Her poor memory.
  b ☐ Making a song to help her revise.
  c ☐ Her marks in the Physics exam.
6 What is Marsha's problem?
  a ☐ She is confused by a subject.
  b ☐ She doesn't want to study a subject.
  c ☐ She has to take a subject again next year.

c Write to somebody giving advice about how he or she can get better exam results.

⊙ Review and extension

1 GRAMMAR

Correct the sentences.

1 You shouldn't to drink coffee before you go to bed.
  You shouldn't drink coffee before you go to bed.
2 I think he should doing some exercise every day.
3 You should read a book for to help you relax.
4 She asked me drive her to the station.
5 My father taught me how play the guitar.
6 What I should do if I can't sleep very well?

2 VOCABULARY

Correct the sentences.

1 The football match was really excited. It finished 3 – 3.
  The football match was really exciting. It finished 3 – 3.
2 I was thinking in that TV programme I saw last night.
3 My uncle paid the tickets and he bought popcorn for us as well.
4 I can't afford to spend a lot of money in a holiday this year.
5 My little sister isn't very interesting in fashion.
6 I didn't hear the phone because I was listening some music.
7 I didn't think that horror film was frightened. What about you?
8 I didn't have any money, so I had to borrow £20 to my brother.

3 WORDPOWER verb + to

Complete the sentences with the words in the box.

read   sold   paid   wrote   lent
described   ~~explained~~   brought

1 She ___explained___ the problem to her parents.
2 I _____ £200 to Jack so he could buy a phone.
3 He _____ lots of CDs with him to the party.
4 Gianni _____ an email to the school to ask for information about their language classes.
5 We _____ £500 to the builder who fixed our roof.
6 She _____ the story very quietly to her class, closed the book and put it back in the cupboard.
7 They _____ their car to their neighbour for £1,500.
8 Laura _____ her new house in Australia to me.

⊙ REVIEW YOUR PROGRESS

Look again at Review your progress on p.66 of the Student's Book. How well can you do these things now?
3 = very well   2 = well   1 = not so well

I CAN ...

give advice on common problems	☐
describe extreme experiences	☐
ask for and give advice	☐
write an email giving advice.	☐

39

Vox pop video

Unit 1: Communicating

🎥 Where do you usually meet new people?

a Watch video 1a and underline the correct words to complete the sentences.

1 Helen usually meets new people *through friends / at parties / on trains or buses*.
2 Ian usually meets new people *through cycling / through friends / at parties*.
3 Carla usually meets new people *at language classes or dance classes / through friends / through cycling*.
4 Jen usually meets new people *on trains or buses / at parties / at language classes or dance classes*.
5 Maria usually meets new people *on trains or buses / through cycling / through friends*.

🎥 What's a good first question to ask someone?

b Watch video 1b. Match 1–4 with a–d to make sentences.

1 [b] Helen's first question is usually about
2 [   ] Carla's first question is usually about
3 [   ] Jen's first question is usually about
4 [   ] Maria's first question is usually about

a the weather or where the person is from.
b something in the news or the weather.
c the person's hobbies.
d the person's free-time activities.

🎥 How do you keep in touch with your family?

c Watch video 1c and tick (✓) the correct answers.

1 Helen uses Skype or email to keep in touch with …
   a ☐ her parents.
   b ☐ her brother.
   c ✓ her son.
2 Ian usually communicates with his family …
   a ☐ by phone.
   b ☐ by letter.
   c ☐ on Facebook.
3 Maria keeps in touch with her family …
   a ☐ by letter.
   b ☐ on the Internet.
   c ☐ by text.
4 Carla contacts her family …
   a ☐ on her phone.
   b ☐ in person.
   c ☐ on her laptop.
5 Jen keeps in touch with her family by …
   a ☐ seeing them face to face.
   b ☐ sending them texts.
   c ☐ phoning them.
6 Maria communicates with her family …
   a ☐ face to face.
   b ☐ by phone.
   c ☐ on Facebook.

Unit 2: Travel

🎥 What was your last holiday like?

a Watch video 2a and tick (✓) the correct answers.

1 Jenny travelled around the USA by …
   a ☐ car.
   b ☐ train.
   c ✓ coach.
2 John spent his last holiday in …
   a ☐ London and Wales.
   b ☐ London and Scotland.
   c ☐ Scotland and Ireland.
3 Suzanne went to Mexico for …
   a ☐ one week.
   b ☐ two weeks.
   c ☐ three weeks.
4 For Rebecca's last holiday, she went to …
   a ☐ the USA.
   b ☐ South America.
   c ☐ Scotland.

🎥 Did you do any sightseeing?

b Watch video 2b and tick (✓) the correct answers.

1 Jenny visited …
   a ☐ New York and Boston.
   b ☐ Chicago and Los Angeles.
   c ✓ San Francisco and Las Vegas.
2 John visited …
   a ☐ Big Ben and the Houses of Parliament.
   b ☐ Buckingham Palace and Westminster Abbey.
   c ☐ the Tower of London and Big Ben.
3 When she was in Mexico, Suzanne …
   a ☐ did lots of sightseeing.
   b ☐ didn't do any sightseeing.
   c ☐ spent most of her time relaxing.
4 When she went to Chicago, Rebecca …
   a ☐ went on a bus tour.
   b ☐ saw the Hollywood sign.
   c ☐ didn't do much sightseeing.

Vox pop video

2c ◀ Did you bring back any souvenirs?

c Watch video 2c. Match 1–4 with a–d to make sentences.
1 [d] When she went on her last holiday, Jenny
2 [ ] When he went on his last holiday, John
3 [ ] When she went on her last holiday, Suzanne
4 [ ] When she went on her last holiday, Rebecca

a didn't bring back any souvenirs.
b brought back lots of souvenirs.
c brought back some presents for his daughters.
d brought back a 'dream catcher'.

Unit 3: Money

3a ◀ What three things have you bought recently?

a Watch video 3a. Complete the sentences with the names in the box.

Darren   Colin   ~~Lauren~~   Carolyn

1 _Lauren_ recently bought some food, some shoes and a magazine.
2 _____ recently bought some shoes, a T-shirt and a holiday.
3 _____ recently bought a dress, a fancy-dress costume and some bike lights.
4 _____ recently bought some spaghetti, some tomato sauce and a house.

3b ◀ Is there anything you've bought in the last year but haven't used yet?

b Watch video 3b and underline the correct words to complete the sentences.
1 Lauren has some *shirts* / *shoes* / *jeans* she's never worn.
2 Carolyn bought a black dress *six months ago* / *last weekend* / *a year ago* in the sales.
3 Colin *never buys* / *doesn't usually buy* / *often buys* things he doesn't need.

3c ◀ What are good ways to raise money for charity?

c Watch video 3c. Match the ideas for raising money 1–4 with the people who mentioned the ideas a–d.
1 [d] My favourite way of making money is to sell cakes to people.
2 [ ] A friend of mine raised money by cycling across Morocco.
3 [ ] You can cycle from London to Brighton to raise money for charity.
4 [ ] You can cut your hair really short to raise money for charity.

a Lauren
b Darren
c Colin
d Carolyn

Unit 4: Social Life

4a ◀ What's the best party you've ever been to?

a Watch video 4a and tick (✓) the correct answers.
1 The best party Seb's ever been to was …
  a [ ] his brother's birthday party.
  b [ ] his school's Christmas party.
  c [✓] his friend's birthday party.
2 The best party Lucy's ever been to was …
  a [ ] her best friend's birthday party.
  b [ ] her own party.
  c [ ] her father's 50th birthday party.
3 The best party Wiktoria's ever been to was …
  a [ ] Simon's leaving party.
  b [ ] Simon's birthday party.
  c [ ] Simon's end-of-year party.
4 One of Solyman's favourite parties was when …
  a [ ] he was about 6.
  b [ ] he was about 16.
  c [ ] he was a student.

4b ◀ What do you usually do to celebrate your birthday?

b Watch video 4b and underline the correct words to complete the sentences.
1 Last year Seb *had a party* / *did two special activities* / *went to a restaurant* with his friends.
2 Lucy usually has a *big party with all her friends* / *meal with her friends* / *meal with her family*.
3 Wiktoria usually has a *barbecue with her friends* / *barbecue with her family* / *party with her friends*.
4 Solyman *doesn't celebrate* / *always celebrates* / *sometimes celebrates* his birthday.

4c ◀ What are your plans for the weekend?

c Watch video 4c. Match 1–4 with a–d to make sentences.
1 [b] This weekend Seb is
2 [ ] This weekend Lucy is
3 [ ] This weekend Wiktoria is
4 [ ] This weekend Solyman is

a doing some gardening.
b watching films with some friends.
c getting ready to go on holiday.
d going to London.

Unit 5: Work

5a ◁ Do you work?

a Watch video 5a and tick (✓) the correct answers.

1 Jen is a teacher of _____.
   a ☐ English
   b ☐ German
   c ✓ Russian

2 Christian shows _____ around Cambridge colleges.
   a ☐ teachers
   b ☐ tourists
   c ☐ students

3 Precious is working with children at a _____ school.
   a ☐ language
   b ☐ Sunday
   c ☐ summer

4 Helen visits _____ and clients two or three days a week.
   a ☐ hospitals
   b ☐ hostels
   c ☐ hotels

5b ◁ What qualifications or abilities are necessary for your job?

b Watch video 5b and underline the correct words to complete the sentences.

1 In Jen's job you need to be able to *write / speak / understand* the language you're teaching.
2 In Christian's job you have to be good at *listening to / working with / talking to* people.
3 In Precious's job you need to be very *friendly / funny / creative*.
4 People who do Helen's job often have a background in *engineering / computing / science*.

5c ◁ What do you think makes people happy at work?

c Watch video 5c. Match 1–4 with a–d to make sentences.

1 [b] Jen thinks that people like their jobs if
2 ☐ Christian thinks that people like their jobs if
3 ☐ Precious thinks that people like their jobs if
4 ☐ Helen thinks that people like their jobs if

a they get on well with their colleagues.
b there is a nice atmosphere at work.
c they are doing something they really enjoy.
d they get personal satisfaction from their work.

Unit 6: Problems and Advice

6a ◁ When you have a problem, who do you prefer to talk to about it?

a Watch video 6a. Match 1–4 with a–d to make sentences.

1 [d] When Mark has a problem, he prefers to discuss it with his
2 ☐ When Laurence has a problem, he prefers to discuss it with his
3 ☐ When Maibritt has a problem, she prefers to discuss it with her
4 ☐ When Colin has a problem, he prefers to discuss it with his

a husband, sister or friends.
b dad, girlfriend or mum.
c girlfriend or friends.
d best friend.

6b ◁ What advice would you give to a student who is worried about exams?

b Watch video 6b. Complete the sentences with the names in the box.

| Maibritt | Mark | Colin | ~~Laurence~~ |

1 __Laurence__ would tell the student not to get too worried about the exam.
2 _____ would tell the student not to panic because it's just an exam.
3 _____ would tell the student the exam isn't as important as it seems.
4 _____ would tell the student to relax and do their best.

6c ◁ What advice would you give to someone who can't sleep?

c Watch video 6c and tick (✓) the correct answers.

1 Maibritt thinks it's a good idea to read a _____ before you go to sleep.
   a ☐ magazine
   b ✓ book
   c ☐ newspaper

2 Colin thinks you should get plenty of exercise in the _____.
   a ☐ morning
   b ☐ afternoon
   c ☐ evening

3 Laurence thinks you shouldn't _____ before you go to sleep.
   a ☐ look at your phone
   b ☐ watch TV
   c ☐ play computer games

4 Mark thinks you should drink _____ before you go to sleep.
   a ☐ coffee
   b ☐ tea
   c ☐ milk

This page is intentionally left blank

Audioscripts

Unit 1

1.1
1 birthday
2 bank
3 cinema
4 food
5 party
6 silly
7 music
8 sport
9 friendly
10 blog

1.2
ALICE What's Sarah doing in that shop?
NAOMI She's buying some postcards to send to her family.
A Really? I don't generally send postcards. I usually write a message on my Facebook wall. And sometimes I put a few photos of my holiday on my wall.
N Yes, me too, but Sarah's grandparents don't have a computer, so she sends them postcards instead.
A Oh, and what are Tom and Jack doing this morning?
N They're spending the day at the beach.
A But Tom doesn't like swimming in the sea. He says the water's too cold.
N Yes, but it's really hot today!

1.3
SAM Hi, James! Long time no see! How are you?
JAMES Hi, Sam. I'm fine, thanks. What a lovely surprise! Great to see you!
S Yes, it's really nice to see you, too.
J Where are you living these days?
S Oh, not far from here. In Park Road, near the sports centre.
J Oh, how nice!
S And this is my wife, Jackie.
J Your wife – wow! That's fantastic news! Nice to meet you, Jackie.
JACKIE Nice to meet you, too.

1.4
1 Sea View Road? Oh, how nice!
2 Your husband – wow! That's fantastic news!
3 We really must go. We're late.
4 What a lovely surprise!
5 Say hello to Roger for me.
6 Long time no see!
7 It was really nice to meet you.
8 We must meet up soon.
9 It was great to see you again.
10 When did we last see each other?

1.5
1 I'm pretty sure it was two months ago.
2 What a lovely surprise!
3 It was really nice to meet you.
4 I'm sorry, but I really must go.
5 Where are you living these days?
6 I'm late for a meeting.

1.6
PRESENTER When you move to a new school or town or start at university, it's important to make new friends. But it isn't easy. On today's programme new students at Princeton University tell us about how they are making friends during the first few weeks of term. First up is Richard.
RICHARD I don't particularly like going to parties and I hardly ever go to bars and discos so it was difficult for me to make friends. I like people who I have something in common with so I joined the university walking club. We meet every Sunday and normally go for a walk into the forests or by the river near the university. It's good fun and I talk to lots of people.
PR Joining a club is a great way to meet new people. But there are other ways. Let's hear from Sophia, a nineteen-year-old student.
SOPHIA I'm studying Drama so I like talking to people. I'm not particularly interested in joining a club, as I generally prefer to meet people who like lots of different things. I posted a message on an online student network saying 'I'm looking for some friends. No rude or serious people. We can meet for a drink in the students' café every Tuesday.' About 10 people come each week. It's great fun and everyone is different.
PR But if you don't want to start your own group, there are other ways. Over to Peter.
PETER I don't really like using Facebook to make friends. I'm living in a large student house with about thirty other people so in the first week I knocked on everyone's bedroom door and said hello. Everyone here is friendly. Now I'm rarely on my own and there is often someone to talk to or go out with in the evenings.

Unit 2

2.1
depart   departed   look   looked
love   loved   post   posted
listen   listened   invite invited
hate   hated   enjoy   enjoyed
sound   sounded   like   liked

2.2
1 Were /wə/ you waiting for the bus?
2 I wasn't driving the car.
3 They were /wə/ watching TV.
4 We weren't having dinner.
5 She was /wəz/ talking on her phone.
6 Was /wəz/ she listening?
7 He wasn't smoking.
8 They weren't playing chess.

2.3
1 Is there anything else I can help you with?
2 Could you tell me where the information desk is?
3 How much is a return ticket to Edinburgh?
4 How often do the buses leave for the airport?
5 What time is the next coach to Barcelona?
6 Can I pay for my ticket in euros?
7 Where can I buy a sandwich for the journey?
8 How much does it cost to get a taxi to the airport?

2.4
A Excuse me.
B Yes, how can I help you?
A Could you tell me which platform the next train to London leaves from?
B Certainly, madam. It leaves from Platform 2.
A OK, thanks. And what time does it leave?
B It leaves at 10:32, in twelve minutes.
A Brilliant. Thanks.
B Is there anything else I can help you with?
A Actually, there is one more thing. Where can I buy a cup of coffee? Is there a café near here?
B Yes, there is. There's a café on the platform, over there.
A Great. Thanks so much.
B No problem. Have a good journey.

2.5
1 When did you check into your hotel?
2 How can I help you?
3 Did you get a visa when you went to China?
4 What time did you set off from home?
5 What time is your plane?
6 How much is a return ticket to Bath?

2.6
STEVE And now we go over to Susie with today's traffic and travel news. I hear it is particularly bad on the M3 and M4 motorways?
SUSIE Thanks, Steve, that's right. The heavy rain this morning caused problems on the M3. Four cars hit each other and because of that, there were long delays between London and Guildford. It doesn't look very good on the M4. A lorry broke down near Swindon about three hours ago and there was a huge traffic jam half an hour later. Peter from Bristol just texted on eight seven six six three two to say that there is a queue now. So if you need to get to Swindon this evening, you might want to go off the motorway and go on the main road – the A429. The M1 is looking a lot better today. There were no delays when I last checked, which is great for anyone who is going to the big music festival in Leeds tomorrow. However, the police have said that you must not hitchhike on the motorway. But if you haven't booked accommodation, you can take a tent and stay on a campsite in the park.
Unusually, there aren't many problems on the trains today, but if you are going away this weekend, lots of trains aren't working normally, so check before you go. If you are flying from Gatwick Airport, please phone your airline before you set off. The computer systems at the airport weren't working this morning and many flights were cancelled today. The computers are working now but there are long delays and even longer queues! Jackie and Bob phoned to say their flight to India was delayed by over twelve hours and they had to check into a hotel at the airport for the night. But I'm pleased to say that they've boarded their plane now and are on their way.
ST Well, I hope they've got a visa or they'll have another long queue when they arrive!
SU I hope so, too! It sounds like they're going to have a real adventure. Back to you, Steve.
ST Thanks, Susie. And here's the latest song by …

Unit 3

3.1
A Good morning. Can I help you?
B Er, yes. I'm looking for a present for my wife.
A Are you looking for anything in particular?
B Well, she loves earrings.
A Really? How about these earrings? They're really beautiful. A perfect present …
B Do you have anything cheaper?
A Well, these earrings here are cheaper. They're only £50 with the discount.
B Yes, I suppose she might like them. On second thoughts, maybe I should get something else.
A OK. Er, let me see … what about this necklace?
B Yes, it's lovely. OK, I'll take it.

3.2
1 Can you show us something else?
2 Can you enter your PIN, please?
3 I'm looking for a present for my husband.
4 Do you have any black jeans?
5 Thanks. I'll take it.
6 Actually, I think we should buy her a book.

3.3
DJ And now it's time for today's talking point. What's the nicest thing you have ever done for someone? Have you given something expensive away to someone or just made someone smile? Call, text or email me now. First on is Anita from Perth.
ANITA Hello, Baz. My neighbour hasn't got a job at the moment and it's her daughter's thirteenth birthday today. I know she couldn't afford to have a party so I thought I could help.
DJ And what have you done?
A I've borrowed a stereo from my brother and some disco lights from my friend. And we've turned part of her back garden into a beach with lots of sand I got at the local beach. Lots of the neighbours have given some food and we're going to have a beach party and disco this evening.
DJ That must have made your neighbour smile. Thanks for your call, Anita, and have a great night. What a nice woman. Next we have Gary from Adelaide. What's the nicest thing you've done?
GARY Hi, Baz. Last year I was in the city centre when a tourist asked me how to get to the museum. I gave him directions and then we started talking. He was from Greece and he was really friendly. Then it started raining really hard. He didn't have a coat so I lent him my umbrella. I asked him to bring it to my house when he was leaving Adelaide and then I forgot about it. Four days later he brought it to my house. I certainly didn't expect that. I invited him in and we had a cup of tea together. We got on well and we

82

Audioscripts

became friends. When he left, he invited me to visit him in Greece next summer. I've been saving up all year and I've just booked my ticket. I can't wait!

DJ That's a great story, Gary. Enjoy your holiday! Before we go, I've had an email from Mike in Darwin. He has started a group called 'Give someone a hug, make someone smile'. Every Sunday he walks around the city centre with his friends, giving people hugs and hopefully making them smile. Good luck with that, Mike – and be careful!

Unit 4

▶ 4.1
A So what have you arranged for this evening?
B Well, my parents are arriving at the station on the 6:30 train from Paris.
A So, are you meeting them at the station?
B Yes, we are. We're taking a taxi from our house at 6:00. I booked it this morning.
A Good. So where are they staying?
B At the Hilton Hotel. They've got a double room with a balcony.
A Great. And what about the restaurant?
B I've reserved a table for eight at eight o'clock. Everyone's coming to the restaurant at 7:45 so we can all be there when they arrive.
A Brilliant. Have you told the restaurant that it's your father's birthday?
B Yes, they've made him a special cake with HAPPY 60TH on it. They're bringing it to our table at ten o'clock, together with the coffee.
A And what about tomorrow?
B They aren't flying to Scotland until the afternoon, so there's plenty of time. Their flight's at 3:30.
A Great, so it's all arranged. I have to go now because I'm meeting Sally for a coffee in ten minutes. See you later!

▶ 4.2
1 Are you going to go out tonight?
2 What are you going to do for your birthday?
3 He isn't going to have a holiday this year.
4 We're going to try to find a taxi.
5 I'm going to have a shower after breakfast.
6 They aren't going to do their homework.
7 She's going to phone her brother.
8 I'm not going to go to Ibiza this year.

▶ 4.3
1 We want to go swimming today.
2 They won't take you to the old castle.
3 I won't go to that restaurant again.
4 You want to wait for the next train.
5 I want to study English again next year.
6 Tom and I won't invite him to our party.

▶ 4.4
A Are you doing anything on Wednesday? Would you like to go for a coffee?
B Oh, that sounds nice. I'll just check. No, sorry, I can't do Wednesday. I'm going shopping with my mother.
A Oh, OK, never mind. How about Friday? Is that OK for you?
B Friday … hang on a minute … no, sorry. I'm going to London for the day. This week's really busy for me.
A OK, so you can't do this week. What are you doing next Monday?
B Next Monday? Just a moment, I'll just check. Nothing! I can do next Monday. Perfect!
A Great! So we can meet for a coffee on Monday?
B Yes, Monday's fine. Where shall we go?
A Shall we meet at The Coffee Place at 11.00?
B Brilliant! 11 o'clock. See you then.

▶ 4.5
1 Would you like me to bring anything?
2 Are you doing anything this Saturday?
3 This week's really busy for us.
4 What time shall we come round?
5 What are you doing on Tuesday next week?
6 Would you like to come round for lunch?
7 I can't do Thursday this week.
8 Is this Sunday OK for you?

▶ 4.6
1 I can't meet you tomorrow.
2 He can meet us at the station.
3 I didn't understand him.
4 She hasn't seen that film.
5 I must start cooking dinner.
6 They don't like basketball.

▶ 4.7
ISAAC What are your plans when you finish university this summer, Giles?
GILES Well, my brother Alex is getting married in July.
I That's great news. Where is the wedding?
G His fiancée Laura is Italian so it's going to be in her town in Tuscany in this magnificent old church there. The town is really pretty.
I That sounds wonderful. Is it going to be a big wedding?
G The party is in the town hall, which is huge. Laura's got a really big family.
I Have you got to do anything at the wedding?
G Yes, I have! I'm going to read a poem I wrote.
I Brilliant! That's exciting. I guess you're going to need a new suit for that.
G Yes, I've got to look my best, especially in front of all those Italian guests.
I Really?
G Yes, they always have great outfits. My dad's going to buy me a new suit if I pass my exams. Something really nice.
I Great! Can you speak any Italian?
G Si. Un po'! But I'm starting lessons next week. The Italian boy in our class, Gavino, is teaching me.
I That's a good idea. How long are you going to Italy for?
G I'm going for two weeks. I'm flying to Rome with my parents on the fourteenth of July and we're going to go sightseeing for a few days. My mum wants to see all the ancient buildings.
I I love Rome. You can walk down a street of really cool modern buildings, then turn a corner and see something that's two thousand years old. It's amazing.
G Wow, I can't wait to go.
I Anyway, I've got to go. I'm going on a date tonight and I want to go to the hairdresser's before it closes.
G OK, well make sure you have a shave before you meet her, Isaac.
I Don't worry, I will. See you tomorrow then.
G OK, see you.

Unit 5

▶ 5.1
1 Shall I lend you some money for the bus?
2 Maybe you should ask your manager for the day off.
3 I'll look up the train times on the Internet.
4 Do you want me to book a taxi for our guest?
5 Why don't I drive you to the airport?
6 How about arranging a meeting in Milan?
7 Why don't you borrow some money from your father?
8 You could catch a direct flight to Rome.

▶ 5.2
1 A Shall I book a room for your meeting?
   B Yes, good idea.
2 A Would you like me to drive you to the station?
   B No, I'll be fine. Don't worry about it. I can take the bus.
3 A But you won't be able to have any lunch.
   B Oh, never mind. I'm not really hungry.
4 A I'm really sorry. I can't come to the cinema tonight.
   B Oh, it doesn't matter. We can go another time.
5 How about asking your boss if you can have more time for the report?
6 Why don't I book the train tickets on the Internet?
7 Maybe you should invite your boss to the meeting, too.
8 You could send her some flowers for her birthday.

▶ 5.3
1 Would you like a coffee?
2 Yes, I would. Thanks.
3 Could you help me with my report?
4 Yes, of course I could.
5 You should get a taxi.
6 Yes, you're right. I should.
7 Shall I book a meeting room?
8 Well, what do you think? Shall I?

▶ 5.4
INTERVIEWER Thank you for coming, Josh. First of all, I'd like to talk about your CV. You have some good qualifications, but you've had a lot of different jobs in the last five years. Can you talk about those?
JOSH Yes, I worked as a postman when I finished university. I enjoyed working outside, but I had to work many hours each day and start early in the morning, which I hated, so I decided to look for other jobs.
I So, you don't like working long hours then. Hmm. Tell me about your next job. You worked as a hairdresser, didn't you?
J Yes, I did. I learned a lot of skills while I was there and I really liked the place. But I didn't like having to talk to people every day. I had to talk to the customers and make coffee.
I Hmm. OK. What about your last job? You were an IT worker.
J Yes, that was great. I earned a good salary and I worked with a nice team of people. Sometimes when we were busy I had to work at weekends, which wasn't great, but I usually just worked Monday to Friday. I didn't have to work with people so much, and I could often just sit at my desk and use the Internet, when we weren't busy, of course. And my manager didn't mind what time I started work.
I And at what time did you usually start work?
J The latest I could start was 10:30 am.
I OK, Josh, so why would you like to work as a bank clerk for Mainland Bank?
J I'd like to work in a team, and get some good experience of working in a bank. It looks like a nice environment to work in. And it also pays really well, too.
I But you don't like working hard or dealing with people every day. Those are important parts of the job.
J Well …
I I'm sorry, Josh, but I don't think you're what we're looking for. Thanks for coming in today and good luck.
J Oh. OK. I thought this would be a good job for me.
I I don't think so. But good luck with your search. Goodbye.
J Bye.

Unit 6

▶ 6.1
1 We took my grandmother to the theatre.
2 The children wanted to go to the zoo.
3 Where did you lose your mobile phone?
4 Would you like a cup of coffee?
5 Who did you invite to the party?
6 I don't think you should go to work today.
7 Could I borrow £5, please?
8 What did you think of the food?

▶ 6.2
1 A I think it's a good idea to book a table. The restaurant might be full.
   B Yes, I suppose so. Saturday night can be very busy.
2 A Someone stole my handbag when I was at the beach this afternoon.
   B How awful! I'm really sorry to hear that.
3 A I'd speak to your boss about it.
   B I don't think I should do that. She'll be angry with me.
4 A I wouldn't worry too much. You can get a new passport at the embassy.
   B Yes, you're right. I can go there one day next week.
5 A Do you think I should invite Steve to the surprise party?
   B No, I don't think that's a very good idea. Anna doesn't like him very much.
6 A What do you think I should do?
   B I think you should go to the police station.
7 A I didn't get the job in marketing.
   B Oh, what a pity. I'm sure you'll get another job soon.
8 A I broke my finger on Saturday.
   B Oh, that's a shame. So that means you can't play tennis today?

▶ 6.3
1 Which job do you think I should apply for?
2 I think you should ask your colleagues.
3 I'm really sorry to hear that.

83

4 Do you think I should look for a new job?
5 I think it's a good idea to speak to your boss.
6 I'd talk to your parents about it.
7 I wouldn't apply for the new marketing job.
8 I don't think you should leave your job.

▶ 6.4

1 You're from Canada, right?
2 Elena works in the Spanish Embassy.
3 Would you like to work in London?
4 We're having a surprise party for Anna.
5 My boss wants to speak to me.

▶ 6.5

MARSHA Hi, Georgia. How are you?
GEORGIA Hi. Not so good. I'm getting really annoyed with my little brother Jim at the moment. I'm trying to revise for my exams and he keeps stopping me from working. Sometimes he listens to his music very loudly late at night, sometimes he borrows something from me that I need to study, like my dictionary or laptop. I can't concentrate on my work for more than a few minutes. It's terrible.
MAR You should go and study in the library. It's really quiet there and you won't have to deal with the interruptions. I go there most weekends to study.
MAX You shouldn't have to go somewhere else. Ask your parents to deal with your brother. Your exams are more important than your brother. Your parents understand that.
G That's a good idea, Max. I'll ask my dad for help tonight. My brother will listen to him. And I'll also think about going to the library at the weekend. It's nice to have a change sometimes when you're studying. How's your revision going, Max?
MAX My problem is I just can't remember anything from History. I read a page and then ten minutes later I've forgotten it.
MAR That's not unusual. You should try writing down what you've just read. It's amazing how much more you will remember that way.
G And you should also record yourself speaking your notes and then you can listen to them on your MP3 player. You'll be surprised how much you can remember.
MAX Yes, I'll definitely try those ideas.
G Sometimes I even sing my notes. It's a bit embarrassing, but it will help you to remember lots of information.
MAX That's a brilliant idea.
MAR Any advice to help me understand Physics? It's so confusing. I look at it, I can read it, I can remember it, but when I think about it, I just don't understand it.
G It doesn't sound like Physics is your subject, Marsha. Perhaps you should do something else!
MAX That's not very nice, Georgia. I'm really interested in Physics. I'm happy to help you with it if you like, Marsha. I think you just need someone to explain it to you.
MAR Thanks, Max. I think that Georgia might be right, but I really want to pass the Physics exam this year, so I don't have to do it again next year. Are you free this weekend?
MAX No, I'm afraid not. I need to record all my history notes on to my MP3 player!

Answer key

Unit 1

1A

1

a 2 serious 3 delicious 4 gorgeous 5 silly 6 lovely

b 2 delicious 3 perfect 4 strange 5 **B** alright 6 awful 7 amazing 8 rude

2

a 2 did you meet 3 Did he grow up 4 was the film like 5 did you pay 6 Why did she go 7 did he make 8 was your holiday

b 2 Does he work in a bank?
3 Why did you go to New York last month?
4 What is that new Brazilian restaurant like?
5 Who was that man with your sister?
6 What type of TV programmes do you watch?
7 Which university did you go to?
8 How much did the tickets cost?

1B

1

a 2 I particularly enjoy watching old Hollywood movies.
3 She absolutely hates it when people are late for meetings.
4 We generally go to Italian restaurants, but sometimes we also go to Turkish ones.
5 We're pretty sure his flight arrives at Terminal 2, but I need to check it.
6 I really hope she brings her gorgeous brother to the party!

b 2 hardly ever 3 normally 4 fairly 5 really 6 rarely 7 mainly 8 pretty

2

a long vowel: 3, 4, 5, 7, 8

3

a 2 go 3 'm reading 4 wants 5 are you waiting 6 visit 7 's studying 8 're playing

b 2 's buying 3 don't 4 send 5 write 6 put 7 don't have 8 sends 9 are Tom and Jack doing 10 're spending 11 doesn't like 12 's

1C

1

a 2 What a 3 to see you 4 these days 5 far from 6 how 7 this is 8 news 9 meet 10 too

c 2 news 3 must 4 surprise 5 hello 6 time 7 meet 8 up 9 again 10 last

2

a 2 lovely, surprise 3 really, nice, meet 4 sorry, must, go 5 Where, living 6 late, meeting

1D

1

a c

b True: 2, 5; False: 1, 3, 4, 6

2

a 2 Yesterday we visited the Palace of Versailles near Paris.
3 In the mornings, I usually go to the beach with my Portuguese friends.
4 I hope you're having a lovely time in Canada with your family.
5 Their English is very good, but we always speak in German.

3

a **Suggested answer:**
Hi Paul
Hope you're having a good holiday in Ireland.
I'm spending two weeks with my brother and his family here in Turkey. I don't speak Turkish, but my brother's wife and his three children speak very good English, so communication isn't a problem.
They live about 30 km from Istanbul in a small town on the Bosphorus. It's very hot at the moment, but they have a lovely swimming pool near their house, so we go swimming there every day.
I'm visiting lots of amazing places with my brother's family. Yesterday we went to the Grand Bazaar in the centre of Istanbul. It's an enormous indoor market and there are over 3,000 shops. I'm sending you a photo of it. I bought a lovely leather handbag.
My brother's house has a big garden, so we usually have dinner outside in the evenings, when it isn't so hot. We normally eat at about ten o'clock. My sister-in-law's a brilliant cook, so the food is delicious!
I'm having a lovely time in Turkey.
See you back at work next month.
Becky

Reading and listening extension

1

a 2 c 3 a

b 2 b 3 c 4 c 5 a 6 b

2

a 2 a 3 b

b 2 a 3 b 4 c 5 a 6 b

Review and extension

1

2 At the moment, she's working in the café by the station. / At the moment, she is working in the café by the station.
3 Why did you miss the bus?
4 I can't talk to you now because I'm doing my homework.
5 What kind of music do you usually listen to?
6 They're waiting for the bus to London. / They are waiting for the bus to London.

2

2 We really enjoyed the film last night.
3 We had a lovely time at the party last night.
4 I think our History lessons are so boring.
5 I think that man's a bit strange. Look, he's talking to himself.
6 New York's all right, but I prefer living in London, actually. / New York's alright, but I prefer living in London, actually.

3

2 h 3 a 4 c 5 g 6 f 7 b 8 d

Unit 2

2A

1

a 2 I slept very badly on the plane, so I felt very tired the next day.
3 Did you take the train from New York to Washington?
4 Correct
5 They spent two nights in a hotel and then they stayed at a friend's house for three days.
6 I didn't enjoy my trip to Scotland because the weather wasn't very good.
7 Correct
8 Correct

b 1 **B** didn't sleep, weren't 2 **A** did you do **B** didn't have, decided
3 **A** did Ben go **B** went 4 **A** Did you bring **B** did, bought
5 **A** Did you meet **B** did, met 6 **A** Did you visit **B** didn't have

2

a 2 e 3 a 4 f 5 h 6 b 7 c 8 g

b 2 passport 3 backpack 4 guidebook 5 foreign currency 6 suitcase

3

a hated, sounded, posted, invited

87

2B

1

a 2 hitchhiked 3 gave 4 set off 5 missed 6 took off 7 landed 8 boarded 9 changed 10 got to

b 1 **B** crash 2 **A** miss **B** got lost 3 **A** long delays **B** strike 4 something wrong 5 queue, broke down 6 **B** turbulence

2

a 2 was snowing 3 Were you flying 4 were you driving 5 were you standing 6 wasn't working

b 2 was driving 3 broke down 4 missed 5 bought 6 were waiting 7 started 8 decided 9 took 10 bought

3

a 1: c, e, f; 2: b, g; 3: d, h

2C

1

a 2 Could you tell me where the information desk is?
3 How much is a return ticket to Edinburgh?
4 How often do the buses leave for the airport?
5 What time is the next coach to Barcelona?
6 Can I pay for my ticket in euros?
7 Where can I buy a sandwich for the journey?
8 How much does it cost to get a taxi to the airport?

c 2 can 3 Could you 4 from 5 what time 6 anything else 7 Actually 8 near here 9 over there 10 Have

e 2 b 3 f 4 d 5 h 6 g 7 e 8 a

2

a 2 a 3 a 4 b 5 a 6 a

2D

1

a 1 d 2 c

b True: 2, 3, 5; False: 1, 4, 6

2

a 2 because 3 but 4 and 5 because 6 When 7 so 8 but

3

a Suggested answer:
Carlos and I got to New York at 14:30 this afternoon. It was a very long flight from Madrid and we were very tired when we arrived because we couldn't sleep on the plane. When we got off the plane the first thing we noticed was the cold – minus six degrees! It was freezing! Everything they say about New York is true! The people at the airport weren't very friendly and we couldn't understand them because they spoke so quickly. In the end we took the subway from JFK Airport to the city centre. We're staying at The Crowne Plaza Hotel near Central Park. The hotel is full of European tourists and everyone was very friendly and helpful. Carlos is telling me to get ready to go and eat, so I have to finish now – more tomorrow.

Reading and listening extension

1

a 2 a, c 3 a, d

b 2 Carl and Sam 3 Carl and Sam 4 Ashish and Bryony 5 Ashish and Bryony

c 2 sunny 3 lift 4 cost 5 morning

2

a 2 e 3 c 4 d 5 b

b 2 c 3 a 4 b 5 b 6 a

Review and extension

1

2 When we got to the station, the train was just arriving.
3 My wife phoned me while I was waiting for my plane.
4 A man took my wallet while I was waiting in the queue for my ticket.
5 Last year, we went on holiday to Greece for two weeks.
6 I was driving to the airport when I saw the accident.

2

2 My journey from Berlin to London took fifteen hours.
3 Last week, I went to Rome on a business trip.
4 The traffic was terrible because it was the rush hour.
5 By the time they checked out of the hotel, it was 2 pm.
6 In the afternoon, they went sightseeing in the old town.

3

2 set 3 took 4 fell 5 75% 6 drove 7 I'm 8 are

Unit 3

3A

1

a 2 Have you ever been to the carnival in Rio de Janeiro?
3 I have given money to charity twice this week.
4 You have never helped me with my homework.
5 Have they ever done any volunteer work?
6 She has never left a big tip for the waiter.
7 Have you ever given any money to a homeless person?
8 I have visited my grandmother several times this month.

b 1 **B** gave
2 **A** Has she ever done **B** did
3 **A** Have you ever helped **B** helped
4 **A** 've left / have left **B** did you leave
5 **A** Has he ever bought **B** bought

2

a 2 h 3 e 4 b 5 g 6 c 7 f 8 a

b 2 give 3 did 4 gave 5 do 6 made 7 doing 8 given

3B

1

a 2 g 3 a 4 h 5 e 6 c 7 d 8 b

b 2 into 3 bank account 4 afford 5 lend 6 borrow 7 spend 8 loan 9 back

2

a 2 yet 3 just 4 already 5 **B** just 6 already 7 just 8 yet

b 2 He's already borrowed £2,000 from his bank. / He has already borrowed £2,000 from his bank.
3 Have you paid Louise back yet?
4 Sue has already spent the money she borrowed from me. / Sue's already spent the money she borrowed from me.
5 We've just bought a new TV in the sales. / We have just bought a new TV in the sales.
6 Has she saved enough money to buy a tablet yet?
7 I've already bought a present for my wife. / I have already bought a present for my wife.
8 They've just opened a new bank account in France. / They have just opened a new bank account in France.

3C

1

a 8, 1, 6, 9, 10, 3, 2, 5, 4, 7

c 2 for 3 in 4 next 5 On second thoughts 6 enter 7 size 8 something else

d 2 I think I'm a size 14.
3 Do you have the same one in blue?
4 Can you tell me how much it is?
5 That's a bit too expensive.
6 Do you have a cheaper one?

2

a 2 enter, PIN 3 present, husband 4 black, jeans 5 Thanks, take 6 Actually, book

3D

1

a c

b True: 2, 3; False: 1, 4

88

Answer key

2
a 7, 5, 2, 4, 1, 3, 6

3
a Suggested answer:
Hello everyone
This email is to say a big 'Thank you!' to everyone who helped us to raise money for Save the Children over the past twelve months. We have successfully raised £495!
Most of you came to the Save the Children sports day in September. That was a brilliant event and we all had lots of fun. A lot of you also came to our 1990s karaoke evening in October. And, of course, next week there's our popular quiz night with big prizes for the winning team.
Save the Children will use our money to save children's lives and to give them a future. Last year, Save the Children helped ten million children around the world. A small amount can make a big difference. For example, just £3 can save the lives of eight children with stomach virus.
Would you like to help us raise more money for Save the Children? Email us and we can tell you about our future events. Thanks again for all your help.

Reading and listening extension

1
a 2 100 3 13 million 4 10 million
b True: 1, 3, 5; False: 2, 4
c 2 wrote 3 cost 4 called 5 spend 6 get 7 borrow 8 save 9 bought

2
a 2 Anita 3 Mike 4 Anita 5 Gary
b 2 b 3 a 4 b 5 c 6 b

Review and extension

1
2 Have you ever given money to charity?
3 I went to China on business last year.
4 I've just bought a new mobile phone. / I have just bought a new mobile phone.
5 I haven't bought a birthday present for my brother yet.
6 I've already spent £200 this weekend. / I have already spent £200 this weekend.

2
2 Can you lend me 50 euros, please?
3 Joe made a really funny joke, but nobody laughed.
4 James is saving up for a new computer.
5 Our taxi driver was very friendly, so we gave him a big tip.
6 I bought a new laptop in the sales – it was only £150!
7 Have you ever done any volunteer work?
8 Tony owes me £50, but he hasn't paid it back yet.

3
2 in time 3 under 4 like 5 about 6 over 7 spoken 8 a beginner

Unit 4

4A

1
a 2 tie 3 jumper 4 sweatshirt 5 earrings 6 tights 7 tracksuit
8 underwear 9 sandals 10 high heels 11 bracelet 12 flat shoes

2
a 2 Are you going to invite your cousin to your wedding?
3 They aren't going to get married this year.
4 What are you going to do after university?
5 We're going to visit my relatives in Spain next year.
6 What are you going to wear to the party?

b 2 are 3 meeting 4 're taking 5 are 6 staying 7 's coming
8 're bringing 9 aren't flying 10 'm meeting

3
a 2 gonna 3 going to 4 going to 5 gonna 6 gonna 7 going to 8 going to

4B

1
a 2 h 3 g 4 b 5 f 6 a 7 d 8 e
b 1 B 'll 2 B 'll 3 shall 4 won't 5 A Shall B 'll 6 won't 7 Shall 8 B 'll

2
a Across: 5 indoor 7 high 8 ordinary 10 peaceful; Down: 1 modern
2 narrow 3 magnificent 6 noisy 9 huge
b 2 pretty 3 outdoor 4 quiet 5 modern 6 high

3
a 2 won't 3 won't 4 want to 5 want to 6 won't

4C

1
a 3, 10, 5, 2, 1, 6, 7, 4, 9, 8
c 2 Are you doing anything this Saturday?
3 This week's really busy for us.
4 What time shall we come round?
5 What are you doing on Tuesday next week?
6 Would you like to come round for lunch?
7 I can't do Thursday this week.
8 Is this Sunday OK for you?

e 2 Mum 3 to the cinema 4 work conference 5 in Blackpool
6 Saturday

2
a 2 meet, station 3 didn't, understand 4 hasn't, seen, film
5 must, start, dinner 6 don't, like, basketball

4D

1
a d
b True: 2, 4; False: 1, 3, 5

2
a 2 Thanks for inviting me to your party.
3 It would be lovely to see you.
4 We're free on Saturday and we'd love to come.
5 This is just to say that we're having a party on Saturday.
6 We haven't seen you for ages!

3
a Suggested answer if she can go:
Hi Sam
Lovely to hear from you. Yes, I'm fine, thanks. My new job is brilliant, but I'm working very hard.
Thanks for inviting me to your birthday party. I'm free next Saturday and I'd love to come. Don't worry. I'll bring a huge salad! I'm looking forward to seeing you and having a nice chat.
All the best
Jess

Suggested answer if she can't go:
Hi Sam
Nice to hear from you. Yes, I'm fine, thanks. My new job is brilliant, but I'm working very hard.
Thanks for inviting me to your birthday party on Saturday. I'm really sorry, the party sounds like fun but I'm afraid I can't come. I'd love to come, but I'm visiting my cousin in Paris next weekend.
Hope you have a nice birthday party. See you soon anyway.
Love
Jess

Reading and listening extension

1
a 6, 4, 5, 3, 2, 1
b True: 2, 3, 5; False: 1, 4
c 2 going to have, hasn't bought / has not bought
3 is going to / 's going to
4 is getting ready / 's getting ready
5 is arriving / 's arriving

2
a 2 Alex 3 Gavino 4 Alex's mum 5 Isaac
b 2 b 3 b 4 c 5 b

Review and extension

1
2 Don't worry. I will pay the money back tomorrow. / Don't worry. I'll pay the money back tomorrow.
3 He's going to buy a new car next month. / He is going to buy a new car next month.
4 Shall I come to your house in half an hour?
5 Shall we go to that café for a cup of tea?
6 Are you going to do your homework this evening?

2
2 Are you going to buy a new suitcase in the sales?
3 I love it here in the country. It's so peaceful!
4 He always wears a tie when he goes for a job interview.
5 I love coming to this park because you can't hear the traffic. It's so quiet here.
6 That restaurant's so noisy. It's really hard to talk there.

3
2 for 3 forward 4 after 5 around 6 up

Unit 5

5A

1
a 2 hairdresser 3 plumber 4 scientist 5 banker 6 electrician 7 lawyer 8 accountant 9 dentist 10 nurse

b 2 salary 3 training 4 environment 5 team 6 university degree 7 people 8 self-employed 9 skills 10 qualifications

2
a 2 can't 3 can't 4 have to 5 have to 6 can't

b 2 can't 3 don't have to 4 have to 5 doesn't have to 6 has to 7 has to 8 mustn't 9 has to 10 doesn't have to

5B

1
a 2 h 3 a 4 g 5 b 6 f 7 e 8 d

b 2 might 3 won't 4 might not 5 will / 'll 6 A will / 'll B will 7 might 8 won't

2
a 2 carer 3 computer programmer 4 vet 5 designer 6 architect 7 musician 8 actor 9 journalist 10 postman 11 shop assistant 12 politician

b 2 builder 3 musician 4 architect 5 shop assistant 6 actor 7 carer 8 computer programmer 9 journalist 10 designer 11 postman 12 politicians

5C

1
a 2 Maybe you should ask your manager for the day off.
3 I'll look up the train times on the Internet.
4 Do you want me to book a taxi for our guest?
5 Why don't I drive you to the airport?
6 How about arranging a meeting in Milan?
7 Why don't you borrow some money from your father?
8 You could catch a direct flight to Rome.

c 1 B idea 2 A Would B fine, worry 3 B mind
4 A sorry B matter 5 about 6 don't 7 Maybe 8 could

2
a 2 strong vowel 3 weak vowel 4 strong vowel 5 weak vowel 6 strong vowel 7 weak vowel 8 strong vowel

5D

1
a c

b True: 1, 3, 4, 6; False: 2, 5

2
a 2 f 3 d 4 a 5 h 6 c 7 b 8 e

3
a Suggested answer:
Dear Sir/Madam,
I am writing to apply for the job of sales assistant, which you advertised in The Argus newspaper.
I am a student at the University of Sussex and I am available to work from October.
A job with you will be an exciting opportunity for me to learn new skills and to work in a new environment. I have a lot of experience of working in sales. Last summer I worked for three months in a very busy shop selling mobile phones and tablets and I think this experience will be very useful in this job.
I attach a copy of my CV with more details about my previous employment. Could you give me more information about the salary and working hours, and also more details of your training programme?
I look forward to hearing from you.
Yours faithfully,

Reading and listening extension

1
a 1 a 2 c 3 d 4 b

b 2 is doing something they love
3 gets paid well, is doing something they love, (sometimes) has to work many hours every day
4 gets paid well, works and studies, is doing something they love, has to work many hours every day

c 2 b 3 a 4 c 5 a, d

2
a 2 Postman, Hairdresser, Bank clerk 3 Hairdresser
4 IT worker, Bank clerk 5 IT worker, Bank clerk

b 1 early
2 skills, people/customers/clients
3 starting, weekends

Review and extension

1
2 Excuse me, sir. You mustn't smoke on the plane. It's against the law. / Excuse me, sir. You must not smoke on the plane. It's against the law.
3 Do you have to wear a suit to work?
4 When I finish school, I might go to university. It depends on my grades. / When I finish school, I may go to university. It depends on my grades.
5 I have to start work at 7 o'clock in the morning in my new job!
6 I'll take my umbrella. It might rain this afternoon. / I'll take my umbrella. It may rain this afternoon.

2
2 My sister works as a shop assistant in a big department store.
3 You need good qualifications if you want to become a doctor.
4 He works as a designer for a top fashion magazine.
5 If you want to become a plumber, you'll need to go to college.
6 My brother wants to become a professional musician.

3
2 job 3 work 4 work 5 work 6 work 7 work 8 jobs 9 work

Unit 6

6A

1
a 2 go 3 Don't sit 4 shouldn't have 5 Eat 6 shouldn't drink 7 don't use 8 should read 9 should have 10 should go

b 2 Eat lots of fruit and vegetables every day. / You should eat lots of fruit and vegetables every day.
3 Don't use your computer for very long in the evenings. / You shouldn't use your computer for very long in the evenings.
4 You should try to relax for an hour before you go to bed. / Try to relax for an hour before you go to bed.
5 I think she should get more exercise during the day.
6 You shouldn't go swimming immediately after lunch.
7 When you've got a headache, take an aspirin. / When you've got a headache, you should take an aspirin.
8 Don't stay at work after 6 o'clock.

2
a 2 h 3 d 4 g 5 f 6 a 7 b 8 c

b 2 on 3 for 4 about 5 for 6 on 7 from 8 for

# Answer key

3
a 2 long 3 long 4 short 5 long 6 short 7 short 8 long

6B
1
a 2 exciting 3 interested 4 shocked 5 annoyed 6 tiring 7 amazing 8 embarrassed

b 2 confused 3 interesting 4 surprising 5 frightened 6 disappointed 7 shocking 8 excited

2
a
2 It was interesting to learn about sharks.
3 Can you tell us where to park our cars?
4 It is dangerous not to wear a seat belt.
5 She had a bath to help her relax.
6 They went to the station to meet their aunt.
7 She phoned her father to ask him for some money.
8 He didn't know what to wear to the party.

b
2 He asked me how to get to the airport.
3 She was annoyed not to receive an invitation to his wedding.
4 They went to the supermarket to buy some food for dinner.
5 We couldn't remember which bus to catch for the airport.
6 John and Angela decided not to have their wedding in Scotland.
7 It was embarrassing to fail my driving test again.
8 She went to the library to borrow a book on dinosaurs for her son.

6C
1
a 2 e 3 f 4 g 5 c 6 h 7 a 8 b

c
2 I think you should ask your colleagues.
3 I'm really sorry to hear that.
4 Do you think I should look for a new job?
5 I think it's a good idea to speak to your boss.
6 I'd talk to your parents about it. / I'd talk about it to your parents.
7 I wouldn't apply for the new marketing job.
8 I don't think you should leave your job.

2
a 2 a 3 b 4 b 5 a

6D
1
a c

b True: 3, 5; False: 1, 2, 4

2
a
2 It's a good idea to read something in English every day. For example, you can read the BBC news pages on the Internet.
3 Why don't you do something relaxing this evening, such as going for a swim after work?
4 There are more enjoyable ways of preparing for an exam. For example, you could revise with a friend on the same course.
5 You could start a new hobby to help you relax, such as dancing or swimming.

3
a **Suggested answer:**
Dear Kento
Thanks for your message and I'm glad that you've written to me to ask for some ideas.
I remember when I was learning Japanese, listening was the most difficult thing for me, too. I could understand when my teacher was talking to me, but it was very hard to understand when other people were speaking. Here are some ideas to help you improve your listening in English.
First of all, don't worry if you don't understand every word you hear. That's impossible! You should concentrate only on the most important words.
Secondly, try to get extra listening practice outside the classroom. For instance, you can go to the study centre and practise listening with their CDs, such as the CDs from your Student's Book. You should also listen to the radio in English and watch English or American TV. It's a good idea to watch films with the subtitles.
Next, you can also practise listening to podcasts from the Internet. It's easy to download short stories onto your computer or tablet. Finally, it's a good idea to listen to pop songs while you read the words at the same time. There are lots of internet sites that give you the words of the most popular pop songs.
I hope this helps and please feel free to talk to me after class next week.
Best wishes
Tina

Reading and listening extension
1
a 2 Petra 3 Petra 4 Petra 5 customers 6 Sue

b 2 b 3 a 4 c 5 c

c 2 b 3 a 4 d 5 e

2
a 2 Marsha 3 Max 4 Georgia 5 Max

b 2 c 3 c 4 b 5 b 6 a

Review and extension
1
2 I think he should do some exercise every day.
3 You should read a book to help you relax.
4 She asked me to drive her to the station.
5 My father taught me how to play the guitar.
6 What should I do if I can't sleep very well?

2
2 I was thinking about that TV programme I saw last night.
3 My uncle paid for the tickets and he bought popcorn for us as well.
4 I can't afford to spend a lot of money on a holiday this year.
5 My little sister isn't very interested in fashion.
6 I didn't hear the phone because I was listening to some music.
7 I didn't think that horror film was frightening. What about you?
8 I didn't have any money, so I had to borrow £20 from my brother.

3
2 lent 3 brought 4 wrote 5 paid 6 read 7 sold 8 described

Vox pop video
Unit 1
a 2 through cycling 3 through friends 4 at language classes or dance classes 5 on trains or buses

b 2 c 3 d 4 a

c 2 a 3 b 4 a 5 c 6 a

Unit 2
a 2 b 3 b 4 a

b 2 b 3 c 4 a

c 2 c 3 a 4 b

Unit 3
a 2 Darren 3 Carolyn 4 Colin

b 2 six months ago 3 doesn't usually buy

c 2 c 3 b 4 a

Unit 4
a 2 b 3 c 4 a

b 2 meal with her friends 3 barbecue with her family 4 doesn't celebrate

c 2 c 3 d 4 a

Unit 5
a 2 b 3 c 4 a

b 2 talking to 3 friendly 4 science

c 2 c 3 d 4 a

Unit 6
a 2 c 3 a 4 b

b 2 Maibritt 3 Colin 4 Mark

c 2 b 3 a 4 c

91

Acknowledgements

The authors and publishers acknowledge the following sources of copyright material and are grateful for the permissions granted. While every effort has been made, it has not always been possible to identify the sources of all the material used, or to trace all copyright holders. If any omissions are brought to our notice, we will be happy to include the appropriate acknowledgements on reprinting.

The publisher has used its best endeavours to ensure that the URLs for external websites referred to in this book are correct and active at the time of going to press. However, the publisher has no responsibility for the websites and can make no guarantee that a site will remain live or that the content is or will remain appropriate.

The publishers are grateful to the following for permission to reproduce copyright photographs and material:

Key: L = left, C = centre, R = right, T = top, B = bottom

p.5: Getty Images/4FR; p.6(B): Alamy/OJO Images Ltd; p.6(T): Shutterstock/StockLite; p.7(B): Alamy/Gaertner; p.7(T): Shutterstock/Kkulikov; p.8: Shutterstock/Baranq; p.9: Shutterstock/Lucky Business; p.10(TL): Getty Images/Holly Harris; p.10(TR): Shutterstock/Kodentseva; p.11(B): Getty Images/Adrian Dennis; p.11(T): Alamy/Prisma Bildagentur AG; p.13(B): Shutterstock/Martin Froyda; p.13(T): Alamy/SFL Travel; p.14: Shutterstock/Dolomite-Summits; p.15: Shutterstock/Adrian Reynolds; p.16: Shutterstock/Monkey Business Images; p.17(BC): Alamy/Incamerastock; p.17(BL): Shutterstock/Sergey Mironov; p.17(BR): Alamy/Paul Rapson; p.18(B): Shutterstock/VannPhotography; p.18(T): Shutterstock/Dmitry Kalinovsky; p.20: Shutterstock/Artem_Ka; p.21: Shutterstock/Maxim Blinkov; p.22(1): Shutterstock/Sagir; p.22(2): Shutterstock/PhotoBlink; p.22(3): Thinkstock/Thomas Northcut; p.22(4): iStockphoto/Gsermek; p.22(5): Shutterstock/Elnur; p.22(6): iStockphoto/PeJo29; p.22(7): Shutterstock/Petar Djordjevic; p.22(8): Thinkstock/Olga Sapegina; p.22(9): Shutterstock/Ivaschenko Roman; p.22(10): Shutterstock/Jacek Bieniek; p.22(11): Shutterstock/Coprid; p.22(12): Shutterstock/Bernashafo; p.22(TR): Shutterstock/Auremar; p.23: Alamy/Andrew Rubtsov; p.24: Shutterstock/Blvdone; p.25(B): Alamy/Jiri Hubatka; p.25(T): Alamy/Kzenon; p.26: Shutterstock/Radu Razvan; p.27: Shutterstock/Viacheslav Lopatin; p.29(1): Shutterstock/Andreas G Karelias; p.29(2): Alamy/Peter Titmuss; p.29(3): Alamy/AberCPC; p.29(4): Shutterstock/Monkey Business Images; p.29(5): Thinkstock/Slavenko Vukasovi; p.29(6): Shutterstock/Chad McDermott; p.29(7): Shutterstock/Faraways; p.29(8): Alamy/Geraint Lewis; p.29(9): Alamy/Zoonar GmbH; p.29(10): Alamy/David J Green - Lifestyle themes; p.29(11): Shutterstock/Dmitry Kalinovsky; p.29(12): Corbis/Ocean; p.29(B): Shutterstock/Monkey Business Images; p.31(B): Shutterstock/Dotshock; p.31(T): Alamy/James Osmond Photography; p.33: Shutterstock/Edhar; p.34: Shutterstock/Stockkete; p.36: Alamy/Tetra Images; p.37(B): Shutterstock/Kzenon; p.37(T): Thinkstock/Shironosov; p.38: Shutterstock/Tyler Olson; p.39: Shutterstock/Alexander Raths.

Commissioned photography by Gareth Boden: p.19.

Video stills by Rob Maidment and Sharp Focus Productions: p.3, p.12(B), p.12(T), p.30, p.76, p.78.

Illustrations by Javier Joaquin p.32; Dusan Lakicevic p.10; Gavin Reece p.4, 34, 35; Sean Sims p.28

This page is intentionally left blank

This page is intentionally left blank

This page is intentionally left blank